PREFACE

The earlier version of *A Key to Adult Males of British Chironomidae* by Clive Pinder (FBA Scientific Publication No. 37, 1978) has been out of print for some time, and numerous advances in the taxonomy of chironomids make a new edition eminently desirable. In fact, this completely new edition is the result of more than ten years of painstaking collaboration between Drs Peter Langton and Clive Pinder. Peter is widely acknowledged as the foremost expert on identifying the pupal stages of chironomids in the British Isles; in addition, like his co-author he is also an expert on the adults. We are very fortunate to have the combined fruits of their wide and long experience.

The long period of gestation for this publication is partly due to changes in taxonomy and much new research on the chironomids of western Europe, necessitating frequent alterations and additions to an ever-expanding text. Indeed, just when a suitable text had been finally prepared and agreed for publication, yet more important changes to nomenclature and further additions to the British list posed a difficult problem for the authors and editor. Incorporation of this latest work would have required substantial rearrangements of text and line-drawings accompanying couplets in several keys – a mammoth undertaking! Therefore, to expedite publication, we decided to add some of the new material in a supplement to Volume 2, with brief cross-references at appropriate places in the main text. This solution is not ideal but provides updated information (to late 2005) concerning 16 newly-recorded species. Altogether, this publication identifies males of 591 species from the British Isles, compared with 439 species in the 1978 key, an increase of one-third. To accommodate the increased number of species, the authors provide nearly 1400 individual line-drawings arranged in 276 text-figures. A list of the 140 genera is provided on pages 22-25, to be used for guidance and orientation when working through the keys, especially with the complex subfamilies Orthocladiinae and Chironominae. Beginners and others unfamiliar with the plethora of names that characterise the Chironomidae, may also find the guide to pupal exuviae by Wilson & Ruse (2005) very helpful for familiarising themselves with the basic taxonomy of the family.

Finally, I wish to thank the authors for their extraordinary patience with my requests and demands as editor, particularly as the past decade has included major upheavals in their lives. Despite this, the senior author has provided many new drawings to illustrate his keys; quite an achievement for a teacher with only limited time and facilities available for this work.

David Sutcliffe

4

CONTENTS

KEYS TO THE ADULT MALE
CHIRONOMIDAE OF
BRITAIN AND IRELAND

by

P. H. LANGTON AND L. C. V. PINDER

Illustrated by

ANGELA M. MATTHEWS AND P. H. LANGTON

'ES

:, Cambridge,
'52 1JN.

4NX, England.

Published by the Freshwater Biological Association, The Ferry House,
Far Sawrey, Ambleside, Cumbria LA22 0LP, UK

ISBN 978-0-900386-75-6

ISSN 0367-1887

INTRODUCTION

The Chironomidae, sometimes called non-biting midges, are the most widely distributed and often the most abundant insects in fresh water. The family also includes many species that are terrestrial or semi-terrestrial and others that thrive in brackish water and intertidal pools. Larval chironomids occur in almost every imaginable freshwater habitat and some are remarkably tolerant of high levels of pollution. In some situations, for example where oxygen levels are severely depressed or there are high concentrations of heavy metals, chironomids may be the only insects present in the sediment (Armitage *et al.* 1995).

It has been estimated that there are as many as 15,000 species of chironomids worldwide, many of which remain undescribed or undiscovered. Cranston (1995) points out that such estimates need to be treated with caution, but agrees that there is good evidence to support an estimate in excess of 10,000 species. The earlier edition of this key (Pinder 1978) dealt with 439 species known, at that time, to occur in Britain and Ireland, about 50 more than the number known to Coe (1950). Since 1978 many more species have been found, including several that were new to science, and this new edition identifies males of 591 species, an increase of 35% since 1978; 6 new species per year on average. This gives an indication of the large amount of interest in Chironomidae that exists within Britain and Ireland. To some extent this interest is driven by the potential of chironomids – with their high diversity and wide range of tolerances – to be useful as biological indicators of water quality (e.g. Wilson 1987, 1996; Wilson & Ruse 2005), and also because of the important part which they play in freshwater ecosystems, as consumers of primary production and as food for fish and other predators (Armitage *et al.* 1995). However, for many people the fascination of chironomid taxonomy is simply attributable to the family's high level of species diversity, and the ever-present possibility of discovering a species not previously recorded from a particular region, or even one new to science.

The amount of literature dealing with aspects of chironomid biology and ecology is vast, as may be seen from the extensive bibliographies produced by Fittkau *et al.* (1976) and Hoffrichter & Reiss (1981). There have been two major attempts to summarise the literature. Thienemann's monumental review, published in 1954, remains a classic, whilst the review edited by Armitage *et al.* (1995) concentrates mainly on more recent literature. Short reviews by Oliver (1971) and Pinder (1986) also provide useful introductions to the ecology and biology of the Chironomidae.

Pinder (1978) referred to problems with generic nomenclature and diagnosis, arising, in part, from the early development of different systems of nomenclature applied to adults and immature stages. Publication of the three volumes of keys and diagnoses for the genera of Holarctic Chironomidae, covering immature stages and adult males (Wiederholm 1983, 1986, 1989) has gone a long way towards establishing a more universally accepted system. The present keys closely follow the generic nomenclature used in the Wiederholm publications, necessitating several changes from the names used by Pinder (1978). A number of species names have also been altered, mostly as a result of synonymies published during the intervening period. Such changes are indicated in the index provided at the end of Volume 1, which conveniently acts as a checklist for the 591 species for which adult males have been recorded so far from Britain and Ireland. A list of subfamilies, tribes, genera and number of species (updated to November 2005) is provided on pages 22–25. This includes 16 new additions, which are described briefly in a Supplement to Volume 2 (pp. 152–168). Another recent record for Britain, *Pseudosmittia arenaria* Strenzke, is fully parthenogenetic and is therefore not keyed out in this publication on adult males.

CLASSIFICATION

Members of the family Chironomidae (non-biting midges) belong to the Suborder Nematocera of the Order Diptera: i.e. they are true flies, with a single pair of wings, the hind pair being modified as *halteres* which are concerned with the maintenance of stability in flight. The Chironomidae and Ceratopogonidae (biting midges) together form a sister group to the Simuliidae (blackflies; see Bass 1998). These three families, along with the small families Dixidae (meniscus midges) and Thaumaleidae (trickle midges) (see Disney 1999), and the superfamily Culicoidea (mosquitoes; see Cranston *et al.* 1987), together constitute the infraorder Culicomorpha (Cranston 1995).

The family Chironomidae is subdivided into a number of subfamilies, of which ten are currently recognised worldwide. Two of these subfamilies are absent from the Holarctic region, but the remaining eight are represented in Britain and Ireland. Relationships between some of the subfamilies are a subject of continuing debate and are briefly summarised by Cranston (1995). Several subfamilies have been further subdivided into tribes. Those referred to later in the keys, and all of the genera found in Britain and Ireland, are listed on pages 22–25 of this volume.

MORPHOLOGY

Adult male chironomids are slender-bodied and vary considerable in size, with wings ranging in length from about 0.7 mm to 7 mm or more, depending on species. Males of most species have plumose antennae, in which they resemble both Ceratopogonidae and also Culicidae (mosquitoes). They can be distinguished easily from mosquitoes by the absence of an elongate proboscis. The wing venation of Chironomidae is also much simpler than that of Culicidae and lacks the appressed scales that are characteristic of the wing veins of the latter. Ceratopogonidae may be distinguished from Chironomidae by the presence of a distally forked vein M_{1+2}, which in Chironominae is simple (see Fig. 5, p. 13).

The following description of the external morphology of adult males is largely restricted to characters that are used diagnostically in the keys. More detailed descriptions may be found in Sæther (1980), Wiederholm (1989) and Armitage *et al.* (1995*).* The main external features of a typical adult male chironomid are shown in Fig. 1. The terminology used in the present key is mostly consistent with that used by Pinder (1978) but some changes have been made in order to conform with the recommendations of Sæther (1980), which were also adopted by Wiederholm (1989). These differences are summarised below in Table 1.

Table 1. Main differences between the terminology employed in this publication and the terminology used by Pinder (1978).

Body part	This publication	Pinder (1978)
Antenna:	Flagellomere	Flagellar segment
Legs:	Tarsomeres (1–5)	Tarsal segments (1–5)
Wing venation:	M_{1+2} M_{3+4} Cu_1	M Cu_1 Cu_2
Hypopygium (Chironominae only):	Superior volsella Inferior volsella Median volsella Digitus	Appendage 1 Appendage 2 Appendage 2a Appendage 1a

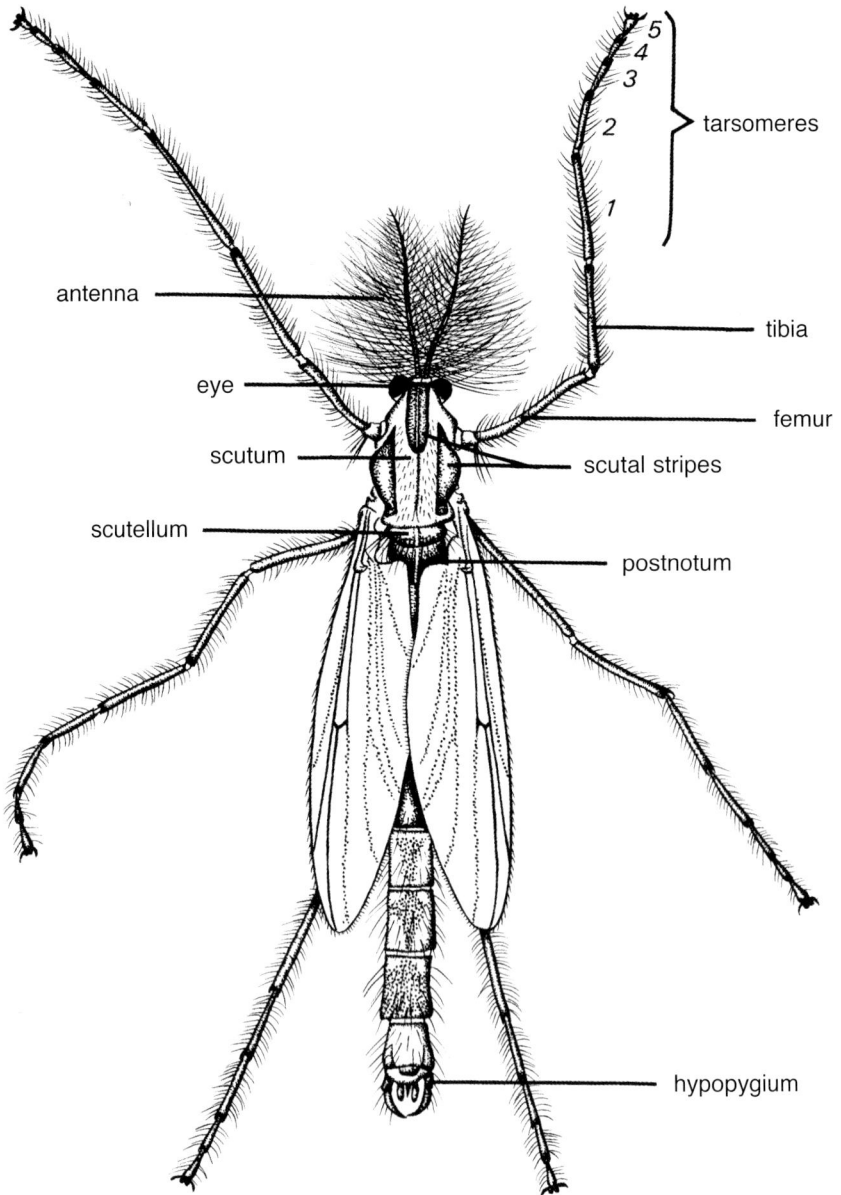

Fig. 1.   Dorsal view of a male chironomid.

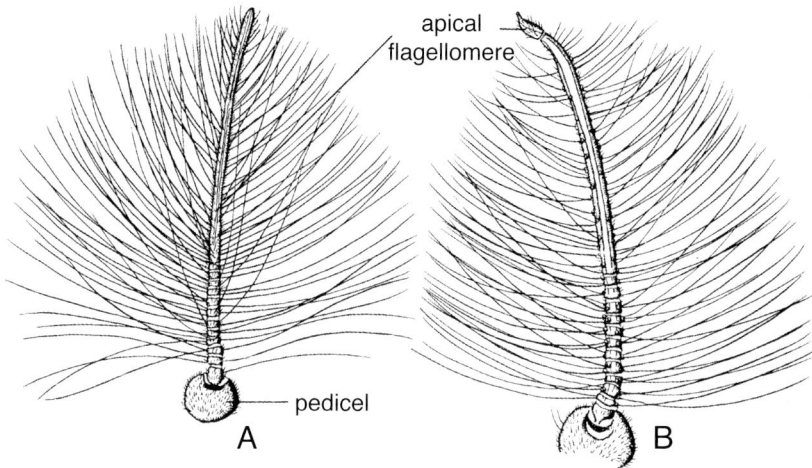

Fig. 2.   Male antennae of: **A**, *Orthocladius thienemanni*   (Orthocladiinae);
B, *Procladius choreus* (Tanypodinae).

Head. The *antenna* of the male chironomid (Figs 2A,B) consists of a reduced
basal segment, the *scape,* which is usually hidden beneath the large globular
second segment or *pedicel.* Distally the pedicel bears a *flagellum,* usually
consisting of between 11 and 14 *flagellomeres* (see Table 1). In subfamilies
Orthocladiinae and Chironominae the terminal flagellomere is the longest (Fig.
2A), whereas in subfamilies Tanypodinae and Podonominae the penultimate
flagellomere is the longest (Fig. 2B). The *antennal ratio* is sometimes a useful
specific character and is defined as the length of the longest flagellomere (plus
the length of any more distal flagellomeres), divided by the combined length
of the preceding flagellomeres.

   In males the flagellomeres normally carry whorls of long setae, giving
male antennae their characteristic plumose appearance. Antennae of female
chironomids are shorter, with fewer flagellomeres and shorter, more sparse
setae. However, in the subfamily Telmatogetoninae, the number of flagellomeres
and setae is also reduced in males (see Fig. 12, p. 28), and similar, female-like
antennae also occur in males of a few species in other subfamilies (Wiederholm
1989). *Frontal tubercles* (Fig. 3A) are present in many Chironominae, dorsal
to the antennae, and may be of diagnostic importance.

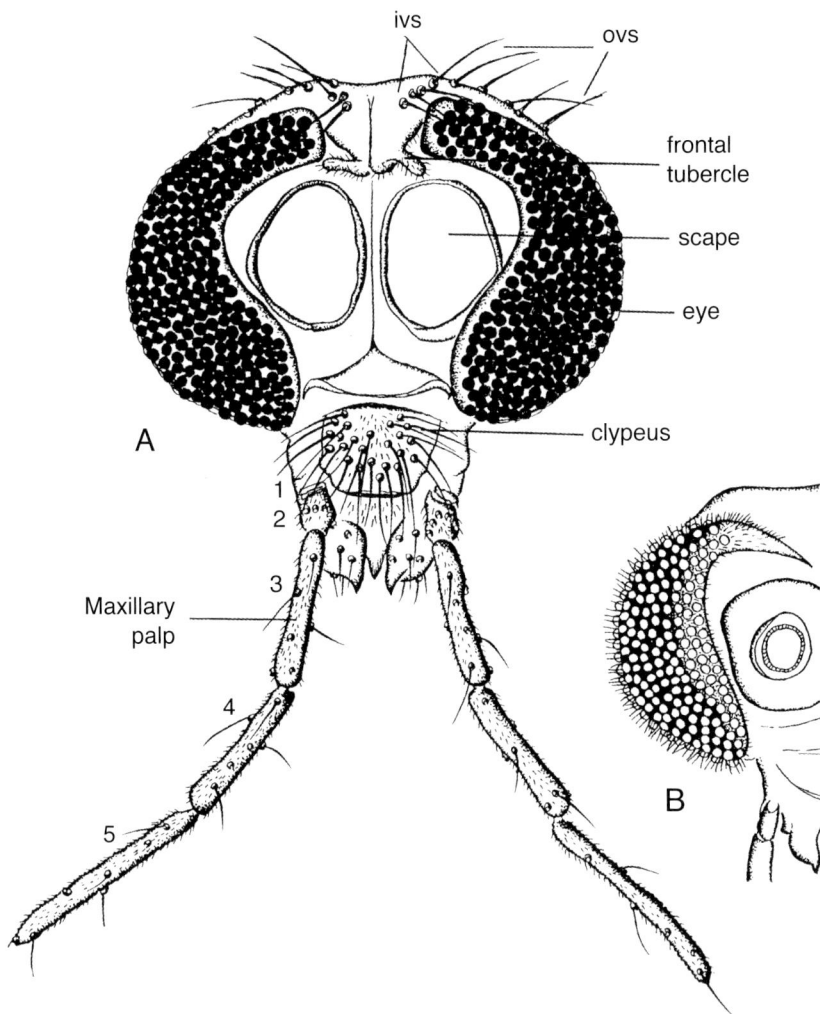

Fig. 3.   Heads of chironomids: **A,** anterior view of male (antennae removed);
           B, head with *hairy* eye (setae project beyond the lenses) (when setae do not
           project, eyes are described as *pubescent*). ivs = inner vertical setae; ovs =
           outer vertical setae; 1–5 = maxillary palp segments 1–5.

The *compound eyes* are very large and in males are often strongly produced dorsally (Fig. 3A). In many species, fine microtrichia are present between the individual lenses (Fig. 3B). Such eyes are referred to as *hairy*, when the length of the microtrichia is greater than the height of the ommatidial lenses, (as in Fig. 3B) or *pubescent* when they are shorter than this.

Adult Chironomidae are often stated to have reduced mouthparts and it is true that functional mandibles are usually lacking, having been recorded only in females of the southern hemisphere genus *Archaeochlus*. Other mouthparts are present, however, with the hypopharynx, labium and soft labella combining to form a food canal, leading to the cibarial pump (Cranston 1995; Burtt *et al.* 1986). The *maxillary palps* are well developed and usually consist of five *segments* (Fig. 3) (although the basal segment may be difficult to discern), but in some species the number of segments is less than five.

The head bears several groups of setae but only the *vertical setae* are referred to in the following keys. These are situated dorsally, between the mid-line of the head and the dorsal part of the eye. They may be separated into groups of *inner vertical setae* and *outer vertical setae*, by virtue of size and/or relative position.

Thorax. The main subdivisions of the thorax are shown in Figs 4A and 4B. As in all Diptera, the thorax is dominated by the *mesonotum*, which contains the flight muscles. The main dorsal component of the mesonotum is the *scutum*, posterior to which is a narrow, rounded lobe, the *scutellum* and, behind this, a well developed *postnotum,* usually with a *median groove* or *keel*. The scutum sometimes has a *median tubercle*, and usually a median row of *acrostichal setae* and mediolateral rows of *dorsocentral setae* are present. In many species median and mediolateral *scutal bands* or *stripes* are visible, sometimes separated, as shown in Fig. 1 (p. 8), and sometimes fused.

The scutal bands are often darker than the surrounding area of the scutum and therefore are conspicuous, but in species with a uniformly coloured scutum they are more difficult to see. Anterior to the scutum is a narrow, bilobed projection, the *antepronotum,* which in some species is visible only when viewed laterally.

In addition to the setae borne on the scutum, the thorax frequently bears other groups of setae that are sometimes useful in identification. These are shown in a generalised way in Figs 4A and 4B and are illustrated more specifically at appropriate points in the keys.

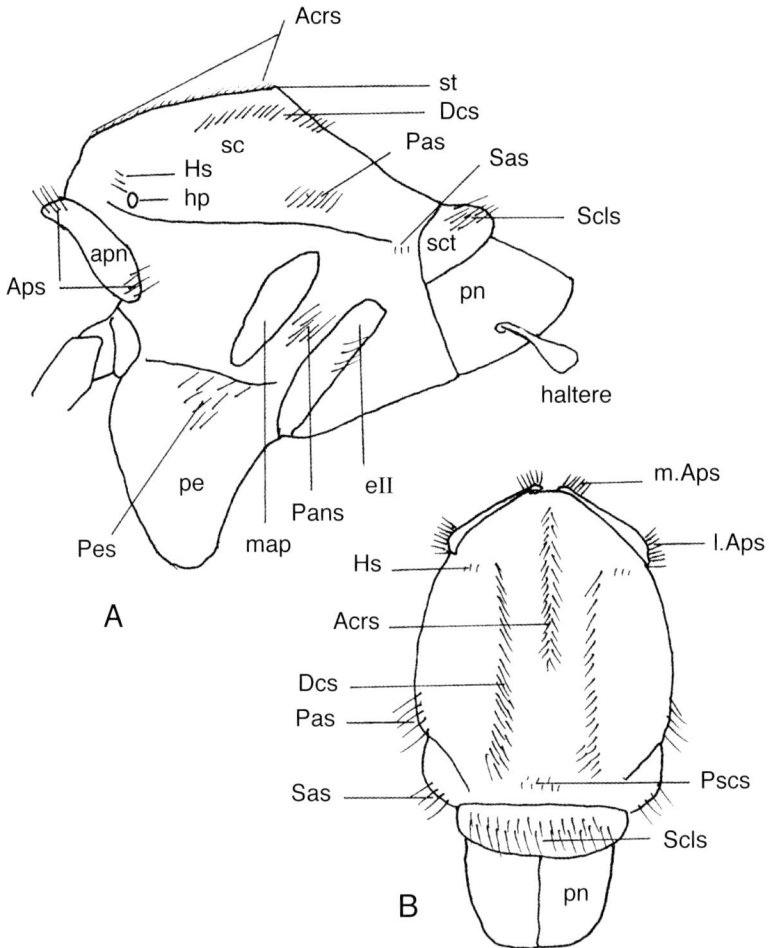

Fig. 4. Generalised thorax of adult chironomid: **A,** lateral view; **B,** dorsal view.
apn = antepronotum; eII = epimeron II; hp = humeral pit; map = median
anepisternum; pe = pre-episternum; pn = postnotum; sc = scutum; sct =
scutellum; st = scutal tubercle.
Setal groups as follows: Acrs = acrostichals; Aps = antepronotals (l.Aps =
lateral antepronotals; m.Aps = median antepronotals); Dcs = dorsocentrals;
Hs = humerals; Pans = posterior anepisternals; Pas = prealars; Pes = pre-
episternals; Pscs = prescutellars; Sas = supra-alars; Scls = scutellars.

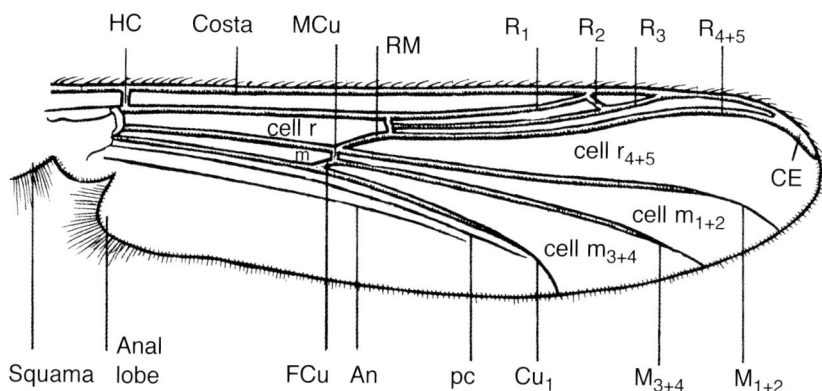

Fig. 5.   Wing of *Psectrotanypus varius* (Tanypodinae) (pigmentation and macrotrichia omitted), showing nomenclature applied to wing venation and cells, as used in the keys: R_{1-5} = radial veins; CE = costal extension; Cu = cubitus; pc = post cubitus; An = anal vein; FCu = cubital fork; HC = humeral cross-vein; MCu and RM are also cross-veins.

Wings. The wing venation of Chironomidae is much reduced from the basic dipteran pattern (Cranston 1995). The nomenclature applied to the wing venation and cells (Fig. 5) is slightly modified from that used by Pinder (1978), in order to conform with Sæther's (1980) interpretation and nomenclature used in Wiederholm (1989). Vein R_2 is present only in some species of the subfamily Tanypodinae and even in this subfamily it may be only weakly developed or absent. The cross-vein MCu is present in subfamilies Tanypodinae, Podonominae, Diamesinae, Prodiamesinae and Buchonomyiinae, but absent in Telmatogetoninae, Orthocladiinae and Chironominae. The wing margins and several of the veins are usually fringed with macrotrichia. The genera *Corynoneura* and *Thienemanniella* (Orthocladiinae) have a distinctive pattern of wing venation, in which veins R_1 and R_{4+5} are apically fused with the costa to form a thickened *clavus* (see Fig. 34F, p. 65) that extends to no more than half the length of the wing.

The wing membrane may be bare or invested to a varying extent and density with macrotrichia. Some apparently bare wing membranes, when examined under high magnification, may be found to be covered with very fine microtrichia. In a number of species the wings are distinctively marked, as a result of differential distribution of pigment or macrotrichia, or a combination of both.

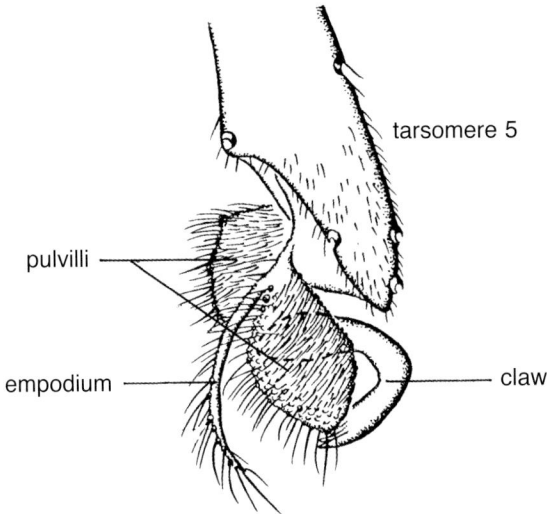

Fig. 6.   Apex of tarsus of *Psectrocladius* sp., showing large pulvilli.

Legs. The legs are made up of a basal *coxa*, followed by the *trochanter*, *femur*, *tibia* and *tarsus*, as shown in Fig. 1 (p. 8). The tarsus is made up of five *tarsomeres* and apically bears a pair of claws, which may be simple or occasionally 'toothed', and a central bristle-like *empodium*. Paired pad-like *pulvilli* also may be present between the claws and these are sometimes well developed and conspicuous (Fig. 6). The tibiae and tarsomeres, particularly of the fore-leg, frequently bear a longitudinal *beard* of conspicuously long setae.

Ratios based on leg measurements are often used for identification and, unless it is stated otherwise, such ratios, when used as key characters, refer to the fore-legs. The *leg ratio* (length of tarsomere 1 divided by length of tibia) is often useful in identification, as is the *beard ratio* (length of the longest tarsal seta divided by the width of the relevant tarsomere). Usually this relates to tarsomere 1 of the fore-legs but, occasionally in the keys, specific reference is made to other tarsomeres.

The mid- and hind-tibiae are usually equipped with distal *spurs* and/or *combs*, the form of which differs between and within subfamilies (Fig. 7). Combs consist of groups of strong setae or spines, which may be separated (Figs 7A,B) or fused basally, as in Fig. 7C. The combs may be distinctly paired, although the division may be very slight, and one or both (as in Fig. 7C) may include a particularly long 'tooth' or spur.

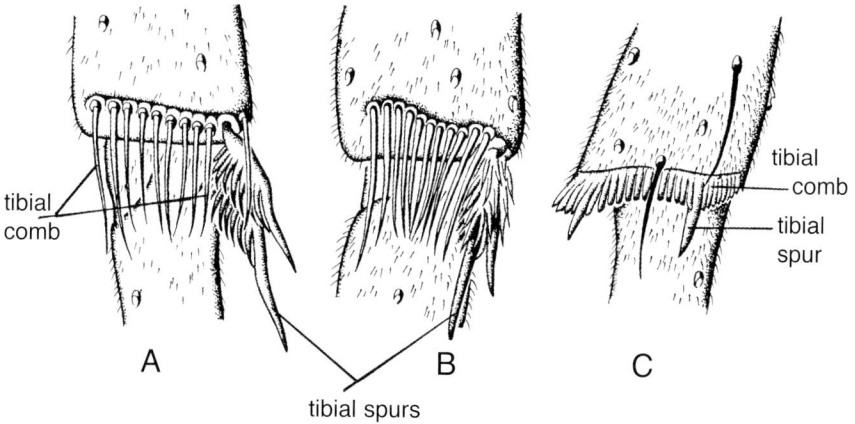

Fig. 7.   Examples of tibial combs and spurs in three subfamilies: **A,** Tanypodinae; **B,** Orthocladiinae; **C,** Chironominae.

Abdomen. The first seven abdominal segments of male chironomids are dorsoventrally flattened and of little help for identification, although abdominal coloration and patterns of setae on the dorsal tergites are sometimes helpful. In most species segment VIII is similarly unremarkable, but in *Polypedilum* and many Tanytarsini it tapers anteriorly to form a narrow waist where it articulates with segment VII. This allows the main external genitalia (*hypopygium*) to be rotated through 180 degrees, a feature that is primarily associated with mating on substrata, rather than the more usual habit of aerial mating (Fittkau 1971).

Characters associated with the external genitalia (hypopygium) of the male are very important in chironomid identification (Fig. 8). Hypopygia of British and Irish species are illustrated in Volume 2. Tergite IX often has a posteromedian projection, the *anal point.* However, the most conspicuous features are the paired claspers, which consist of a basal *gonocoxite* and a distal *gonostylus.* The gonocoxite carries a variable number of mesal appendages, called *volsellae*, and these are named with reference to their relative positions or shape. Cranston (1995) points out that the establishment of homologies for volsellae, across rather widely differing subfamilies, is difficult and potentially confusing. For this reason the descriptive neutral terms that were used by Pinder (1978), such as 'dorsal lobe of gonocoxite', have been retained for most subfamilies in the keys presented here. An exception is made for the subfamily Chironominae (Table 1, p. 7), in which the *superior volsella, inferior volsella* and *median volsella,* together with the *digitus*, are generally well developed and easily distinguishable (Fig. 8).

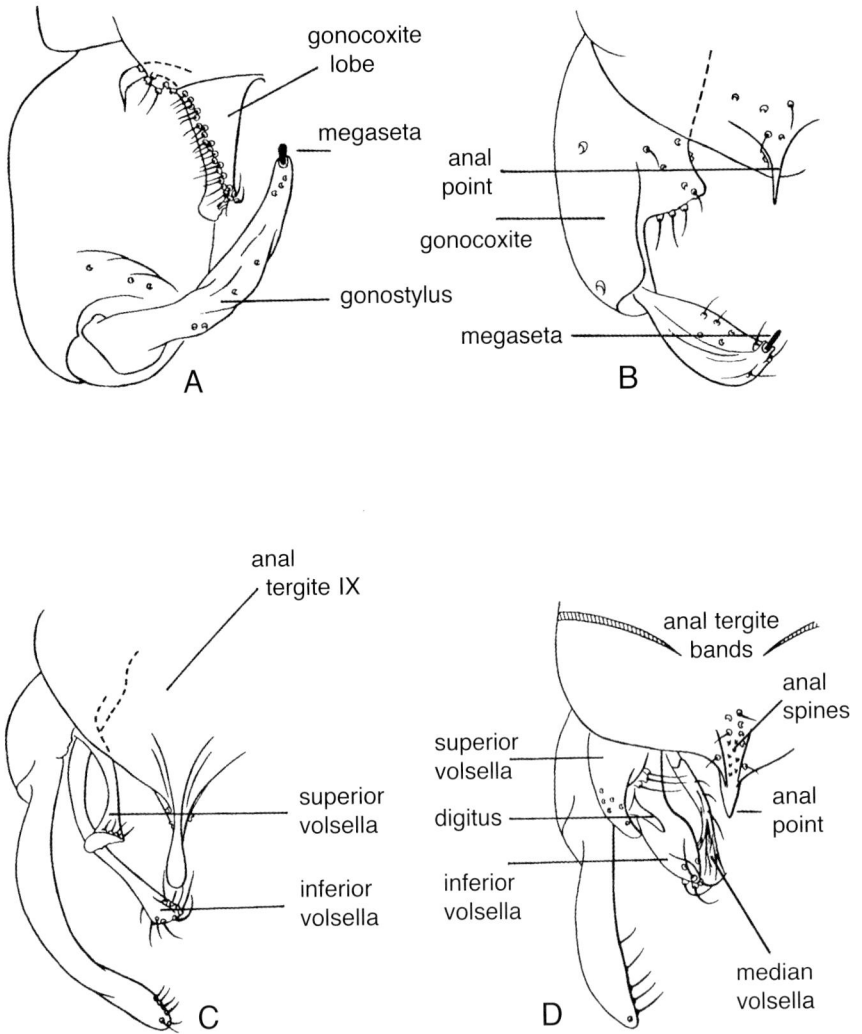

Fig. 8.   Dorsal views of hypopygia of: **A,** *Arctopelopia* sp. (Tanypodinae); **B,**
Chaetocladius sp. (Orthocladiinae); **C,** *Dicrotendipes* sp. (Chironominae, tribe
Chironomini); **D,** *Cladotanytarsus* sp. (Chironominae, tribe Tanytarsini).

In most subfamilies the gonostylus is movably articulated with the posterior margin of the gonocoxite. However, in Chironominae the connection is more rigid and the junction may be indistinct, although in some genera a degree of movement is possible. In many species the gonostylus carries an apical *megaseta* (Fig. 8), and sometimes more than one, but a megaseta is never present in Chironominae. In Orthocladiinae a sclerotised, apicodorsal lamella is often present, proximal to the megaseta; this is known as the *crista dorsalis* and it frequently takes the form of a distinct spine or rounded lobe.

In some genera, internal structures associated with the genitalia are of diagnostic importance. Chief among these are the internal skeletal structures or *apodemes* (Fig. 9). These consist of a *sternapodeme*, which may be divided into a transverse section and posteriorly directed lateral parts; these connect with the paired *coxapodemes* and articulate with the *phallapodemes*. The latter form the anterior margins of a hyaline structure called the *aedagus*, which passes a package of sperms to the female. The phallapodemes act as levers that evert the *endophallus* (penis). In Orthocladiinae the penis cavity may contain a sclerotised structure, known as the *virga*, which is everted by the action of the phallapodemes (Cranston 1995). When present it is visible as a median, internal, sclerotised rod-like structure. In a small number of cases the form of the virga is of diagnostic importance.

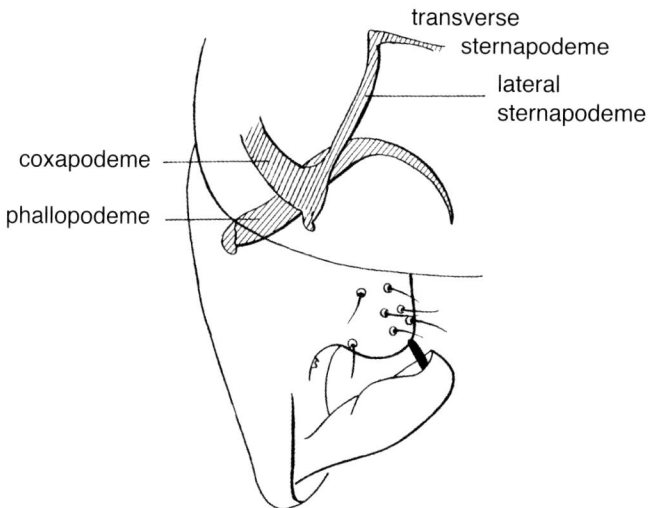

Fig. 9.   Dorsal view of hypopygium of *Thienemanniella* sp., illustrating important endoskeletal structures (apodemes).

METHODS

COLLECTION OF MATERIAL

The following descriptions of methods for collecting and preserving adult chironomids are based largely on those recommended in Wiederholm (1989). Hand-netting from swarms and sweep-netting of vegetation are the most commonly used methods for collecting adult midges but a variety of other methods have been used, and are useful in some situations, depending on the objectives of the study.

Emergence trapping, using traps such as those described by Mundie (1956), is a useful method for obtaining information on spatial and temporal patterns of adult emergence and was successfully used by Mundie (1955) to study the seasonal emergence of Chironomidae from a London reservoir.

Sticky traps provide a cheap means of collecting large numbers of individuals, but removal of the insects from the traps is rather laborious and has to be carried out carefully, using a suitable solvent in order to avoid damaging them. Mason & Sublette (1971) successfully used floating sticky traps, instead of traditional emergence traps, to capture adult midges emerging from the Ohio River. Pinder (1974) used grease bands (designed to protect apple trees from pests such as winter moth) wrapped around plastic cylinders, to collect chironomids above a chalk stream, with the objective of producing a species list for the stream and obtaining information on flight periods. In a single transect of traps, across a small chalk stream in Dorset, he collected more than 70 species. The species composition of the catch was strongly influenced by the distance of the trap from the stream margins and their height above the water surface. For example, traps placed adjacent to the banks and below bank height collected large numbers of *Rheotanytarsus curtistylus*, a species that, until then, had not been recorded from Britain, but which selected this inconspicuous location for swarming.

Light trapping is also an effective method for collecting large numbers of individuals, and was used by Dejoux (1968) in a study of Lake Chad. Ali *et al.* (1994) investigated the attractiveness of different wavelengths of light to adult *Chironomus salinarius,* using incandescent lights of seven colours. White and yellow light attracted most midges whilst red was the least effective. However, they also found a strong relationship between light intensity and numbers caught.

During his investigation of transantarctic relationships, Brundin (1966) collected a large amount of chironomid material using stream drift nets. Material of a similar nature also may be collected on a more casual basis, using pond nets to skim surface scum from eddies and snags at the margins of rivers and streams, and from lake shores and similar situations (Langton 1991). Such material mainly consists of pupal exuviae but a few of these will have partly emerged adults attached to them, and some adults and mature pupae (some with attached larval exuviae) are also likely to be present. Material collected in this way can thus be very useful taxonomically.

REARING LARVAE TO ADULTS

Substantial progress has been made in chironomid taxonomy in recent years, especially in respect of increased accessibility to information (e.g. Cranston 1982; Langton 1984, 1991; Wiederholm 1983, 1986, 1989). But, for taxonomic purposes and also to accurately identify larvae to species, it is often necessary to rear larvae through to adults for specific identification. Identification may then be achieved using either the imago or pupal exuviae. Exuviae have the advantage that both sexes of the vast majority of British and Irish chironomids can be identified to species using Langton's (1991) key to the Palaearctic fauna, whereas with adults this is generally only possible with males.

A simple method for rearing larvae was described by Cranston (1982). This involves sorting larvae in the field, to remove most of the associated substratum, after which they are placed in a thermos flask, together with water from the collection site. Cranston was primarily concerned with Orthocladiinae and found that even the more sensitive larvae survived for up to a day after collection. On returning to the laboratory, larvae are placed individually in shallow water, from the thermos flask, in 50-mm disposable plastic petri-dishes. Disposal of the dishes after use reduces the likelihood of harmful fungal growths, while the large surface to volume ratio in the dishes ensures that oxygen concentrations are adequate and the microbial film that develops on the bottom of the dish eliminates the need to provide an extraneous food source. Many larvae, especially among the subfamilies Orthocladiinae and Diamesinae, are cold stenotherms and, for Orthocladiinae, Cranston (1982) found that the optimum temperature lies between 10 and 14°C. Most Diamesinae are adapted to lower temperatures than this while, in general, Chironominae will tolerate somewhat higher temperatures.

In order to avoid possible confusion between the developmental stages of several species present in collected samples, it is essential to rear larvae individually. However, good results also may be obtained by rearing batches of larvae when these are hatched from a single egg mass, using a similar methodology.

PRESERVATION AND MOUNTING SPECIMENS ON SLIDES

For detailed examination, especially of hypopygial structures, adults must be cleared, dissected and mounted on slides. For this reason, preservation in 70% ethanol or propanol is strongly recommended. A 4% formaldehyde solution is sometimes used as a preservative (taking care not to inhale harmful fumes) but this fixes the muscles so that they become impossible to clear. It is then difficult or impossible to observe structural details, especially those of the hypopygium.

A detailed methodology for preparing slides of adult midges is given in Wiederholm (1989). This is an improvement on the slightly simpler method described by Pinder (1978), and it allows scope for larval and pupal exuviae to be mounted on the same slide as the adult, when reared series are available. It is recommended that the methodology should be followed for specimens intended for long-term storage in voucher collections or museums.

For this, the wings, antennae and legs from one side of the body (preserved in 70% ethanol or propanol) are first removed using fine forceps and fine dissecting needles, and are placed in absolute ethanol or isopropanol for a few minutes to dehydrate. They are then transferred to Euparal on a slide, the wings being placed under one coverslip and the legs and antennae beneath a second (at positions 3 and 4 respectively, as shown in Fig. 10). The remainder of the animal, without further dissection, is placed in 10% potassium hydroxide solution and left overnight at room temperature to clear the musculature. Once cleared the carcass is transferred to glacial acetic acid for a few minutes and then into absolute alcohol or isopropanol to complete dehydration. The carcass can then be transferred directly to Euparal at position 7 on the slide (Fig. 10), before dissection.

The next step is to remove the head, using fine needles, and place this in a drop of Euparal at position 5 (Fig. 10), making sure that it is displayed with the anterior surface uppermost before placing the coverslip in position. The abdomen is also removed and placed at position 6 (Fig. 10) with the dorsal side uppermost. The thorax is then displayed laterally, at position 7, with the remaining legs extended so that they do not obscure the thorax. Note that direct placement of coverslips at positions 5 and 7 may compress and distort the underlying structures to an undesirable extent. A simple solution to this problem is to support the coverslip using short lengths of nylon fishing line, which is available in a range of diameters. When they are available, associated larval and pupal exuviae should be mounted at positions 1 and 2 respectively (Fig. 10); otherwise these positions remain vacant. It is advisable to use a slight excess of mountant, to prevent air from being drawn in beneath the

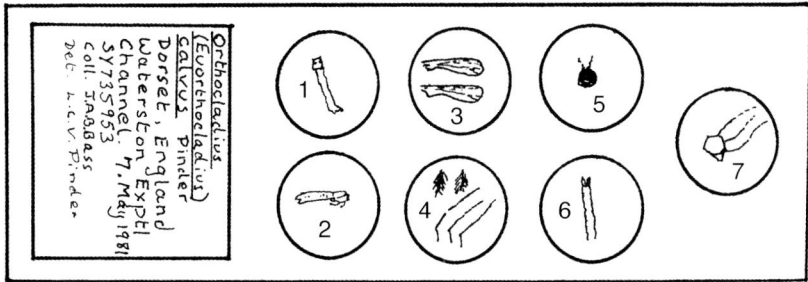

Fig. 10. Microscope slide of male chironomid showing a convenient method of arranging body parts. 1, larval exuviae; 2 pupal exuviae; 3 wings; 4 antennae and legs from one side of body; 5 head; 6 abdomen; 7 thorax with remaining legs. (When associated larval and pupal exuviae are unavailable, positions 1 and 2 are vacant).

coverslip during the drying process. Any excess mountant can be removed easily when the mountant has dried. The drying process may be accelerated by placing the prepared slides in an oven at a temperature of 35 to 50°C.

Canada Balsam may be used an alternative to Euparal. The same procedure applies, except that each body part must be transferred from absolute alcohol through clove oil before mounting.

Other mountants are not recommended for making permanent slides, and Wiederholm (1989) draws particular attention to problems that have arisen in respect of mounts in chloral hydrate (e.g. Berlese fluid). However, when it is necessary to quickly screen large numbers of adult midges (e.g. from light traps, emergence traps or sticky traps), a quicker method of preparation may be advantageous. In such circumstances, mounting directly from 70% alcohol into dimethyl hydantoin formaldehyde (DMHF) is successful. Although this mountant is not recommended for permanent preparations, slides made using this material are still in excellent condition more than 30 years after they were first made.

NOTES ON USE OF THE KEYS

Volume 1 of this two-volume work is divided into sections corresponding with the eight subfamilies that are represented in Britain and Ireland. For speed and ease of identification the couplets in the keys have been kept as brief as possible, commensurate with accuracy. As far as possible qualitative characters have been illustrated on the page facing the relevant couplet. Detailed drawings of hypopygia of each species are contained in Volume 2. Scale-lines that accompany most of the drawings of hypopygia represent a distance of 50 μm (unless otherwise stated), as a guide to relative size. It is recommended that initial identification should be arrived at using only Volume 1 and the detailed illustrations of hypopygia in Volume 2 should be used for confirmation. This is important because there remains a real possibility that new species, additional to those that have been considered in the compilation of these keys, are still to be discovered in the British Isles. Workers are encouraged to send any such records, preferably accompanied by specimens, to Dr Peter Langton.

LIST OF KEYS FOR THE SUBFAMILIES, TRIBES, GENERA AND NUMBERS OF SPECIES OF BRITISH AND IRISH CHIRONOMIDAE
(Suborder Nematocera; Order Diptera; Class Insecta; Phylum Arthropoda)

KEY TO EIGHT SUBFAMILIES
OF CHIRONOMIDAE

1   Wing cross-vein MCu present* (Figs 11A–C)—   **2**

—   Wing cross-vein MCu absent (Figs 11D,E)—   **6**

*See Fig. 5, p. 13, for nomenclature of the wing veins.

2   Gonostylus (Fig. 8, p. 16) comprised of two separate lobes (Fig. 13A, p. 29); dorsal lobe sickle-shaped, without microtrichia; ventral lobe broad, rounded, covered with microtrichia (see hypopygium, Fig. 114A in Vol. 2). Wing vein R_{2+3} absent (cf. Fig. 11B). Wing membrane covered with microtrichia and setae, some scale-like—

                               BUCHONOMYIINAE (p. 28)

—   Gonostylus may be lobed, but not divided to the base (e.g. see Fig. 13B, p. 29). Wing vein R_{2+3} present or absent. Setae of wing membrane never scale-like—   **3**

3   Wing vein R_{2+3} present and simple (i.e. not forked) (Figs 11A,B). Wing membrane bare. Apical flagellomere usually much longer than any of the preceding flagellomeres (except *Protanypus* in which a small incompletely separated terminal segment may be discernible)—   **4**

—   Wing vein R_{2+3} present and forked (Fig. 11C) or absent. Wing membrane often densely covered with macrotrichia. Apical flagellomere much shorter than penultimate flagellomere—   **5**

4   Cubital fork FCu proximal to MCu (Fig. 11A)— DIAMESINAE (p. 54)

—   Cubital fork FCu distal to MCu (Fig. 11B)—PRODIAMESINAE (p. 61)

5(3)   Wing vein R_{2+3} present and forked (Fig. 11C), or absent; when absent, R_1 and R_{4+5} lie in close proximity—   TANYPODINAE (p. 30)

—   Wing vein R_{2+3} absent; R_1 and R_{4+5} well separated—

                               PODONOMINAE (p. 29)

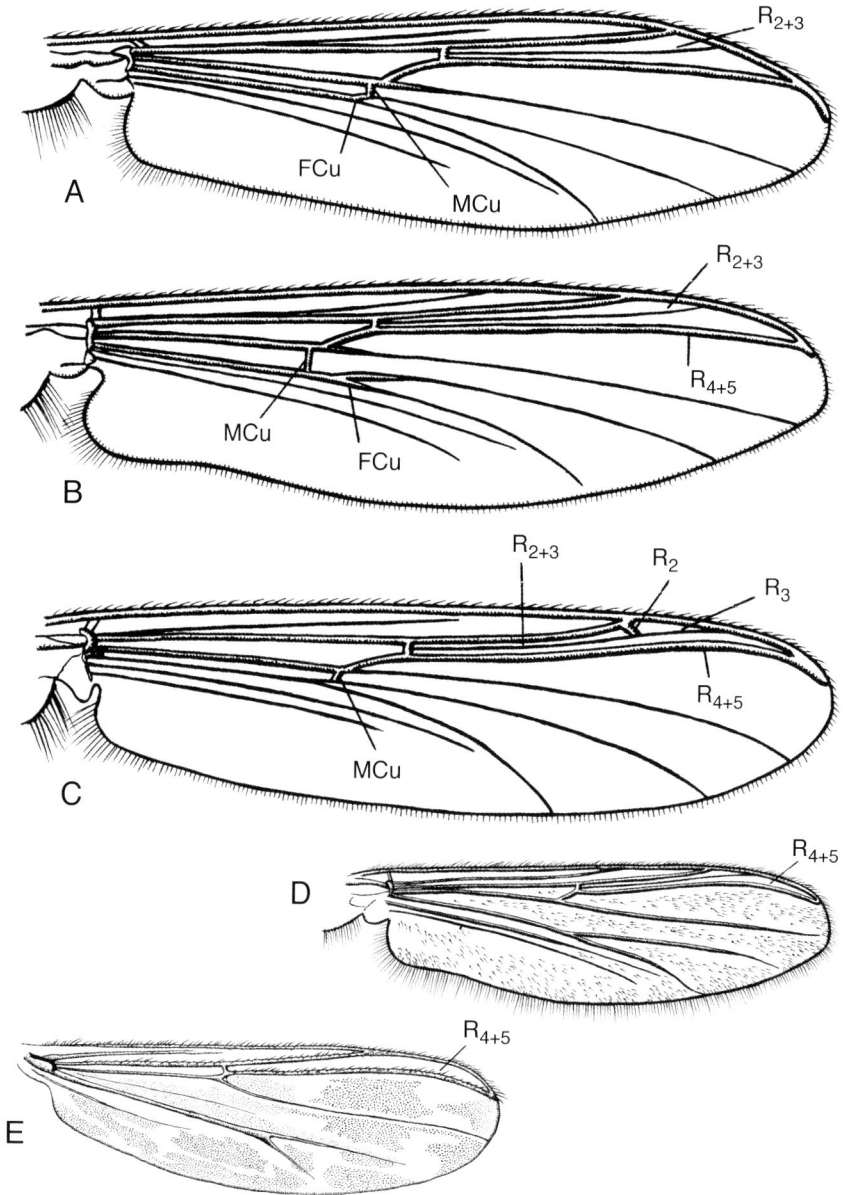

Fig. 11. **A–E:** wings of: A, *Potthastia gaedii* (Diamesinae); B, *Prodiamesa olivacea* (Prodiamesinae); C, *Zavrelimyia nubila* (Tanypodinae); D, *Heterotrissocladius marcidus* (Orthocladiinae); E, *Zavreliella marmorata* (Chironominae).

Fig. 12.   Antenna of *Telmatogeton pectinatus* (Telmatogetoninae).

6(1)   Antennae with 6 flagellomeres (Fig. 12). Postnotum of thorax (Fig. 4, p. 12) without a median keel or groove. Larvae marine—
                                    TELMATOGETONINAE (p. 54)

—   Antennae usually with 10 or more flagellomeres, rarely as few as 7. Postnotum usually with a median groove or keel (except for the marine genus *Clunio*). Larvae mainly fresh water or terrestrial—   **7**

7   Anterior leg ratio <1.0 (see p. 14). Gonostylus movable on the gonocoxite and usually bent inwards, rarely without 1 or more apical megasetae (e.g. Fig. 8B, p. 16)—   ORTHOCLADIINAE (p. 63)

—   Anterior leg ratio usually >1.0. Gonostylus more rigidly attached to the gonocoxite and usually directed backwards; rarely with 1 or more stiff apical setae, but never with a true megaseta (e.g. Figs 8C,D, p. 16)—
                                    CHIRONOMINAE (p. 146)

KEYS TO GENERA AND SPECIES IN EIGHT SUBFAMILIES

SUBFAMILY BUCHONOMYIINAE

Genus BUCHONOMYIA Fittkau

The sole genus included in the subfamily Buchonomyiinae is *Buchonomyia*, represented in England and Ireland by a single species. The gonostylus has two separate lobes (Fig. 13A); other characteristics are given in the key to subfamilies (Couplet 2, p. 26). Hypopygium Fig. 114A—
                                    Buchonomyia thienemanni Fittkau

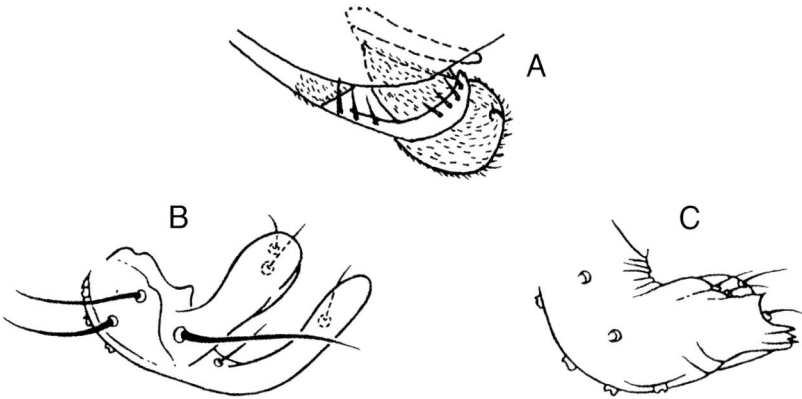

Fig. 13. **A–C:** gonostyli of: A, *Buchonomyia thienemanni*; B, *Parochlus kiefferi*; C, *Lasiodiamesa sphagnicola*.

SUBFAMILY PODONOMINAE

KEY TO 3 GENERA AND SPECIES OF PODONOMINAE

1   Gonostylus with two lobes (Fig. 13B). Hypopygium Fig. 114B —
                                Parochlus kiefferi (Garrett)

—   Gonostylus simple (e.g. Figs 8A–D, p. 16) —   **2**

2   Abdominal tergite IX with an anal point (see p. 15). Gonostylus robust, strongly curved (Fig. 13C). Hypopygium Fig. 114C —
                        Lasiodiamesa sphagnicola (Kieffer)

—   Tergite IX without an anal point. Gonostylus slender, nearly straight. Hypopygium Fig. 114D —   **Paraboreochlus minutissimus** (Strobl)

SUBFAMILY TANYPODINAE

KEY TO 26 GENERA OF TANYPODINAE

1 Fourth tarsomere of all legs bilobed and much shorter than the fifth tarsomere (Fig. 14A)— CLINOTANYPUS Kieffer (p. 40, 1sp.)

— Fourth tarsomere cylindrical, not or only slightly shorter than the fifth— **2**

2 Wing cross-vein MCu proximal to cubital fork FCu (Figs 14B,C)— **3**

— Wing cross-vein MCu distal to cubital fork FCu (Fig. 14D)— **4**

3 Distance between FCu and MCu less than one-third the length of M_{3+4} (Fig. 14B)— TANYPUS Meigen (p. 54, 3spp.)

— Distance between FCu and MCu at least half the length of M_{3+4} (Fig. 14C)— PROCLADIUS Skuse (p. 52, 8spp.)

4(2) Thoracic postnotum covered with setae. Tibial spurs thorn-like, without lateral teeth— ANATOPYNIA Johannsen (p.40, 1sp.)

— Thoracic postnotum with a double row of long, bristle-like setae medially (arrow, Fig. 14E), or bare. Tibial spurs somewhat flattened with a row of lateral teeth (Figs 19B,D,G, p. 39), or lyrate (Fig. 19C)— **5**

5 Thoracic postnotum with a double row of long, bristle-like setae medially (may be abraded: check for presence of sockets) (arrow, Fig. 14E)— **6**

— Thoracic postnotum bare— **9**

6 Large pulvilli *p* present on the apex of the tarsus (Fig. 14F)— **7**

— Pulvilli absent (Fig. 14G)— **8**

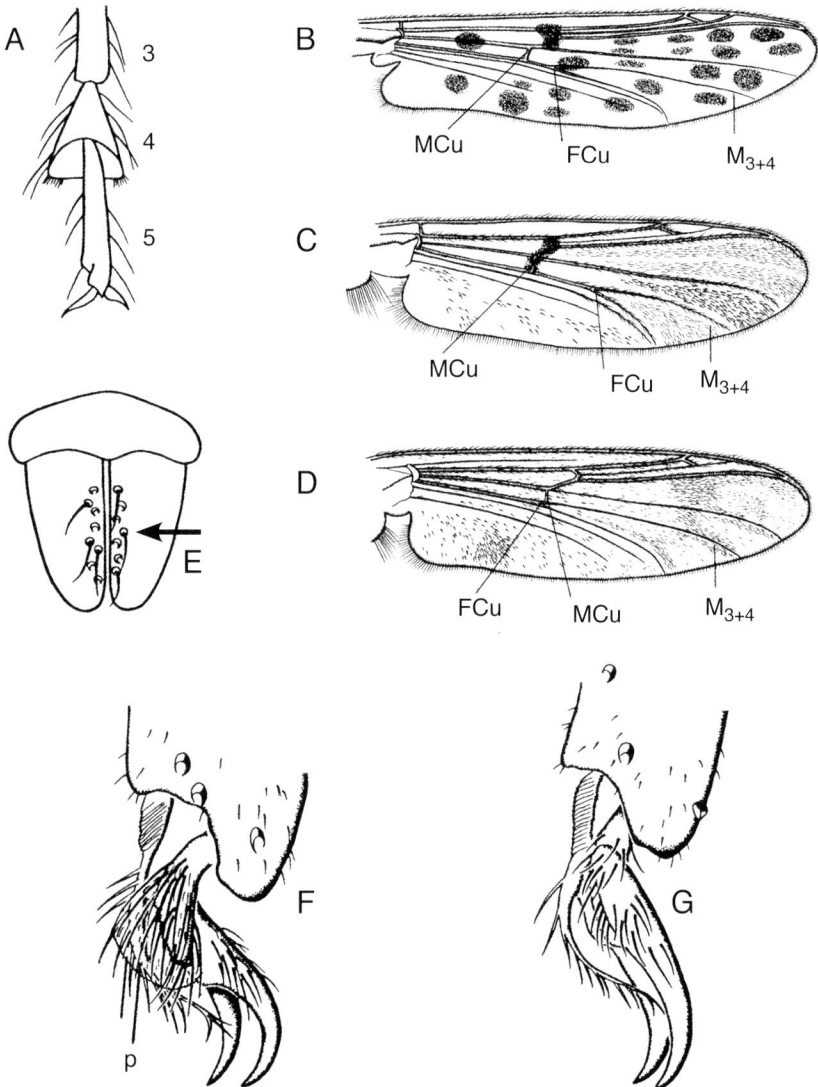

Fig. 14. **A:** terminal segments (3, 4, 5) of the tarsus of *Clinotanypus nervosus*. **B–D:** wings of: B, *Tanypus punctipennis*; C, *Procladius choreus*; D, *Macropelopia nebulosa*. **E:** postnotum of *Psectrotanypus varius*. **F, G:** foot of: F, *P. varius*, G, *M. nebulosa*.

7   Gonostylus *gs* long, about two-thirds length of gonocoxite *gc* (Fig. 15A). Wings with two dark transverse bands (Fig. 15B)—
                      PSECTROTANYPUS Kieffer (p. 41, 1sp.)

—   Gonostylus *gs* shorter, only about half as long as gonocoxite *gc* (Fig. 15C). Wings with three dark transverse bands (Fig. 15D)—
                      APSECTROTANYPUS Fittkau (p. 40, 1sp.)

8   Claws on tarsus are pointed distally (arrows, Fig. 15E). Thoracic scutum (Fig. 4, p. 12) with a small median hump (scutal tubercle *sct*, Fig. 15F)—   MACROPELOPIA Thienemann (p. 40, 3spp.)

—   Claws on tarsus are broad and serrated distally (arrows, Fig. 15G). Thoracic scutum without a median hump—
                      NATARSIA Fittkau (p. 42, 2spp.)

9(5)   Tibiae with three conspicuous dark rings (Fig. 15H). Tip of gonostylus *gs* unusual in form (arrow, Fig. 15I)—
                      ABLABESMYIA Johannsen (p. 42, 3spp.)

—   Tibiae unicolorous or with a single dark ring at one end. Gonostylus not as in Fig. 15I—   **10**

Fig. 15.   *(On page 33).* **A, B:** *Psectrotanypus varius:* A, gonostylus; B, wing. **C, D:** *Apsectrotanypus trifascipennis:* C, gonostylus, D, wing. **E, F:** *Macropelopia notata:* E, claws; F, lateral view of thorax (*sct,* scutal tubercle; see Fig. 4, p. 12). **G:** claws of *Natarsia nugax.* **H, I:** *Ablabesmyia monilis:* H, femur and tibia; I, gonostylus.

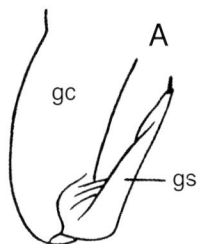

A

gc

gs

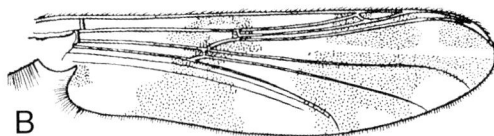

B

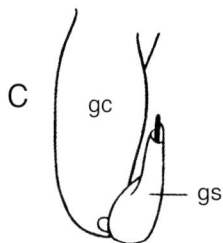

C

gc

gs

D

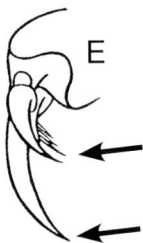

E

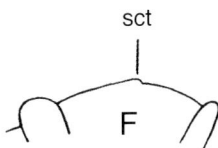

sct

F

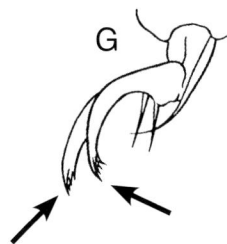

G

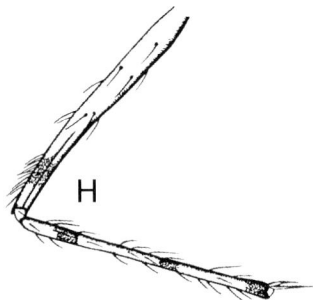

H

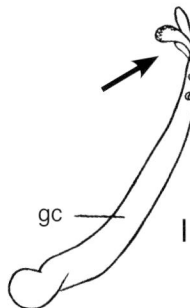

gc

I

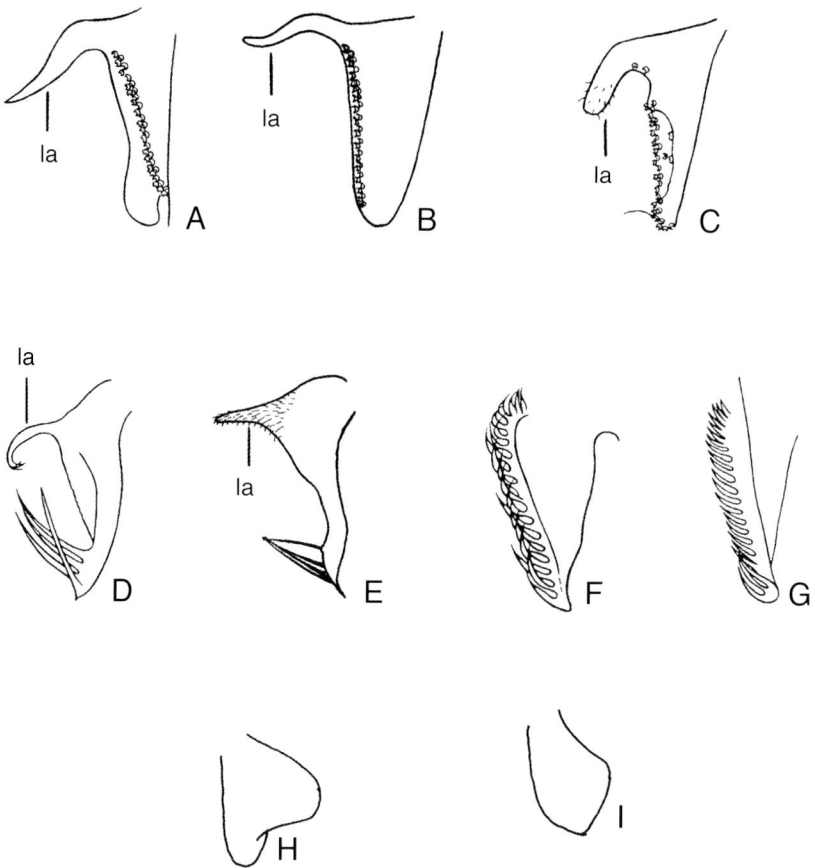

Fig. 16. **A–G:** basal gonocoxite lobes of: A, *Arctopelopia griseipennis*; B, *A. melanosoma*; C, *A. barbitarsis*; D, *Conchapelopia melanops*; E, *C. aagaardi*; F, *C. pallidula*; G, *C. viator*; H, *Thienemannimyia pseudocarnea*; I, *T. carnea*.

10   Gonocoxite with a basal lobe* (some with a lateral arm *la*) (e.g. Figs 16A–I)—   **11**

—   Gonocoxite without a basal lobe*—   **16**

*If in doubt, compare Figs 16A to 16I with the following examples of hypopygia which have basal lobes on the gonocoxite (Volume 2): 118A–D, 119A–C, 120A, 123C,D, 124A–D, 125A,B,D. Examples without basal lobes are Figs 119D, 120B–D, 121A–D, 123A,B, 125C.

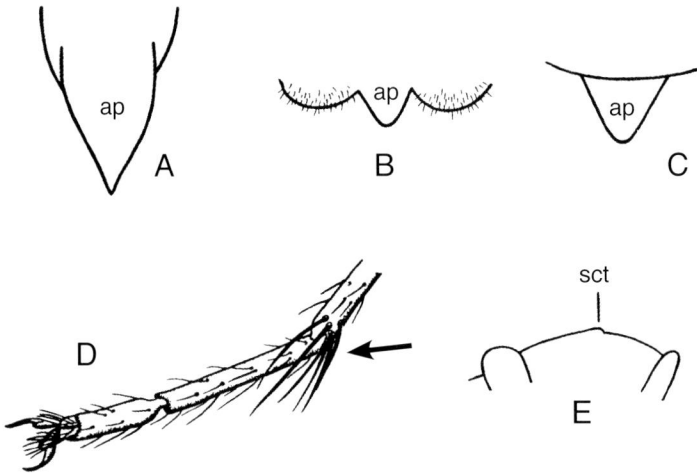

Fig. 17. **A–C:** Anal points of: A, *Xenopelopia nigricans*; B, *Telmatopelopia nemorum*; C, *Krenopelopia binotata*. **D:** tarsus of *Conchapelopia viator*; **E:** lateral view of thorax of *Macropelopia notata*, illustrating the scutal tubercle (*sct*; see Fig. 4, p. 12).

11   Anal point *ap* (Figs 8B–D, p. 16) rather slender, about twice as long as broad (Fig. 17A)—   XENOPELOPIA Fittkau (p. 50, 2spp.)

—   Anal point *ap* not well developed, broader than long (Figs 17B,C)— **12**

12   Third tarsomere of mid-leg with a distal group of strongly developed setae (arrow, Fig. 17D). Maxillary palps pale—   **13**

—   Third tarsomere of mid-leg without a group of particularly robust setae distally. Maxillary palps dark—   **14**

13   Thoracic scutum with a small median hump *sct* (Fig. 17E). Wings only faintly marked or not at all; cross-veins pale—
                              CONCHAPELOPIA Fittkau (p. 44, 6spp.)

—(13) Thoracic scutum without a median hump. Wings distinctly marked and with darkened cross-veins (Fig. 18A, p. 37)—
                              RHEOPELOPIA Fittkau (p. 47, 3spp.)

14(12) Wings with three distinct spots: one around the humeral cross-vein, one around the median cross-vein and one at the junction of R_1 and the costa (Fig. 18B)—   HAYESOMYIA Murray & Fittkau (p. 46, 1sp.)

—   If wings are marked, the markings traverse the membrane, or markings are pale on a dark background—   **15**

15   Hind-tibia with an apical comb (as in Fig. 7A, p. 15). Basal appendage of gonocoxite much less than half as long as gonocoxite (arrow, Fig. 18D)—   THIENEMANNIMYIA Fittkau (p. 48, 8spp.)

—   Hind-tibia without an apical comb. Basal appendage of gonocoxite half as long as gonocoxite (arrow, Fig. 18E)—
                              ARCTOPELOPIA Fittkau (p. 44, 3spp.)

16(10) Wing membrane distinctively patterned with pale spots on a dark background (Fig. 18C)—   GUTTIPELOPIA Fittkau (p. 45, 1sp.)

—   Wings unmarked or with dark areas on a pale background—   **17**

17   Eyes pubescent (see Fig. 3, p. 10)—
                              NILOTANYPUS Kieffer (p. 47, 1sp.)

—   Eyes bare—   **18**

18   Conspicuous pulvilli present on the apex of the tarsus (as in Figs 6, p. 14 and 14F, p. 31). Apex of hind-tibia with 2 spurs, each with 10 or more teeth (Fig. 18F); comb absent—
                              TRISSOPELOPIA Kieffer (p. 50, 1sp.)

—   Pulvilli on apex of tarsus are absent or very small. Apex of hind-tibia with 0–2 spurs, spurs with fewer teeth (Fig. 18G); comb present (Fig. 18G)—   **19**

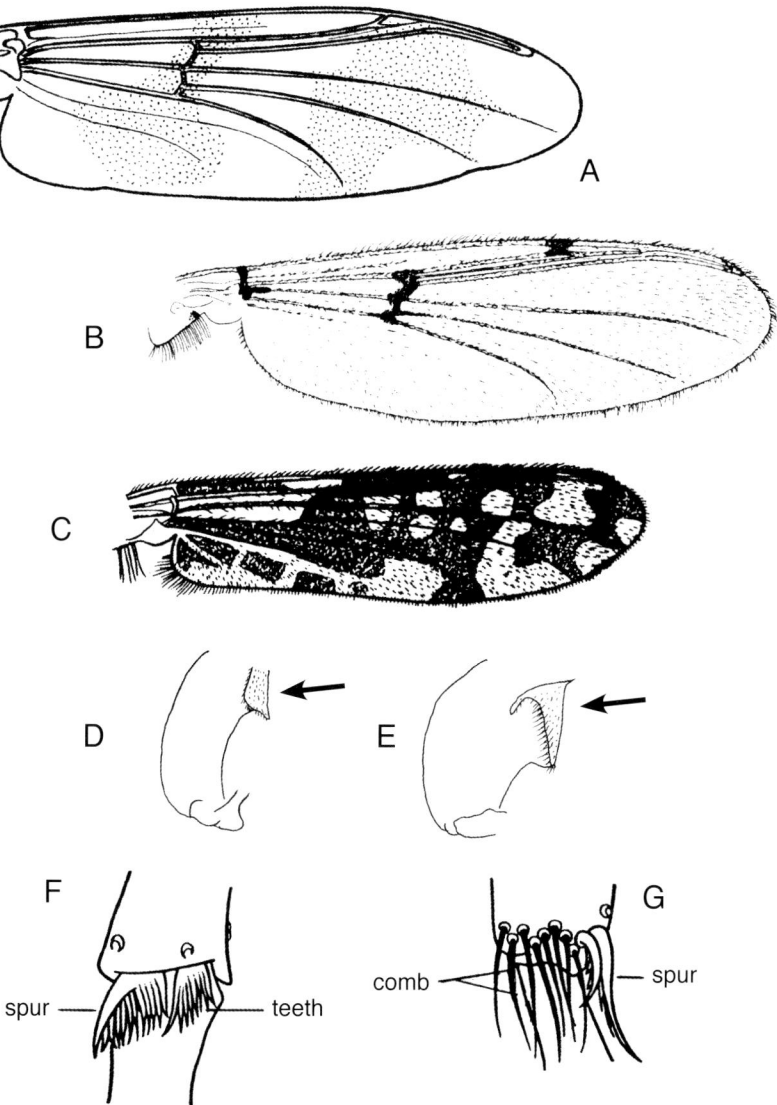

Fig. 18. **A–C:** wings of: A, *Rheopelopia ornata*; B, *Hayesomyia tripunctata*; C, *Guttipelopia guttipennis*. **D, E:** gonocoxites and appendages of: D, *Thienemannimyia fuscipes*; E, *Arctopelopia barbitarsus*. **F:** spurs (2) with teeth on hind-tibia of *Trissopelopia longimana*. **G:** spurs (2) and comb of strong setae on hind-tibia of *Zavrelimyia hirtimana*.

19   Hypopygium with very long darkened phallapodemes (p. 17), extending
      to about half-way along the gonocoxite (Fig. 19A). Apex of hind-tibia
      with two spurs, the smaller spur with an apical tooth and only two small
      lateral teeth (Fig. 19B)—   PARAMERINA Fittkau (p. 47, 2spp.)

—   Phallapodemes not so strongly developed, often small and inconspicuous.
      If hind-tibia with 2 spurs, the smaller spur has more than 3 teeth—   **20**

20   Hind-tibia without an apical spur—
                              LABRUNDINIA Fittkau (p. 46, 1sp.)

—   Hind-tibia with 1 or 2 apical spurs—   **21**

21   Apex of hind-tibia with only 1 spur—
                              MONOPELOPIA Fittkau (p. 46, 1sp.)

—   Apex of hind-tibia with 2 spurs—   **22**

22   Thoracic scutum with a tubercle (cf. *sct* in Fig. 17E, p. 35). Hind-tibial
      spurs of similar size, lyrate (Fig. 19C)— LARSIA Fittkau (p. 46, 2spp.)

—   Thoracic scutum without a tubercle. Inner spur *is* at the apex of hind-tibia
      much larger than the outer spur (Fig. 19D)—   **23**

23   Anal tergite expanded laterally to form a rounded lobe on each side of the
      anal point *ap* (Fig. 19E)—   TELMATOPELOPIA Fittkau (p. 47, 1sp.)

—   Anal tergite with a conical anal point *ap* (Fig. 19F)—   **24**

24   Wing vein R_{2+3}* absent. Thorax black, abdomen distinctively patterned
      with yellow and black bands—
                              SCHINERIELLA Murray & Fittkau (p. 47, 1sp.)

—   Wing vein R_{2+3}* present. Body coloration subdued—   **25**

      *See Fig. 5, p. 13.

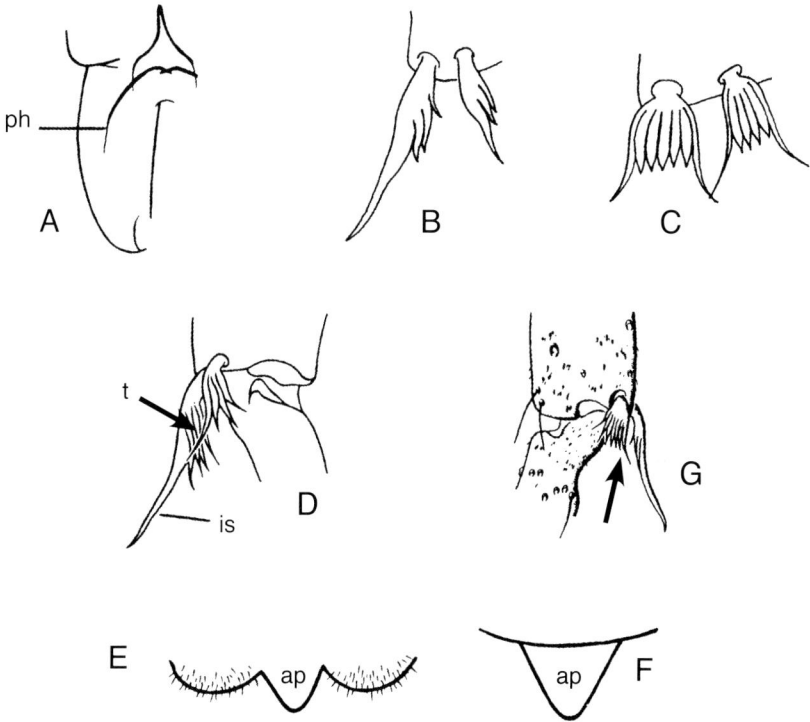

Fig. 19. **A:** gonocoxite of *Paramerina cingulata*, showing the conspicuously darkened phallapodeme (ph). **B–D:** tibial spurs of: B, *Paramerina cingulata*; C, *Larsia curticalcar*; D, *Krenopelopia binotata*. **E, F:** anal points of: E, *Telmatopelopia nemorum*; F, *Krenopelopia binotata*. **G:** tibial spur of *Zavrelimyia nubila*.

25 Wing macrotrichia dark, producing an overall grey effect or distinct transverse bands (see Figs 24C–E, p. 51). Smaller outer spur at the apex of hind-tibia with main 'tooth' short, scarcely longer than the accessory 'teeth' (arrow, Fig. 19G) — ZAVRELIMYIA Fittkau (p. 50, 4spp.)

— Wing macrotrichia pale. Smaller outer spur at the apex of hind-tibia with a long main 'tooth' *t* (Fig. 19D) — KRENOPELOPIA Fittkau (p. 46, 2spp.)

KEYS TO 63 SPECIES IN 26 GENERA OF SUBFAMILY TANYPODINAE

Tribe ANATOPYNIINI

Genus ANATOPYNIA Johannsen

The single species is large (wing length up to 7.5 mm) and distinctive on account of its simple tibial spurs and dense covering of setae on the head and thorax. Hypopygium Fig. 115A—   **Anatopynia plumipes** (Fries)

Tribe COELOTANYPODINI

Genus CLINOTANYPUS Kieffer

Only one species occurs in Britain and Ireland, readily recognisable by the very short, bilobed fourth tarsal segment (Fig. 14A, p. 31). Hypopygium Fig. 115B—   **Clinotanypus nervosus** (Meigen)

Tribe MACROPELOPIINI

Genus APSECTROTANYPUS Fittkau

There is only one European representative of this genus, which should be identified easily from the characters given in the key to genera (p. 32). The wings have three dark bands (Fig. 15D, p. 33). Hypopygium Fig. 115C—
Apsectrotanypus trifascipennis (Zetterstedt)

Genus MACROPELOPIA Thienemann

1   Wing cross-vein RM darkened, wing otherwise unmarked. Gonocoxite without an obvious basal lobe; gonostylus straight, nearly parallel-sided to the apical third, then narrowed to the tip (Fig. 20A). Hypopygium Fig. 115D—   **Macropelopia adaucta** Kieffer

—   Wing membrane with distinct dark markings (but note that in teneral and abraded specimens these may be obscure or absent). *EITHER:* gonocoxite with a basal lobe (Fig. 20C), *OR:* gonostylus narrowed to an attenuated, curved tip from half-way (Fig. 20B)—   **2**

2   Gonocoxite with a small lobe bearing setae (arrow, Fig. 20C). Gonostylus as in *M. adaucta* (Fig. 20A). Wing as in Fig. 20D. Hypopygium Fig. 116A—   **Macropelopia notata** (Meigen)

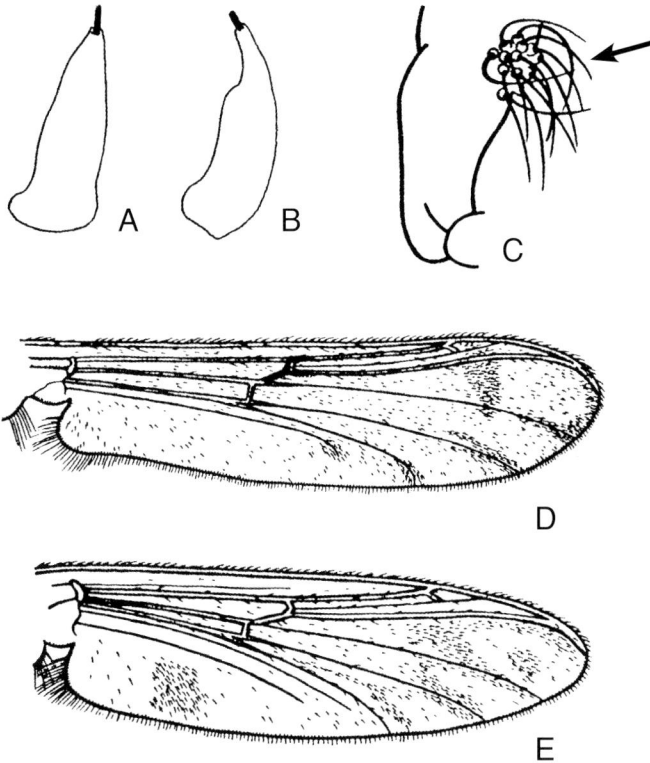

Fig. 20. **A, B:** gonostyli of: A, *Macropelopia adaucta*; B, *M. nebulosa*. **C:** gonocoxite of *M. notata*. **D, E:** wings of: D, *M. notata*; E, *M. nebulosa*.

—(2) Gonocoxite without a lobe; gonostylus narrowed from half-way to an attenuated curved tip (Fig. 20B). Wing as in Fig. 20E. Hypopygium Fig. 116B— **Macropelopia nebulosa** (Meigen)

Genus PSECTROTANYPUS Kieffer

Only one species of this genus is known from Britain and Ireland. The characters given in the key to genera (see p. 32) should suffice to identify it. The wing is shown in Fig. 15B (p. 33). Hypopygium Fig. 116C— **Psectrotanypus varius** (Fabricius)

Tribe NATARSIINI

Genus NATARSIA Fittkau

1   Wings with conspicuous dark markings (Fig. 21A). Gonostylus
     swollen basally (arrow, Fig. 21C). Hypopygium Fig. 116D—
                              Natarsia punctata (Fabricius)

—   Wings unmarked except for a dark fleck around the cross-veins (Fig.
     21B). Gonostylus rounded basally (arrow, Fig. 21D). Hypopygium
     Fig. 117A—   **Natarsia nugax** (Walker)

Tribe PENTANEURINI

Genus ABLABESMYIA Johannsen

This genus is easily distinguished by the presence of three dark rings on the
tibiae of the legs (Fig. 21E) and by the characteristic form of the gonostylus
(Fig. 21F). Basally the hypopygium bears two pairs of appendages, of which
the more ventral pair are more or less spinose (Figs 21G–I) whilst the dorsal
pair are in the form of pubescent pads (Fig. 21G) or brushes (Figs 21H,I).

1   Dorsal appendages of hypopygium pad-like (arrow, Fig. 21G). Antennal
     ratio (p. 9) about 2.5. Hypopygium Fig. 117B—
                              Ablabesmyia phatta (Egger)

—   Dorsal appendages brush-like (arrows, Figs 21H,I). Antennal ratio 2.0 or
     less—   **2**

2   Ventral appendages of hypopygium sinuous, twice as long as the dorsal
     appendages (Fig. 21H). Hypopygium Fig. 117C—
                              Ablabesmyia monilis (L.)

—   Ventral appendages straight, only one-third longer than the dorsal
     appendages (Fig. 21I). Hypopygium Fig. 117D—
                              Ablabesmyia longistyla Fittkau

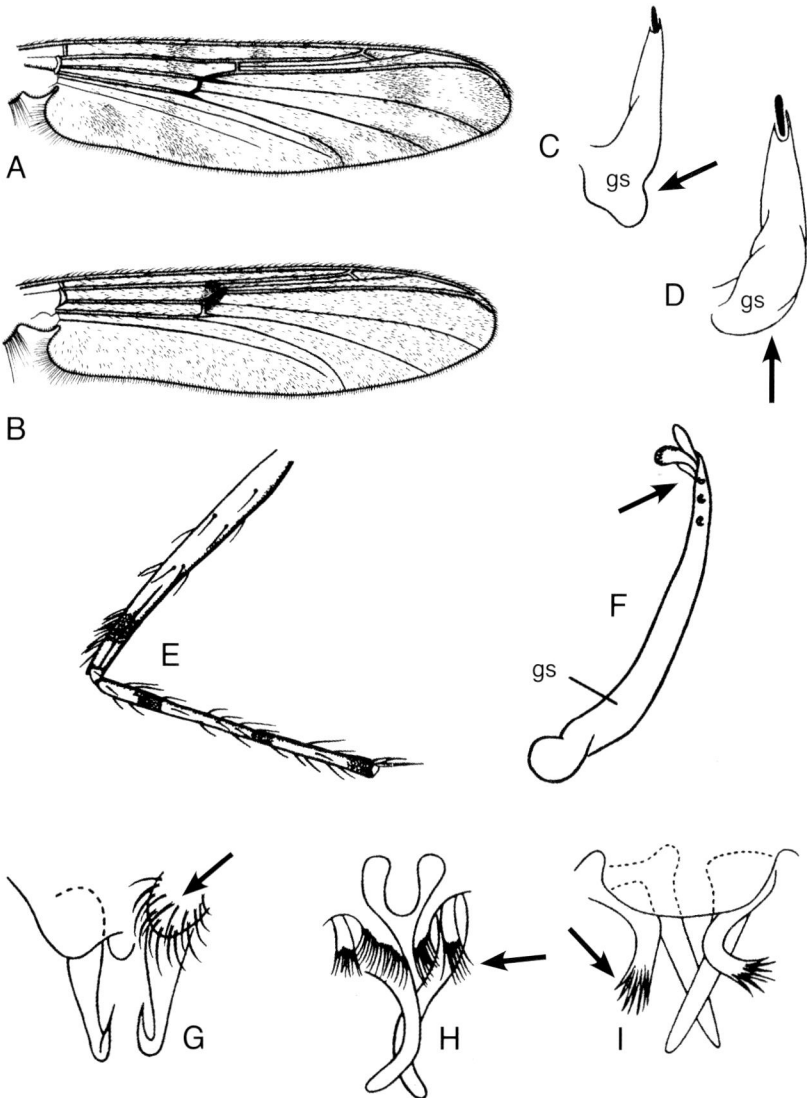

Fig. 21. **A, B:** wings of: A, *Natarsia punctata*; B, *N. nugax*. **C, D:** gonostyli of: C, *N. punctata*; D, *N. nugax*. **E, F:** *Ablabesmyia monilis*: E, tibia and tarsus; F, gonostylus. **G–I:** basal appendages of hypopygium (dorsal view) of: G, *Ablabesmyia phatta*; H, *A. monilis*; I, *A. longistyla*.

Genus ARCTOPELOPIA Fittkau

1   Colour yellowish with darker markings; abdominal tergites II–IV with the anterior third dark. Lobe of gonocoxite with a slender lateral arm *la* which tapers to a point, more than half as long as the elongate triangular main part of the lobe which bears a pronounced tubercle *t* near its apex (Fig. 22A). Hypopygium Fig. 118A—

   Arctopelopia griseipennis (van der Wulp)

—   Colour dark with indistinct darker markings; abdominal tergites with anterior bands extending over anterior half. Lateral arm *la* of gonocoxite lobe pointed or blunt at the tip (Figs 22B,C); if pointed the main lobe is broadly rounded—   **2**

2   Lateral arm *la* of gonocoxite lobe narrowed to a pointed tip, main lobe broadly rounded (Fig. 20B). Pre-episternum (Fig. 4, p. 12) with several setae. Hypopygium Fig. 118B—

   Arctopelopia melanosoma (Goetghebuer)

—   Lateral arm *la* of gonocoxite lobe short and rounded distally, main lobe elongate, triangular (Fig. 22C). Pre-episternum without setae. Hypopygium Fig. 118C—   **Arctopelopia barbitarsis** (Zetterstedt)

Genus CONCHAPELOPIA Fittkau

1   Lobe of gonocoxite subapically with a group of long, tapering processes *tp* and with a lateral arm *la* at the base (e.g. Figs 22D,E)—   **2**

—   Lobe of gonocoxite with shorter processes along the entire lateral margin (arrows, Figs 22F,G)—   **3**

2   Mainly creamy-yellow. Lateral arm *la* of gonocoxite lobe parallel-sided for much of its length, rounded apically and curved posteriorly, with sparse bristly setae (Fig. 22D). Hypopygium Fig. 118D—

   Conchapelopia melanops (Meigen)

—   Mainly brown. Lateral arm *la* of gonocoxite lobe triangularly tapered to the acute tip, pubescent (Fig. 20E). Hypopygium Fig. 119A—

   Conchapelopia aagaardi Murray

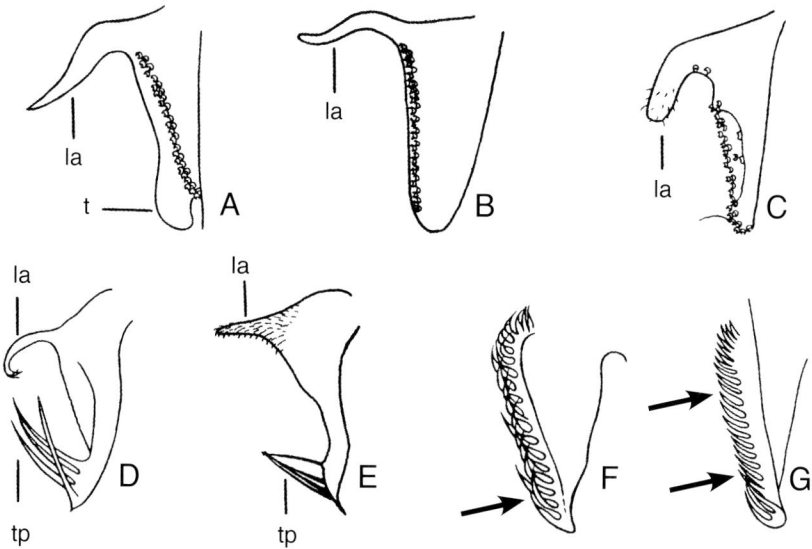

Fig. 22. **A–G:** basal gonocoxite lobes of: A, *Arctopelopia griseipennis*; B, *A. melanosoma*; C, *A. barbitarsis*; D, *Conchapelopia melanops*; E, *C. aagaardi*; F, *C. pallidula*; G, *C. viator*.

3(1) Abdominal tergites VII and VIII mostly brown, remainder of abdomen yellowish. Processes of gonocoxite lobe expanded subapically (arrow, Fig. 22F). Hypopygium Fig. 119B—
Conchapelopia pallidula (Meigen)
and **Conchapelopia hittmairorum** Michiels & Spies [see p. 152, Vol. 2]

— Anterior halves of abdominal tergites VII and VIII brown, remainder pale. Processes of gonocoxite lobe uniformly tapered to the apex (arrows, Fig. 22G). Hypopygium Fig. 119C—
Conchapelopia viator (Kieffer)
and **Conchapelopia triannulata** (Goetghebuer) [see p. 153, Vol. 2]

Genus GUTTIPELOPIA Fittkau

The sole representative of this genus in Britain and Ireland is readily identified from the distinctive pattern of the wing markings (Fig. 18C, p. 37). Hypopygium Fig. 119D—   **Guttipelopia guttipennis** (van der Wulp)

Genus HAYESOMYIA Murray & Fittkau

A single species of this genus is known to occur in Europe. It is easily identifiable from the arrangement of 3 dark spots on the wing membrane (one around humeral cross-vein, one around median cross-vein and one at junction of R_1 and the costa) and by the bifurcate form of the basal lobe of the gonocoxite. Hypopygium Fig. 120A—   **Hayesomyia tripunctata** (Goetghebuer)

Genus KRENOPELOPIA Fittkau

1   Abdomen with a dark fleck close to the anterior margin of abdominal tergites VI and VII. Hypopygium Fig. 120B—
                    Krenopelopia binotata (Wiedemann)

—   Abdominal tergites I and II all white, III to VI with brown anterior margins, VII and VIII more extensively brown. Hypopygium Fig. 120C—   **Krenopelopia nigropunctata** (Staeger)

Genus LABRUNDINIA Fittkau

The single European species is characterised by its small size (wing length 1.5–2.0 mm) and the absence of spurs on the hind-tibiae. Hypopygium Fig. 120D—   **Labrundinia longipalpis** (Goetghebuer)

Genus LARSIA Fittkau

1   Longest ventral setae of hind-femur less than three times as long as the maximum width of the femur. Hypopygium Fig. 121A—
                    Larsia curticalcar (Kieffer)

—   Longest ventral setae of hind-femur four or more times as long as the maximum width of the femur. Hypopygium Fig. 121B—
                    Larsia atrocincta (Goetghebuer)

Genus MONOPELOPIA Fittkau

The single European species is small (wing length 2.0–2.5 mm), differing from *Labrundinia* (see above) in the possession of a short spur on the hind-tibia. Hypopygium Fig. 121C—   **Monopelopia tenuicalcar** (Kieffer)

Genus NILOTANYPUS Kieffer

The only species recorded for Britain and Ireland is easily identified by the presence of pubescent eyes (Fig. 3B, p. 10) and small size (wing length 1.5–2.0 mm). Hypopygium Fig. 121D— **Nilotanypus dubius** (Meigen)

Genus PARAMERINA Fittkau

1 Abdominal tergites II and V pale. Hypopygium Fig. 122A—
Paramerina divisa (Walker)

— Abdominal tergites II and V mainly brown, with narrowly pale anterior margins, or all brown. Hypopygium Fig. 122B—
Paramerina cingulata (Walker)

Genus RHEOPELOPIA Fittkau

1 Large pulvilli present on the apex of the tarsus (see Fig. 6, p. 14). Hypopygium Fig. 122C— **Rheopelopia ornata** (Meigen)

— Pulvilli absent from the tarsus— **2**

2 Tibiae with a dark ring basally. Hypopygium similar to that of the next species— **Rheopelopia eximia** (Edwards)

— Tibiae without a dark basal ring. Hypopygium Fig. 122D—
Rheopelopia maculipennis (Zetterstedt)

Genus SCHINERIELLA Murray & Fittkau

The single species of this genus is easily recognised by its black thorax and black and yellow banded abdomen. Hypopygium Fig. 123A—
Schineriella schineri (Strobl)

Genus TELMATOPELOPIA Fittkau

A monospecific genus, characterised by the unusual shape of the anal point *ap* (Fig. 19F, p. 39). Hypopygium Fig. 123B—
Telmatopelopia nemorum (Goetghebuer)

Genus THIENEMANNIMYIA Fittkau

1   Bases of tibiae and tips of femora each with a dark ring—   **2**

—   Tibial bases not ringed; femora with or without a dark ring—   **3**

2   Anterior margin of abdominal tergite II with three dark spots which may be fused to form a continuous band (Fig. 23A). Hypopygium Fig. 123C—   **Thienemannimyia lentiginosa** (Fries)

—   Anterior margin of abdominal tergite II with one pair of dark spots (Fig. 23B). Hypopygium Fig. 123D—   **Thienemannimyia laeta** (Meigen)

3(1) Tips of femora with a dark ring—   **4**

—   Femora without apical rings—   **5**

4   Wings with a faint shade due to dark hairs from the middle of cell r_{4+5} to the end of vein Cu_1. Hypopygium Fig. 124A—   **Thienemannimyia woodi** (Edwards)

—   Wings unmarked. Hypopygium Fig. 124B—   **Thienemannimyia geijskesi** (Goetghebuer)

5(3) Gonostylus with a short posterior process (arrow, Fig. 23C). Hypopygium Fig. 124C—   **Thienemannimyia fusciceps** (Edwards)

—   Gonostylus lacking such a process—   **6**

6   Gonostylus more or less parallel-sided for basal two-thirds (arrow, Fig. 23D). Dark markings on wing membrane restricted to cross-veins and/or beyond (Fig. 23H)—   **7**

—   Gonostylus robust, expanded medially (arrow, Fig. 23E). Dark markings on wing membrane also present proximal to cross-veins (arrows, Fig. 23I). Hypopygium Fig. 124D—   **Thienemannimyia northumbrica** (Edwards)

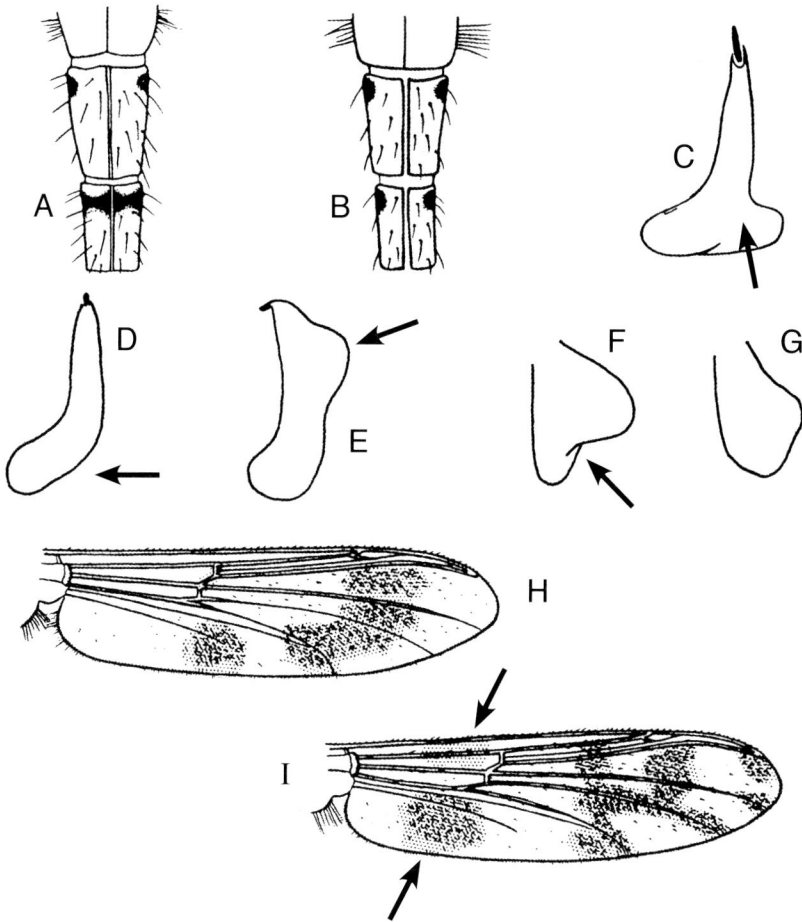

Fig. 23. **A, B:** anterior abdominal tergites I and II of: A, *Thienemannimyia lentiginosa*; B, *T. laeta.* **C–E:** gonostyli of: C, *T. fusciceps*; D, *T. carnea*; E, *T. northumbrica.* **F, G:** basal lobes of gonocoxites of: *T. pseudocarnea*; G, *T. carnea.* **H, I:** wings of: H, *T. carnea*; I, *T. northumbrica.*

7   Gonocoxite lobe concave apically (arrow, Fig. 23F). Hypopygium Fig. 125A—   **Thienemannimyia pseudocarnea** Murray

—   Gonocoxite lobe straight or slightly convex apically (Fig. 23G). Hypopygium Fig. 125B—   **Thienemannimyia carnea** (Fabricius)

Genus TRISSOPELOPIA Kieffer

Only one species has been recorded from Britain and Ireland. It is predominantly reddish-brown in colour, with the scutal stripes scarcely differentiated. Hypopygium Fig. 125C—   **Trissopelopia longimana** (Staeger)

Genus XENOPELOPIA Fittkau

1   Lobe of gonocoxite bearing a row of long, slender processes along the entire median margin (Fig. 24A). Hypopygium Fig. 125D—
                    Xenopelopia nigricans (Goetghebuer)

—   Lobe of gonocoxite bearing two groups of slender processes medially, separated by a short bare section (Fig. 24B). Hypopygium Fig. 126A—
                    Xenopelopia falcigera (Kieffer)

Genus ZAVRELIMYIA Fittkau

1   Wings uniformly dark, without distinct markings. Hypopygium Fig. 126B—   **Zavrelimyia melanura** (Meigen)

—   Wings with two or three distinctly darkened transverse bands (Figs 24C–E)—   **2**

2   Wings with three dark bands distal to the cross-veins (Fig. 24C). Hypopygium as in the next species— **Zavrelimyia hirtimana** (Kieffer)

—   Wings with only two dark bands—   **3**

3   Tip of wing vein Cu_1 surrounded by a separate dark field (arrow, Fig. 24D). Hypopygium Fig. 126C—   **Zavrelimyia barbatipes** (Kieffer)

—   Area surrounding tip of wing vein Cu_1 pale (arrow, Fig. 24E). Hypopygium Fig. 126D—   **Zavrelimyia nubila** (Meigen)

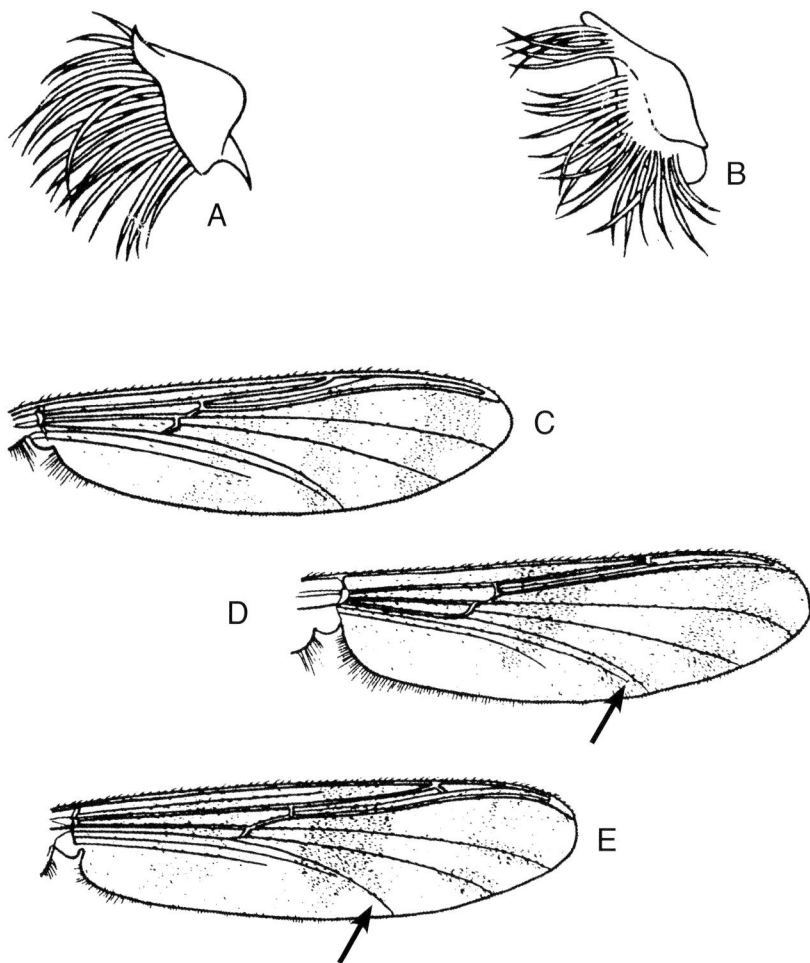

Fig. 24. **A, B:** basal lobes of gonocoxite of: A, *Xenopelopia nigricans*; B, *X. falcigera*. **C–E:** wings of: C, *Zavrelimyia hirtimana*; D, *Z. barbatipes*; E, *Z. nubila*.

Tribe PROCLADIINI

Genus PROCLADIUS Skuse

1   Wing membrane with macrotrichia, at least apically—
(HOLOTANYPUS) **2**

—   Wing membrane lacking macrotrichia—   (PSILOTANYPUS) **6**

2   Gonostylus without a posterior process (Fig. 25A). Hypopygium
Fig. 127A—   **Procladius (Holotanypus) simplicistylus** Freeman

—   Gonostylus with a distinct posterior process (arrows, Figs. 25B–D)— **3**

3   Length of posterior process of gonostylus at least three times its diameter
(arrows, Figs 25C,D). Abdomen black—   **4**

—   Length of posterior process of gonostylus no more than twice its diameter
(e.g. Fig. 25B). Abdominal tergites pale posteriorly—   **5**

4   Phallapodeme *ph* (see p. 17) with a cluster of small 'teeth' distally (Fig.
25H). Hypopygium Fig. 127B— **Procladius (H.) signatus** (Zetterstedt)

—   Phallapodeme simple. Hypopygium Fig. 127C—
Procladius (H.) crassinervis (Zetterstedt)

5(3) Posterior process of gonostylus scarcely as long as broad. Wing without
a dark shade over distal half. Hypopygium Fig. 127D—
Procladius (H.) sagittalis (Kieffer)

—   Posterior process of gonostylus about twice as long as broad (arrow,
Fig. 25B). Wing with a dark shade over distal half (best seen in a fresh
specimen). Hypopygium Fig. 128A—
Procladius (H.) choreus (Meigen)

N.B.   We are unable to separate *P. choreus* (Meig.), sensu Coe (1950), from *P. culiciformis*
(L.) sensu Coe (1950).

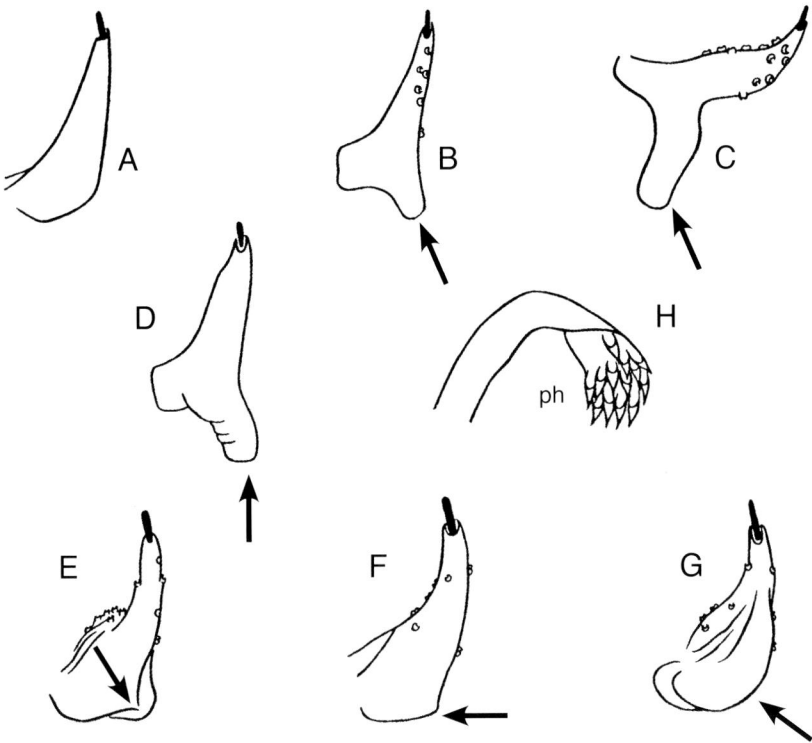

Fig. 25. **A–G:** gonostyli of: A, *Procladius simplicistylus*; B, *P. choreus*; C, *P. signatus*; D, *P. crassinervis*; E, *P. rufovittatus*; F, *P. lugens*; G, *P. flavifrons*. **H:** phallapodeme (ph) of *P. signatus*.

6(1) Gonostylus with a pronounced internal swelling and a short posterior process (arrow, Fig. 25E). Background colour of thoracic scutum yellowish. Hypopygium Fig. 128B—
   Procladius (Psilotanypus) rufovittatus (van der Wulp)

— Gonostylus not as above. Thorax black—   **7**

7 Posterior margin of gonostylus abruptly angled (arrow, Fig. 25F). Hypopygium Fig. 128C—   **Procladius (Ps.) lugens** Kieffer

— Posterior margin of gonostylus smoothly rounded (arrow, Fig. 25G). Hypopygium Fig. 128D—   **Procladius (Ps.) flavifrons** Edwards

Tribe TANYPODINI

Genus TANYPUS Meigen

1   Wings without spots except over cross-veins and, in dark individuals, a streak along middle of M_{1+2} (Fig. 26A). Hypopygium Fig. 129A —
                                                    Tanypus vilipennis (Kieffer)

—   Wings spotted though the spots may be faint —   **2**

2   Wing spots usually dark; spots small, e.g. middle anterior pair in cell r_{4+5} (arrows, Fig. 26B) separated by more than the length of one of them, spot over RM (Fig. 26B) extending little into cells r and r_{4+5}; spots in anal cell distinct, basal spot somewhat circular in shape (Fig. 26B). Tarsomeres 4 and 5 brown. Hypopygium Fig. 129B —
                                                 Tanypus punctipennis Meigen

—   Wing spots usually pale; spots larger, e.g. middle anterior pair in cell r_{4+5} (arrows, Fig. 26C) separated by less than their length, spot over RM (Fig. 26C) oval to circular in shape; spots in anal cell large, more diffuse, tending to amalgamate (Fig. 26C). Tarsomeres 4 and 5 not darkened. Hypopygium Fig. 129C —   **Tanypus kraatzi** (Kieffer)

SUBFAMILY TELMATOGETONINAE

KEY TO 2 GENERA AND 3 SPECIES OF TELMATOGETONINAE

1   Wings greatly reduced. Maxillary palps with one or two distinct segments only. Hypopygium Fig. 130A —   **Telmatogeton pectinatus** (Deby)

—   Wings normally developed. Maxillary palps with four distinct segments. Hypopygium Fig. 130B —   **Thalassomyia frauenfeldi** Schiner
                  and **Telmatogeton japonicus** Tokunaga [see p. 154, Vol. 2]

SUBFAMILY DIAMESINAE

KEY TO 7 GENERA OF DIAMESINAE

1   Antepronotum (pp. 11–12) bearing a group of setae dorsally (arrow, Fig. 26D) —   PROTANYPUS Kieffer (p. 61, 1sp.)

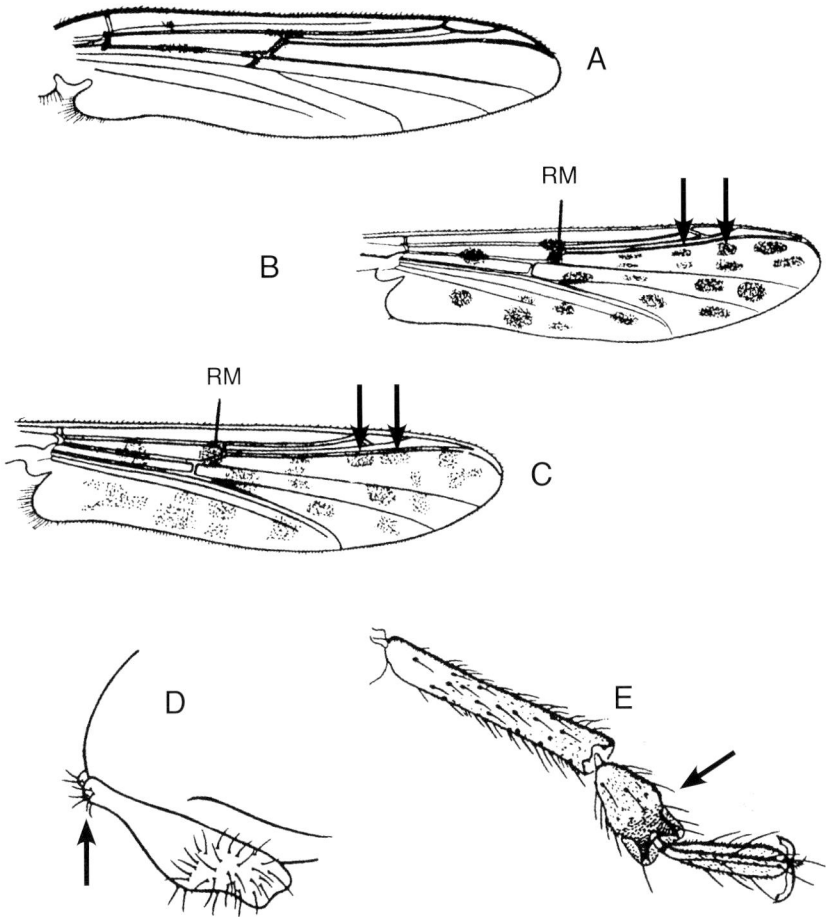

Fig. 26. **A-C:** wings of: A, *Tanypus vilipennis*; B, *T. punctipennis*; C, *T. kraatzi* (macrotrichia are present on the membrane of the *Tanypus* species, but have been omitted from the drawings). **D:** antepronotum of *Protanypus morio*. **E:** distal tarsal segments of *Diamesa cinerella*.

—   Antepronotum bare dorsally—   **2**

2   Fourth tarsomere cordiform (arrow, Fig. 26E)—   **3**

—   Fourth tarsomere cylindrical—   **5**

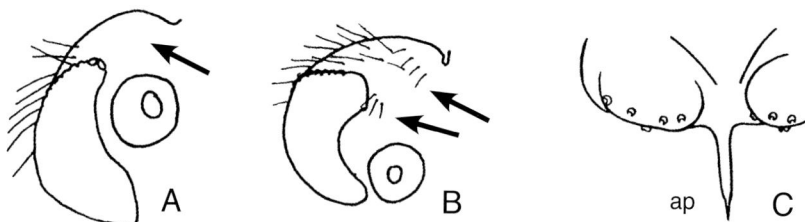

Fig. 27. **A, B:** head setation of: A, *Potthastia gaedii*; B, *Diamesa tonsa*. **C:** anal point of *Pseudodiamesa branickii*;

3   Head without inner vertical setae (arrow, Fig. 27A)—
                              POTTHASTIA Kieffer (p. 58, 4spp.)

—   Head with inner vertical setae (arrows, Fig. 27B)—   **4**

4   Microtrichia present between all ommatidia of the eye—
                              DIAMESA Meigen (p. 57, 7spp.)

—   Microtrichia present only between ommatidia near the inner margin of
       the eye—   PSEUDOKIEFFERIELLA Zavrel (p. 60, 1sp.)

5(2)   Head without inner vertical setae (e.g. arrow, Fig. 27A). Lateral aedeagal
       lobe (p. 17) spiniferous (see Fig. 134A)—
                              SYMPOTTHASTIA Pagast (p. 60, 1sp.)

—   Head with inner vertical setae (e.g. arrows, Fig. 27B). Lateral aedeagal
       lobe without spines—   **6**

6   Hypopygium with an anal point *ap* (Fig. 27C)—
                              PSEUDODIAMESA Goetghebuer (p. 60, 2spp.)

—   Anal point absent—   SYNDIAMESA Kieffer (p. 60, 1sp.)

KEYS TO 17 SPECIES IN 7 GENERA
OF SUBFAMILY DIAMESINAE

Tribe DIAMESINI

Genus DIAMESA Meigen

1   Inner margin of gonostylus expanded basally (arrow, Fig 28A) or medially (arrow, Fig. 28B)—   **2**

—   Inner margin of gonostylus not expanded—   **4**

2   Gonostylus expanded medially (Fig. 28B). Hypopygium Fig. 130C—
                                                          Diamesa insignipes Kieffer

—   Basal half of gonostylus expanded (arrows), distal portion rather slender (Figs 28A,C)—   **3**

3   Gonocoxite lobe with two branches (arrows, Fig. 28D), the longer branch with a tuft of longer setae at the tip. Hypopygium Fig. 130D—
                                                          Diamesa tonsa (Haliday)

—   Gonocoxite lobe unbranched, covered with short setae that are even in length (arrow, Fig. 28E). Hypopygium Fig. 131A—
                                                          Diamesa cinerella Meigen

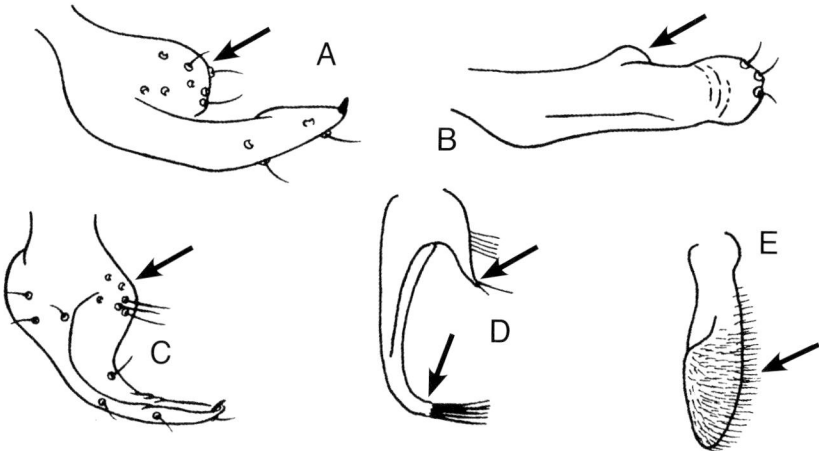

Fig. 28.   **A–C:** gonostyli of: A, *Diamesa tonsa*; B, *D. insignipes*; C, *D. cinerella*. **D, E:** gonocoxite lobes of: D, *D. tonsa*; E, *D. cinerella*.

4(2) Gonocoxite with one or two long, finger-like lobes (arrows, Figs 29A,B)— **5**

— Gonocoxite not as above— **6**

5 Anal point *ap* very long, somewhat swollen in the distal half (arrow, Fig. 29C). Eyes hairy (p. 9). Hypopygium Fig. 131B—
Diamesa bohemani Goetghebuer

— Anal point *ap* relatively slender and parallel-sided (Fig. 29D). Eyes bare. Hypopygium Fig. 131C— **Diamesa latitarsis** (Goetghebuer)

6(4) Anal point absent. Inner margin of gonostylus strongly chitinised distally and produced into a short 'tooth' (arrow, Fig. 29G). Hypopygium Fig. 131D— **Diamesa incallida** Walker

— Anal point *ap* short and triangular, overlying the anal tergite (Fig. 29E). Gonostylus not as above. Hypopygium Fig. 132A—
Diamesa permacra Walker

Genus POTTHASTIA Kieffer

1 Inner margin of gonostylus deeply divided into two lobes (arrows, Fig. 29H). Anal point very small or absent. Hypopygium Fig. 132B—
Potthastia gaedii (Meigen)

— Gonostylus not as above— **2**

2 Short anal point *ap* present (Fig. 23F). Hypopygium Fig. 132C—
Potthastia montium (Edwards)

— Anal point absent— **3**

3 All wing veins pale. In fresh specimens the scutal stripes are dull black, the whole thorax with a whitish bloom. Hypopygium Fig. 132D—
Potthastia longimanus (Kieffer)

— Anterior wing veins blackish. In fresh specimens the scutal stripes are shining black. Hypopygium Fig. 133A—**Potthastia pastoris** (Edwards)

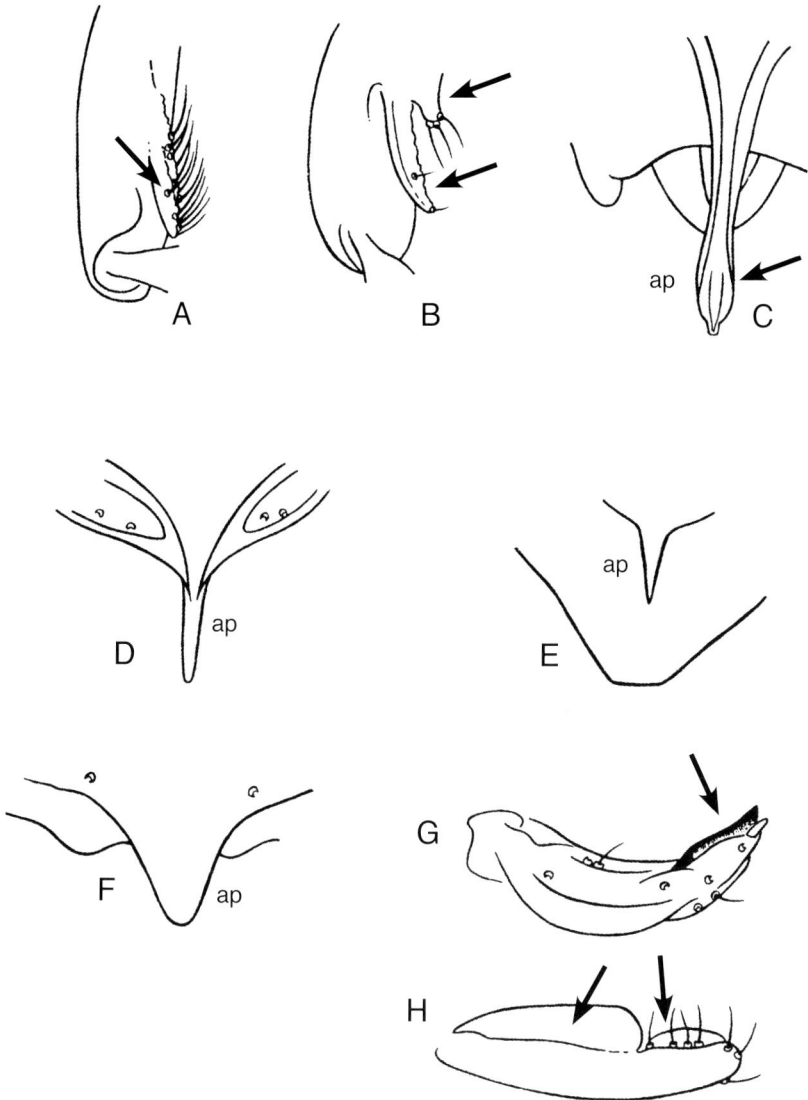

Fig. 29. **A, B:** gonocoxi and gonocoxal lobes of: A, *Diamesa bohemani*; B, *D. latitarsis*; **C–F:** anal points of: C, *D. bohemani*; D, *D. latitarsis*; E, *D. permacra*; F, *Potthastia montium*. **G, H:** gonostyli of: G, *D. incallida*; H, *P. gaedii*.

Genus PSEUDODIAMESA Goetghebuer

1   Wing membrane with macrotrichia distally. Gonostylus not thickened
     basally and with a long slender spine (megaseta) distally (arrow, Fig.
     30A). Hypopygium Fig. 133B— **Pseudodiamesa branickii** (Nowicki)

—   Wing membrane bare. Gonostylus thickened basally, megaseta very short
     (arrow, Fig. 30B). Hypopygium Fig. 133C—
                              Pseudodiamesa nivosa (Goetghebuer)

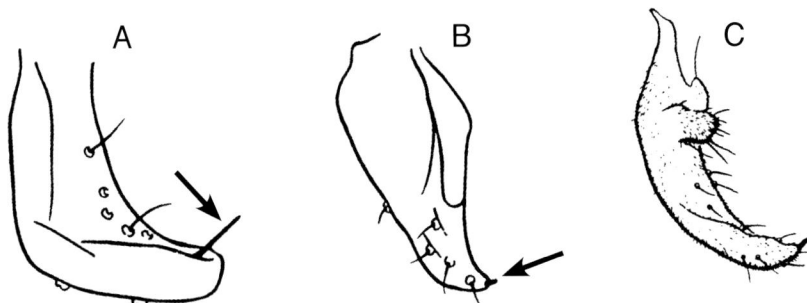

Fig. 30. **A–C:** gonostyli of: A, *Pseudodiamesa branickii*; B, *P. nivosa*; C,
Syndiamesa edwardsi.

Genus PSEUDOKIEFFERIELLA Zavrel

There is one named species, readily identifiable from the characters given
in the key to genera (pp. 54–56) and its characteristic hypopygium (Fig.
133D)—   **Pseudokiefferiella parva** (Edwards)

Genus SYMPOTTHASTIA Pagast

Only one species is referred to this genus. The characters given in the key
to genera (pp. 54–56), together with the illustration of its hypopygium (Fig.
134A), should suffice to identify it—   **Sympotthastia zavreli** Pagast

Genus SYNDIAMESA Kieffer

Only one species has been recorded for Britain and Ireland. It is easily
identified from the form of the gonostylus (Fig. 30C)—
                              Syndiamesa edwardsi (Pagast)

Tribe PROTANYPINI (Subfamily DIAMESINAE)

Genus PROTANYPUS Kieffer

Only one species has been recorded for Britain and Ireland. It is easily recognised by the presence of dorsal setae on the antepronotum (Fig. 26D, p. 55) and by the fact that the gonocoxite is produced well beyond the point of articulation with the gonostylus. Hypopygium Fig. 134B—

Protanypus morio (Zetterstedt)

SUBFAMILY PRODIAMESINAE

KEY TO 3 GENERA OF PRODIAMESINAE

1   Penultimate segment of maxillary palp with a distal 'tooth' (arrow, Fig. 31A)—   ODONTOMESA Pagast (p. 62, 1sp.)

—   Penultimate segment of maxillary palp not toothed—   **2**

2   Base of gonocoxite bearing darkly chitinised elongate appendages, arising from obvious swellings (arrows, Fig. 31B)—

PRODIAMESA Kieffer (p. 62, 2spp.)

—   Basal appendages of gonocoxite pale, not arising from obvious swellings—   MONODIAMESA Kieffer (p. 62, 2spp.)

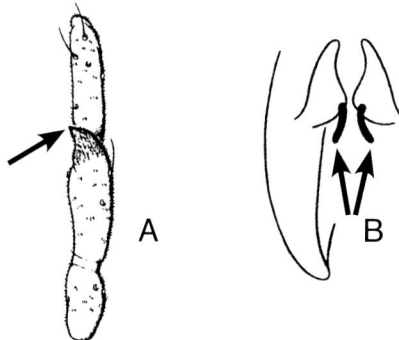

Fig. 31.   **A:** distal segments of the maxillary palp of *Odontomesa fulva.* **B:** ventro-basal appendages of the hypopygium of *Prodiamesa olivacea.*

KEYS TO 5 SPECIES IN 3 GENERA OF PRODIAMESINAE

Genus MONODIAMESA Kieffer

1   Gonocoxite lower lobe *ll* little longer, at most, than the gonocoxite upper lobe *ul* (Fig. 32A). Fore-tarsus with a beard of long setae (but these setae are thinner than the semi-erect setae of the tarsomeres and may project less because they lie at an acute angle and are easily overlooked). Antennal ratio (p. 9) about 3. Hypopygium Fig. 134C—
Monodiamesa bathyphila (Kieffer)

—   Gonocoxite lower lobe *ll* reaching to the origin of the gonostylus (Fig. 32B). Fore-tarsus beard moderate, setae about 4 times as long as width of the tarsomere. Antennal ratio about 2. Hypopygium Fig. 134D—
Monodiamesa ekmani (Brundin)

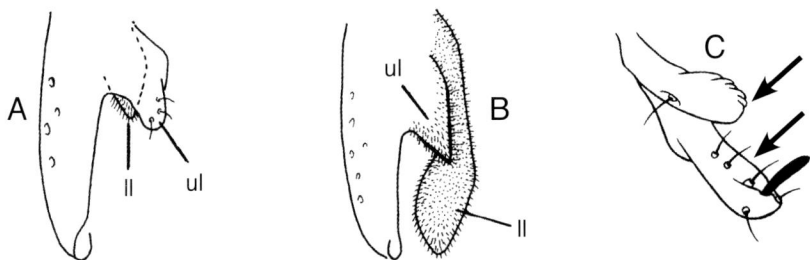

Fig. 32. **A, B:** gonocoxite lobes of: A, *Monodiamesa bathyphila*; B, *M. ekmani*. **C:** gonostylus of *Prodiamesa olivacea*.

Genus ODONTOMESA Pagast

The single European species may be recognised by the presence of a distal 'tooth' on the penultimate segment of the maxillary palp (arrow, Fig. 31A, p. 61). The hypopygium is also distinctive (Fig. 135A)—
Odontomesa fulva (Kieffer)

Genus PRODIAMESA Kieffer

1   Gonostylus bilobed (arrows, Fig. 32C). Hypopygium Fig. 135B—
Prodiamesa olivacea (Meigen)

—   Gonostylus simple. Hypopygium Fig. 135C—
Prodiamesa rufovittata Goetghebuer

SUBFAMILY ORTHOCLADIINAE
KEY TO 51 GENERA

1   Postnotum without a median groove or keel. Larvae marine—
CLUNIO Haliday (p. 88, 1sp.)

—   Postnotum with a median longitudinal groove or keel—   **2**

2   Wing membrane with at least a few macrotrichia near the apex, usually more extensively 'hairy'. Apical flagellomere of antenna without a differentiated seta at the tip—   **3**

—   Wing membrane without macrotrichia, except in one species that has an apical seta on the tip of the antenna—   **12**

Fig. 33. **A, B:** gonostylus of: A, *Brillia flavifrons*; B, *Eurycnemus crassipes*.

3   Gonostylus bifurcate (Figs 33A,B)—   **4**

—   Gonostylus simple—   **6**

4   Gonostylus with a few scattered, short setae that are shorter than the width of the rami (arrow, Fig. 33A)—   BRILLIA Kieffer (p. 78, 2spp.)

—   Gonostylus outer ramus with flattened setae at the apex and with subapical setae longer than the width of the ramus (arrow, Fig. 33B)—   **5**

5   Larger species with wing length 4 mm or more—
EURYCNEMUS van der Wulp (p. 108, 1sp.)

—   Smaller species with wing length less than 3 mm—
EURYHAPSIS Oliver (p. 108, 1sp.?)

6(3) Eyes hairy or pubescent (see pp. 9–10) —
                    THIENEMANNIA Kieffer (p. 142, 3spp.)

—   Eyes bare —   **7**

7   Anal tergite *at* very small, triangular; anal point *ap* weakly developed
     (Fig. 34A) —   HETEROTANYTARSUS Spärck (p. 110, 1sp.)

—   Anal tergite normally developed, with or without a distinct anal point — **8**

8   Anal point minute or absent —
                    GYMNOMETRIOCNEMUS Edwards (p. 108, 2spp.)

—   Anal point well developed —   **9**

9   Costa ending abruptly at tip of wing vein R_{4+5} (arrow, Fig. 34B) —
                    HETEROTRISSOCLADIUS Spärck (p. 110, 3spp.)

—   Costa produced beyond the tip of wing vein R_{4+5} —   **10**

10   Abdominal tergites densely setose. Wing vein Cu_1 almost straight or very
     slightly curved (Fig. 34C) —
                    METRIOCNEMUS van der Wulp (p. 116, 10spp.)

—   Abdominal tergites with reduced setation. Wing vein Cu_1 curved, usually
     conspicuously so (e.g. Fig. 34D) —   **11**

11   Wing vein R_{4+5} ending above tip of M_{3+4} (Fig. 34E) —
                    PARAMETRIOCNEMUS Goetghebuer (p. 127, 2spp.)

—   Wing vein R_{4+5} ending distinctly proximal to tip of M_{3+4} (Fig. 34D) —
                    PARAPHAENOCLADIUS Thienemann (p. 128, 4spp.)

12(2) Wing veins R_1 and R_{4+5} are fused with the costa to form a thickened
     clavus (p. 13) (arrow, Fig. 34F) —   **13**

—   Wing veins R_1 and R_{4+5} are separate from the costa, as usual — **15**

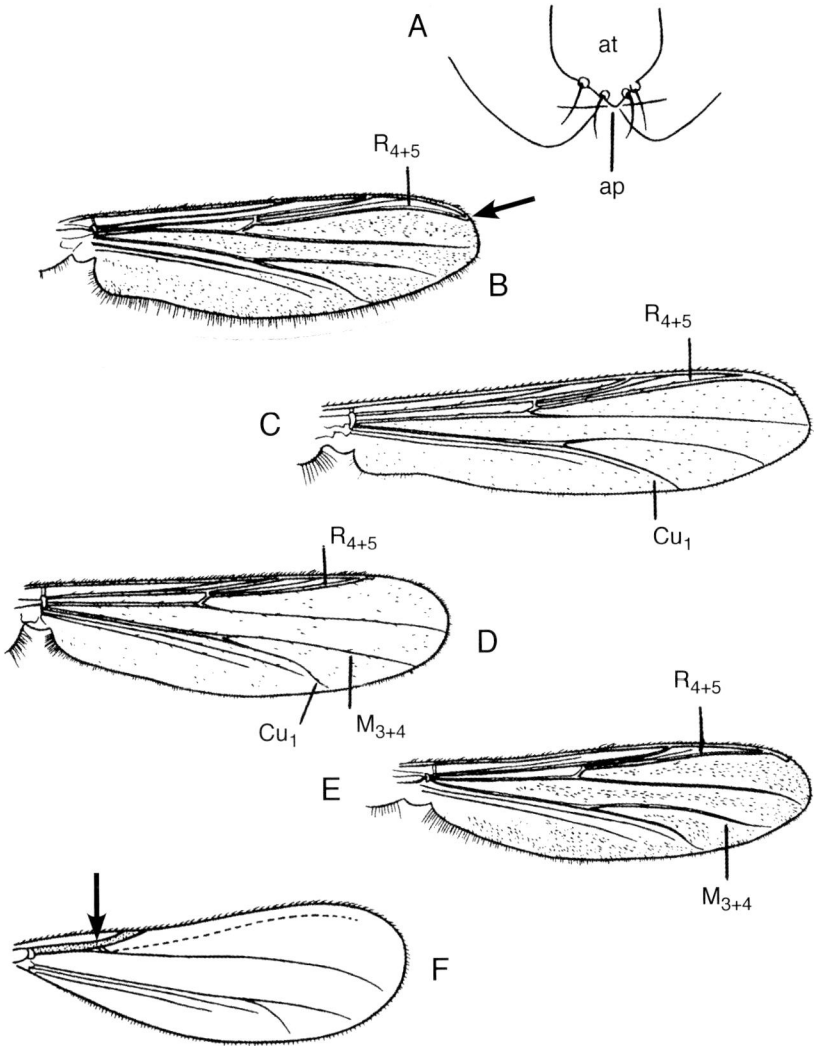

Fig. 34. **A:** anal tergite of *Heterotanytarsus apicalis*. **B–F:** wings of: B, *Heterotrissocladius marcidus*; C, *Metriocnemus eurynotus*; D, *Paraphaenocladius impensus*; E, *Parametriocnemus stylatus*; F, *Corynoneura scutellata*.

13 Hypopygial sternapodemes (see p. 17) inverted V-shaped or U-shaped (Fig. 35A). Hind-tibia strongly expanded distally, apex oblique (arrow, Fig. 35C). Eyes bare —   CORYNONEURA Winnertz (p. 88, 11spp.)

—   Transverse sternapodeme of hypopygium long, with an anteriorly-directed horn at each end (arrows, Fig. 35B). Hind-tibia, at most, a little expanded distally, apex transverse. Eyes pubescent to hairy —   **14**

14 Gonocoxite with a large distal lobe (Fig. 35D) —
                    CORYNONEURELLA Brundin (p. 92, 1sp.)

—   If the gonocoxite has a lobe, it is median in position (e.g. arrows, Figs 35E–G) —   THIENEMANNIELLA Kieffer (p. 142, 7spp.)

15(12) Fourth tarsomere bilobed, much shorter than fifth tarsomere —
                    CARDIOCLADIUS Kieffer (p. 84, 2spp.)

—   Fourth tarsomere cylindrical, usually as long as or longer than the fifth tarsomere —   **16**

16 Antepronotum covered with many small setae in addition to the microtrichia (arrow, Fig. 35H). Squama at base of wing bare* —
                    HELENIELLA Gowin (p. 110, 1sp.)

—   Antepronotum usually without setae dorsally; if setae present, squama* at base of wing with two or more marginal setae —   **17**

*See Fig. 5 on p. 13.

17 Gonostylus bilobed (arrows, Fig. 35I) —
                    DIPLOCLADIUS Kieffer (p. 104, 1sp.)

—   Gonostylus simple —   **18**

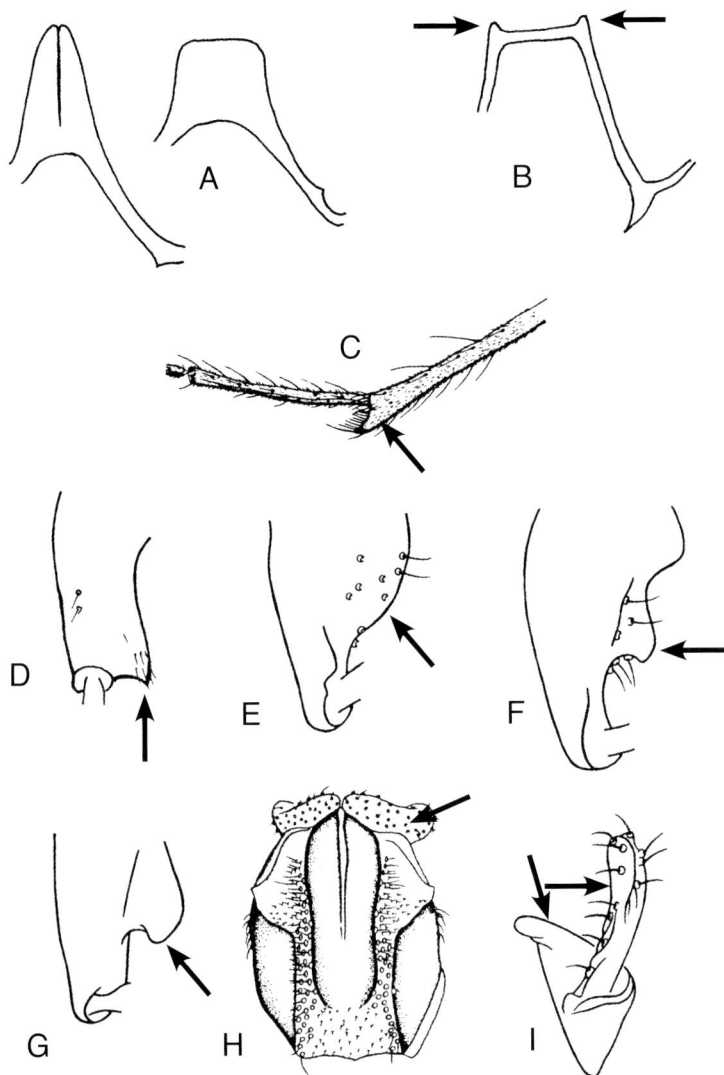

Fig. 35. **A, B:** sternapodemes of: A, *Corynoneura gratias* (left) and *C. coronata* (right); B, *Corynoneurella paludosa*. **C:** tip of hind-tibia and first tarsal segment of *Corynoneura scutellata*. **D–G:** gonocoxite of: D, *Corynoneurella paludosa*; E, *Thienemanniella clavicornis*; F, *T. acuticornis*; G, *T. lutea*. **H:** dorsal view of scutum and antepronotum of *Heleniella ornaticollis*. **I:** gonostylus of *Diplocladius cultriger*.

18   Squama at base of wing bare*. Eyes usually bare or pubescent; if hairy, last antennal flagellomere with a distinct apical seta *s* (Fig. 36A)—   **19**

—   Squama* usually at least partially fringed with setae; when bare, eyes are hairy and last flagellomere is without an apical seta—   **27**

      *See Fig. 5 on p. 13.

19   Eyes pubescent or hairy. Last antennal flagellomere with a distinctly differentiated straight seta *s* apically (Fig. 36A)—
                              SMITTIA Holmgren (p. 140, 11spp.)

—   Eyes usually bare, never hairy; if pubescent, the last antennal flagellomere is without an apical seta. Apical flagellomere rarely with a seta at its tip—   **20**

20   Wing costa very strongly produced beyond vein R_{4+5} (arrow, Fig. 36B)—   **21**

—   Wing costa not or weakly produced (arrow, Fig. 36C) (moderately produced only in *Pseudosmittia albipennis*, which has an anal point pubescent to its tip; see Fig. 36F)—   **25**

21   Anal vein *An* on wing ending well proximal to cubital fork FCu—
                      KRENOSMITTIA Thienemann & Krüger (p. 111, 2spp.)

—   Anal vein on wing ending below or beyond cubital fork FCu (e.g. see Figs 36C,D). (If antennal ratio is 1.2 or more see *Bryophaenocladius*, couplet 34, p. 72)—   **22**

22   Gonocoxite bearing two lobes (arrows, Fig. 36E). Larvae marine—
                      THALASSOSMITTIA Strenzke & Remmert (p. 142, 1sp.)

—   Gonocoxite with only one lobe. Larvae terrestrial or live in fresh water—   **23**

23   Wing vein R_{2+3} ending at, or before, midway between veins R_1 and R_{4+5} (arrow, Fig. 36D). Tip of R_{4+5} above, or scarcely proximal to, tip of M_{3+4} (Fig. 36D)—   EPOICOCLADIUS Sulc & Zavrel (p. 104, 1sp.)

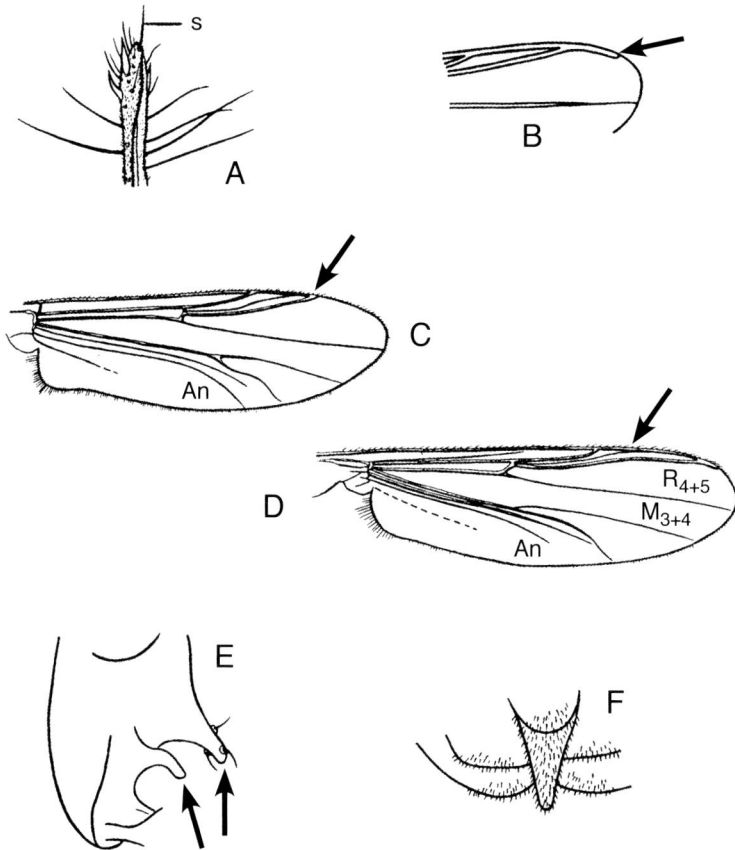

Fig. 36. **A:** tip of antenna of *Smittia leucopogon*. **B–D:** wings of: B, *Krenosmittia camptophleps*, showing the produced costa at the tip of the wing; C, *Camptocladius stercorarius*; D, *Epoicocladius ephemerae*. **E:** gonocoxite of *Thalassosmittia halassophila*. **F:** pubescent anal point on tergite IX of *Pseudosmittia albipennis*.

—(23) Wing vein R_{2+3} ending close to vein R_{4+5}, or fused with it. Tip of R_{4+5} proximal to tip of M_{3+4} — **24**

24   Eyes pubescent—   RHEOSMITTIA Brundin (p. 138, 1sp.)

—   Eyes bare—   PARAKIEFFERIELLA Thienemann (p. 126, 5spp.)

25(20) Fifth tarsomeres flattened dorsoventrally. Wing vein R_{4+5} ending above or beyond tip of M_{3+4} —
$\qquad$ ACAMPTOCLADIUS Brundin (p. 78, 2spp.)

— All tarsomeres are cylindrical. Wing vein R_{4+5} usually ending distinctly proximal to the tip of M_{3+4} — **26**

26   Anal vein *An* very long, reaching almost to wing margin (Fig. 36C, p. 69). Pulvilli present on apex of tarsus—
$\qquad$ CAMPTOCLADIUS van der Wulp (p. 84, 1sp.)

— Anal vein ending well before wing margin. Pulvilli absent from apex of tarsus— $\qquad$ PSEUDOSMITTIA Edwards (p. 135, 8spp.)

27(18) Eyes bare, pubescent or hairy; when hairy, the squama at the base of the wing is bare— **28**

— Eyes hairy. Squama at base of wing is at least partially fringed— **44**

28   Anal tergite swollen medially to form a longitudinal ridge (arrow, Fig. 37A). Costa of wing not produced beyond vein R_{4+5} —
$\qquad$ MESOSMITTIA Brundin (p. 115, 1sp.)

— Anal tergite IX without a longitudinal ridge. Costa on wing either produced or not produced beyond vein R_{4+5} — **29**

29   Wing membrane coarsely granular in appearance (magnification ×200) (cf. Fig. 37B)— **30**

— Wing membrane only very finely dotted (at ×200) — **35**

30   Thoracic epimeron II, posterior median anepisternum II and usually the pre-episternum and antepronotum (see Fig. 4, p. 12) all bearing setae. Thoracic scutum often with scale-like setae (Fig. 37C). Anal point *ap* usually broad and pubescent (Figs 37D,E) or lacking (one species may have a small bare anal point)—   LIMNOPHYES Eaton (p. 111, 13spp.)

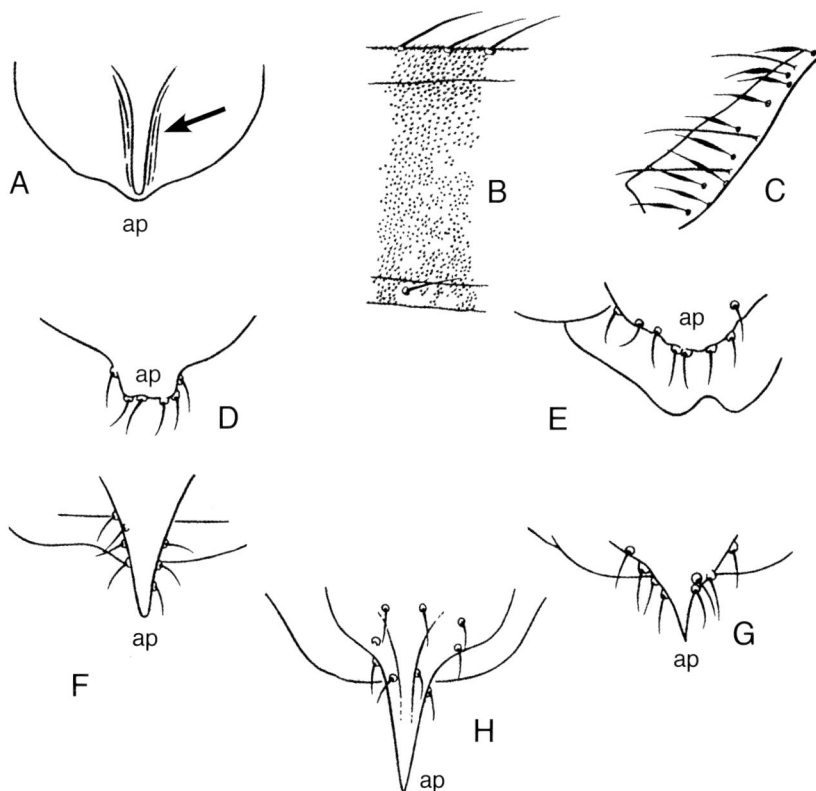

Fig. 37. **A:** anal tergite and median ridge of *Mesosmittia flexuella*. **B:** portion of wing membrane of *Chaetocladius perennis*. **C:** prescutellar setae of *Limnophyes pentaplastus*. **D–H:** anal points of: D, *Limnophyes habilis*; E, *L. natalensis*; F, *Paratrissocladius excerptus*; G, *Trissocladius brevipalpis*; H, *Chaetocladius piger*.

—(30) Thoracic epimeron II, posterior mesanepisternum II, pre-episternum and antepronotum (see Fig. 4, p. 12) without setae. Thoracic scutum with simple setae only. Anal point present, though it may be small—   **31**

31   Anal point *ap* bearing several strong setae laterally (Fig. 37F)—
                    PARATRISSOCLADIUS Zavrel (p. 129, 1sp.)

—   Anal point *ap* without lateral setae (e.g. Figs 37G,H)—   **32**

32   Spurs of mid- and hind-tibiae with strongly projecting apicolateral
      denticles (Fig. 38A). Costa not or scarcely produced beyond wing
      vein R_{4+5}. Vein Cu_1 straight or only weakly curved. Anal point well
      developed, usually robust (e.g. as in Fig. 37H, p. 71) —
                             CHAETOCLADIUS Kieffer (p. 86, 5spp.)

—   Spurs of mid- and hind-tibiae, if denticulate, with the denticles appressed
      to the spurs, not projecting. Costa usually produced well beyond wing
      vein R_{4+5}. Vein Cu_1 straight or curved. Anal point either weak or well
      developed —   **33**

33   Acrostichal setae (see Fig. 4, p. 12) absent from thorax. Anal point very
      small, with a sharp point (Fig. 37G) —
                             TRISSOCLADIUS Kieffer (p. 144, 1sp.)

—   Acrostichal setae present on thorax, though they may be minute. Anal
      point well developed —   **34**

34   Robust acrostichal setae begin at anterior margin of the scutum. Anterior
      leg ratio (p. 14) about 0.5 or more —
                             BRYOPHAENOCLADIUS Thienemann (p. 78, 16spp.)

—   Minute, curved, flattened acrostichal setae restricted to mid region of the
      scutum. Anterior leg ratio about 0.5 or less —
                             PARALIMNOPHYES Brundin (p. 127, 1sp.)

35(29) Distinct, broad pulvilli p present on the apex of the tarsus (Fig. 38B).
      Antenna without a stiff seta at the apex —
                             PSECTROCLADIUS Kieffer (p. 130, 16spp.)

—   Pulvilli on tarsus *EITHER* absent or small, *OR* when pulvilli are well
      developed, antenna has a stiff seta at the apex —   **36**

36   Anal point, including the tip, covered with microtrichia and bearing long
      setae (Fig. 38C) —   **37**

—   Anal point, if present, lacking microtrichia at least apically, though
      lateral setae may be present —   **38**

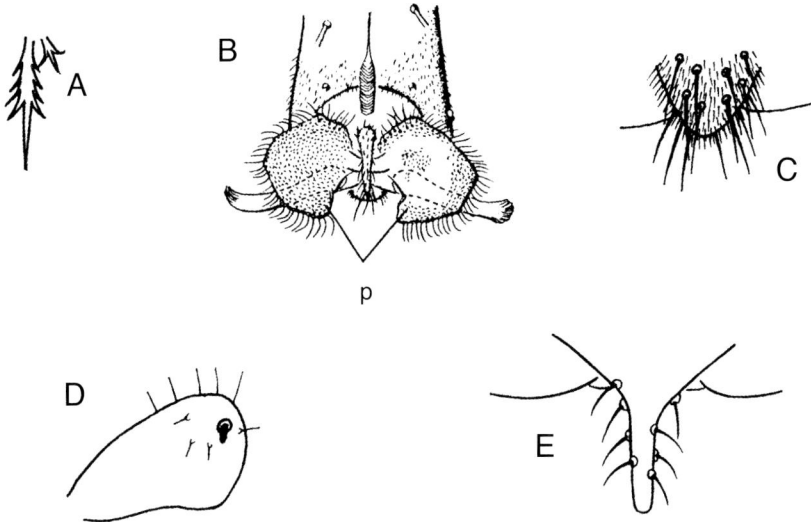

Fig 38.   **A:** tibial spurs of *Chaetocladius perennis*. **B:** ventral view of the foot of
Psectrocladius sp. **C:** anal point of *Georthocladius luteicornis*. **D:** gonostylus
of *Georthocladius luteicornis*. **E:** anal point of *Orthocladius rivulorum*.

37   Gonostylus expanded triangularly towards the apex (Fig. 38D)—
                        GEORTHOCLADIUS Strenzke (p. 108, 1sp.)

—   Gonostylus weakly expanded in apical half or parallel-sided—
                        PSEUDORTHOCLADIUS Goetghebuer (p. 134, 5spp.)

38(36) Anal point with several long lateral setae (e.g. Fig. 38E)—   **39**

—   Anal point, if present, without lateral setae—   **41**

39   Acrostichal setae absent from thorax. Wing vein R_{4+5} ending opposite
      or a little proximal to the tip of vein M_{3+4}. Anal point parallel-sided,
      rounded apically (cf. Fig. 38E)—
                        PARORTHOCLADIUS Thienemann (p. 129, 1sp.)

—(39) Acrostichal setae (Fig. 4, p. 12) present on thorax. Wing vein R_{4+5} ending distal to tip of vein M_{3+4}. Anal point generally tapering to a point (except for subgenus *Euorthocladius* in which the anal point is similar to that of *Parorthocladius*; see Fig. 38E, p. 73)—   **40**

40   Acrostichal setae begin at the anterior margin of the scutum. Gonostylus simple—   ORTHOCLADIUS van der Wulp (p. 118, 22spp.)

—   Acrostichal setae begin some distance behind the anterior margin of the scutum. Gonostylus with an elongate lateral lobe (arrow, Fig. 39A)—
                                              ZALUTSCHIA Lipina (p. 145, 1sp.)

41(38) Anal point short and triangular (arrow, Fig. 39B). Tip of antenna with several long, curved setae (arrow, Fig. 39C)—
                            SYNORTHOCLADIUS Thienemann (p. 142, 1sp.)

—   Anal point either absent or present, and either short or long, though it can be transparent and easily overlooked. Tip of antenna without long, curved setae—   **42**

42   Hypopygium without a distinct virga. Wing vein R_{4+5} ending before the tip of vein M_{3+4}. Anal point absent from tergite IX—
                            EUKIEFFERIELLA Thienemann (p. 105, 12spp.)

—   Hypopygium with a well developed virga (see p. 17) (arrow, Fig. 39D). Wing vein R_{4+5} ending opposite or beyond the tip of vein M_{3+4}. Anal point usually present—   **43**

43   Anal point well developed, but often transparent, projecting from the posterior margin of tergite IX (e.g. Fig. 39E)—
                                              TVETENIA Kieffer (p. 144, 4spp.)

—   Anal point at most small, situated on tergite IX before the posterior margin (Fig. 39F)—   TOKUNAGAIA Sæther (p. 144, 1sp.)

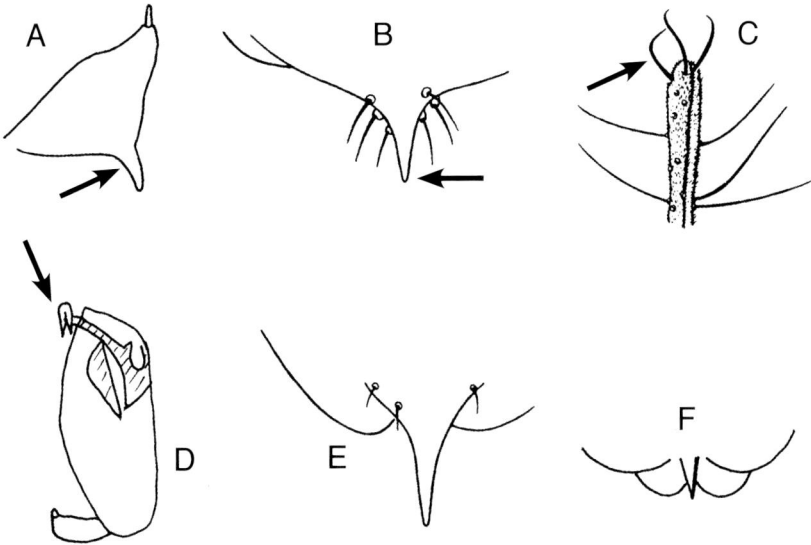

Fig. 39. **A:** gonostylus of *Zalutschia humphriesiae*. **B:** anal point of *Synorthocladius semivirens*. **C:** apex of antenna of *S. semivirens*. **D:** hypopygium of *Tokunagaia tonollii*. **E, F:** anal points of: E, *Tvetenia calvescens*; F, *Tokunagaia tonollii*.

44(27) Hypopygium with a distinct anal point—   **45**

— Anal point minute or absent—   **47**

45 At most 2 acrostichal setae (Fig. 4, p. 12) on the thorax. Anal point lacks setae—   NANOCLADIUS Kieffer (p. 118, 3spp.)

— Acrostichal setae on thorax more numerous. Anal point with lateral setae—   **46**

46 Setae of abdominal tergites in two distinct transverse rows—   PARACRICOTOPUS Thienemann & Harnisch (p. 126, 1sp.)

— Setae of abdominal tergites irregularly arranged—   RHEOCRICOTOPUS Brundin (p. 138, 6spp.)

47(44) Dorsocentral setae (Fig. 4, p. 12) long and upright, arising from distinct pale spots (arrows, Fig. 40A)— **48**

— Dorsocentral setae weak and decumbent, not arising from obvious spots— **49**

48 Antepronotum *apr* unusually large (Fig. 40B). Antennal ratio (p. 9) about 3.0— ACRICOTOPUS Kieffer (p. 78, 1sp.)

— Antepronotum normally developed. Antennal ratio less than 2.0— PARATRICHOCLADIUS Santos Abreu (p. 128, 3spp.)

49(47) Legs usually with a pale ring (Fig. 40C) and/or abdomen with yellow markings. Anterior prealar setae *ap* usually absent (arrow, Fig. 40E), but if present (Fig. 40D), the pale tibial rings are distinct. Anal point usually absent; if present, abdominal tergites III and IV with a few setae medially and a bare area on each side— CRICOTOPUS van der Wulp (p. 92, 34spp.)

— Legs and abdomen without pale markings. Anterior prealar setae *ps* present or absent. If an anal point is present, abdominal tergites are setose with a narrow, mid-longitudinal, bare band— **50**

50 Anterior prealar setae present. Anal point absent. Found on rocky coasts— HALOCLADIUS Hirvenoja (p. 108, 4spp.)

— Anterior prealar setae absent. Hypopygium with a minute anal point. A freshwater species— PARACLADIUS Hirvenoja (p. 125, 1sp.)

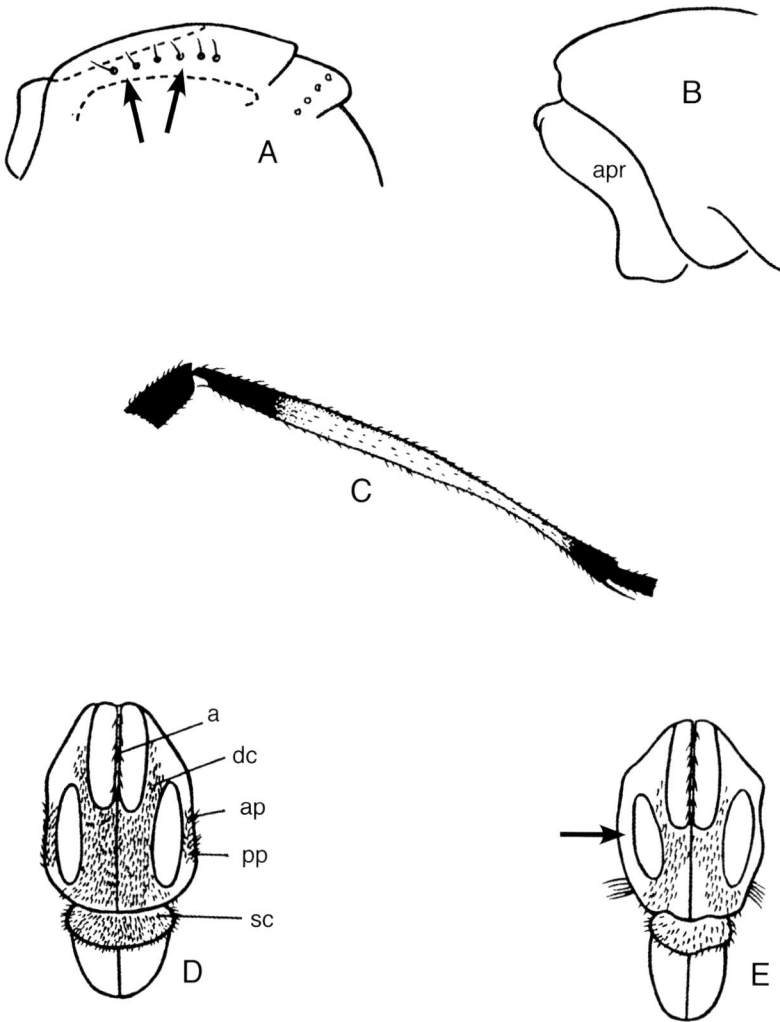

Fig. 40. **A, B:** lateral views of the thorax of *Acricotopus lucens*: A, location of dorsocentral setae; B, anterior part with a large antepronotum (*apr*). **C:** fore-tibia of *Cricotopus sylvestris*. **D, E:** dorsal views of the thorax of: D, *Cricotopus pilosellus* (a = acrostichal setae, dc = dorsocentral setae, ap = anterior prealar setae, pp = posterior prealar setae, sc = scutellar setae); E, *C. polaris*.

KEYS TO 243 SPECIES IN 51 GENERA
OF SUBFAMILY ORTHOCLADIINAE

Genus ACAMPTOCLADIUS Brundin

1   Hypopygium with inner arm of the phallapodeme (p. 17) much shorter than the outer arm (Fig. 41B). Antennal ratio (p. 9) about 1.3. Hypopygium Fig. 136A— **Acamptocladius submontanus** (Edwards)

—   Inner and outer arms of the phallapodeme about equal in length (Fig. 41A). Antennal ratio <1.0. Hypopygium Fig. 136B—
    Acamptocladius reissi Cranston & Sæther

Genus ACRICOTOPUS Kieffer

The only European representative is characterised by its unusually large antepronotum *apr* (Fig. 40B, p. 77) and high antennal ratio (about 3.0). Hypopygium Fig. 136C— **Acricotopus lucens** (Zetterstedt)

Genus BRILLIA Kieffer

1   Outer branch of gonostylus about twice as long as the inner branch (Fig. 41C). Hypopygium Fig. 136D— **Brillia flavifrons** (Johannsen)

—   The two branches of the gonostylus roughly equal in length (Fig. 41D). Hypopygium Fig. 137A— **Brillia bifida** (Kieffer)

Genus BRYOPHAENOCLADIUS Thienemann

1   Gonostylus with 4 megasetae in a row towards the apex (arrow, Fig. 41E). Hypopygium Fig. 137B— **Bryophaenocladius dentatus** (Karl)

—   Gonostylus with 1 megaseta—   **2**

2   Entirely yellow in colour or predominantly yellow with darkened scutal stripes and postnotum. Hypopygium Fig. 137C—
    Bryophaenocladius ictericus (Meigen)

—   Mostly dark brown or blackish species; when ground colour is yellow, the thorax is more extensively darkened than above—   **3**

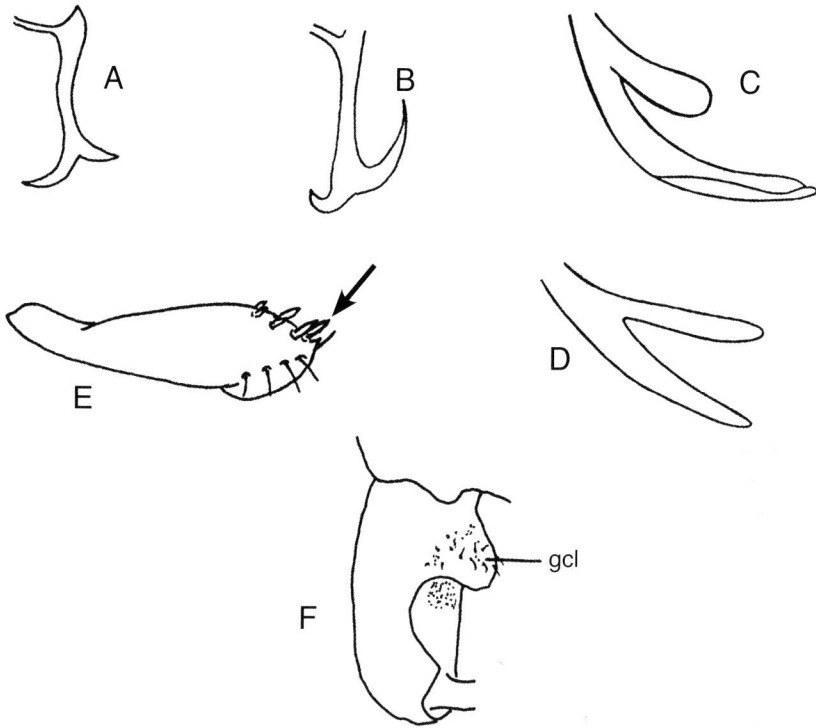

Fig. 41. **A, B:** phallapodemes of: A, *Acamptocladius reissi*; B, *A. submontanus*. **C–E:** gonostyli of: C, *Brillia flavifrons*; D, *B. bifida*; E, *Bryophaenocladius dentatus*. **F:** gonocoxite of *Bryophaenocladius vernalis*.

3   Inner ventral margin of gonocoxite abruptly and deeply concave posterior to the gonocoxite lobe *gcl* (Fig. 41F). Hypopygium Fig. 137D—
Bryophaenocladius vernalis (Goetghebuer)

—   Gonocoxite without this constriction—   **4**

4   Gonocoxite bearing two lobes, of which the posterior, though large, is almost transparent and easily overlooked—   **5**

—   Gonocoxite bearing only a single lobe, with, at most, a weak indication of the posterior lobe—   **7**

5   Anterior lobe of gonocoxite in the form of a small but prominent tubercle
      (arrow, Fig. 42A). Hypopygium Fig. 138A—
                          Bryophaenocladius simus (Edwards)

—   Anterior lobe of gonocoxite not so prominent (arrows Figs 42B,C)— **6**

6   Anal point broad, rounded (arrow, Fig. 42E). Hypopygium Fig. 138B—
                      Bryophaenocladius xanthogyne (Edwards)

—   Anal point triangular (arrow, Fig. 42F). Hypopygium Fig. 138C—
                      Bryophaenocladius sp. cf. **scanicus** (Brundin)

7(4) Lobe of gonocoxite in the form of a small bare papilla (arrow, Fig. 42D).
      Hypopygium Fig. 138D—
                      Bryophaenocladius nitidicollis (Goetghebuer)

—   Lobe of gonocoxite not as above—   **8**

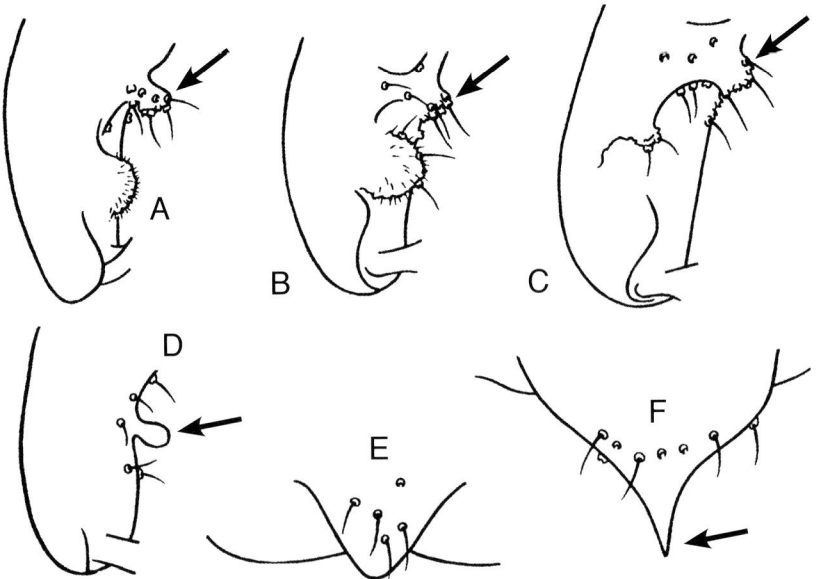

Fig. 42. **A–D:** gonocoxites of: A, *Bryophaenocladius simus*; B, *B. xanthogyne*;
          C, *B.* sp. cf. *scanicus*; D, *B. nitidicollis.* **E, F:** anal points of: E, *B.*
          xanthogyne; F, *B.* sp. cf. *scanicus.*

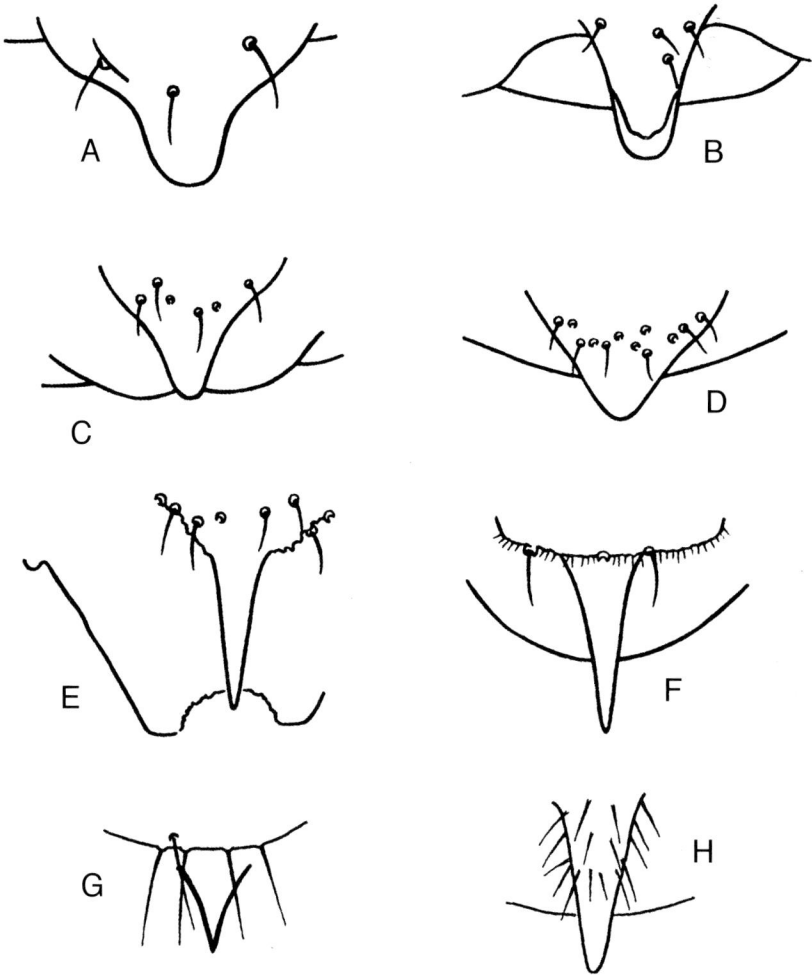

Fig. 43. **A–F:** anal points of: A, *Bryophaenocladius femineus*; B, *B. illimbatus*; C, *B. nidorum*; D, *B. tuberculatus*; E, *B. subvernalis*; F, *B. aestivus*; G, *B. muscicola*; H, *B. flexidens*.

8   Anal point broadly rounded (Figs. 43A–D)—   **9**

—   Anal point with an acute apex, elongate triangular to long and slender (Figs. 43E–H)—   **13**

9   Gonocoxite expanded over basal half into a broad and rounded lobe (arrow, Fig. 44A). Hypopygium Fig. 139A—
                              Bryophaenocladius inconstans (Brundin)

—   Gonocoxite lobe produced posteromedially into a pronounced corner or projecting flap—   **10**

10   Gonocoxite lobe relatively large (arrows, Figs 44B,C)—   **11**

—   Gonocoxite lobe in the form of a small tubercle (arrows, Figs 44D,E)—
                                                                         12

11   Gonocoxite lobe squarish (arrow, Fig. 44B). Outer margin of gonostylus smoothly rounded. Hypopygium Fig. 139B—
                              Bryophaenocladius femineus (Edwards)

—   Gonocoxite lobe rounded (arrow, Fig. 44C). Gonostylus abruptly bent inwards at the tip. Hypopygium Fig. 139C—
                              Bryophaenocladius illimbatus (Edwards)

12(10) Dark brown to black; halteres dark brown. Hypopygium, in addition to the small anterior lobe of the gonocoxite (upper arrow, Fig 44D), also with a very small posterior lobe, which can be squashed in mounts and unrecognisable (lower arrow, Fig. 44D). Hypopygium Fig. 139D—   **Bryophaenocladius nidorum** (Edwards)*

B. nidorum sometimes has a triangular anal point, pointed at the tip; it is separable from *B. aestivus* (couplet 13) by the antennal ratio (p. 9): >1.5 in *nidorum*, <1.5 in *aestivus.*

—   Thorax with yellow ground colour and dark scutal stripes; halteres yellowish. Gonocoxite with no trace of a second lobe (Fig. 44E). Hypopygium Fig. 140A—
                              Bryophaenocladius tuberculatus (Edwards)

13(8) Lobe of gonocoxite conical, projecting (arrow, Fig. 44F). Hypopygium Fig. 140B—   **Bryophaenocladius aestivus** (Brundin)

—   Lobe of gonocoxite curved or bent, apex directed posteriorly—   **14**

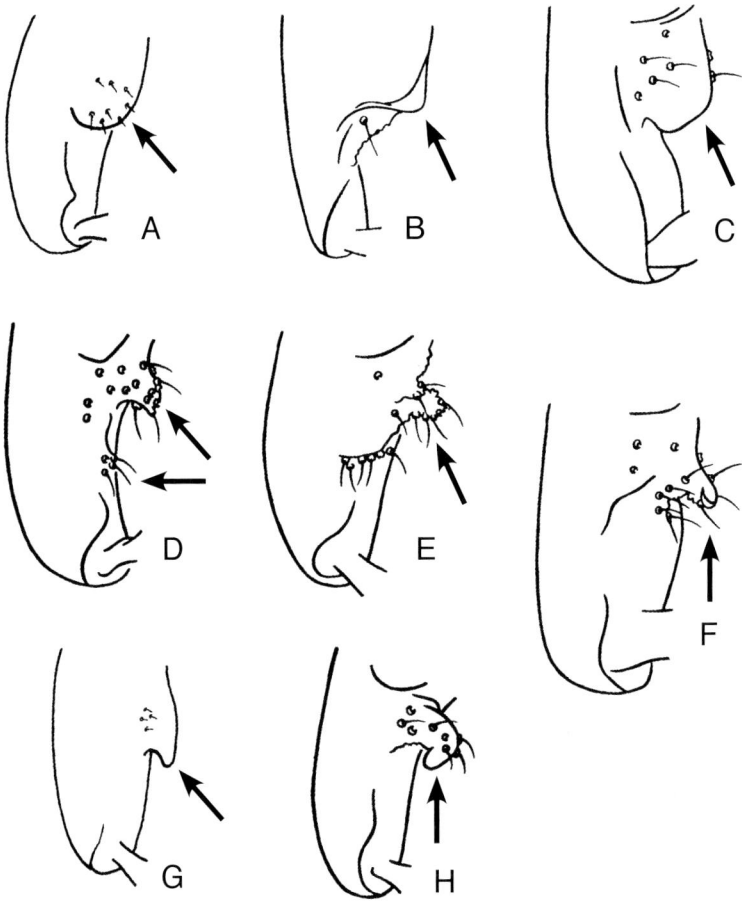

Fig. 44. **A–H:** gonocoxites of: A, *Bryophaenocladius inconstans*; B, *B. femineus*; C, *B. illimbatus*; D, *B. nidorum*; E, *B. tuberculatus*; F, *B. aestivus*; G, *B. muscicola*; H, *B. subvernalis*.

14 Gonocoxite lobe curved posteriorly (arrow, Fig. 44G). Anal point elongate triangular (arrow, Fig. 45A, p. 85). Hypopygium Fig. 140C—
Bryophaenocladius muscicola (Kieffer)

— Gonocoxite lobe strongly bent through a right angle (arrow, Fig. 44H). Anal point longer than above (Figs 45B,C)— **15**

15   Antennal ratio <1.5 (p. 9), apical flagellomere usually expanded towards
     the tip. Wing vein FCu well beyond the cross-vein RM. Anal point long
     and narrow (Fig. 45B). Hypopygium Fig. 140D—
                             Bryophaenocladius subvernalis (Edwards)

—   Antennal ratio >1.5, apical flagellomere parallel-sided. Wing vein FCu
     below RM. Anal point broader (Fig. 45C). Hypopygium Fig. 141A—
                             Bryophaenocladius flexidens (Brundin)

Genus CAMPTOCLADIUS van der Wulp

The single species has antennae with broad, leaf-like setae on the second, third
and terminal flagellomeres (arrows, Fig. 45D). Hypopygium Fig. 141B—
                             Camptocladius stercorarius (De Geer)

Genus CARDIOCLADIUS Kieffer

1   On the hind-legs, the fourth tarsomere is relatively short (Fig. 45E).
     Hypopygium Fig. 141C—   **Cardiocladius fuscus** Kieffer

—   On the hind-legs, the fourth tarsomere is relatively longer, though
     distinctly shorter than the fifth tarsomere (Fig. 45F). Hypopygium Fig.
     141D—   **Cardiocladius capucinus** (Zetterstedt)

Fig. 45. *(On page 85).* **A–C:** anal points of: A, *Bryophaenocladius muscicola*; B, *B.
       subvernalis*; C, *B. flexidens*. **D:** basal segments (below the broken line) and
       the apex (above the broken line) of the antennal flagellum of *Camptocladius
       stercorarius*. **E, F:** distal tarsal segments (3, 4, 5) of hind-legs of: E,
       Cardiocladius fuscus; F, *C. capucinus*.

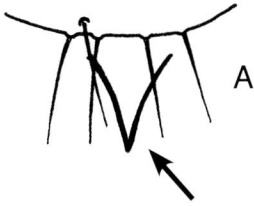

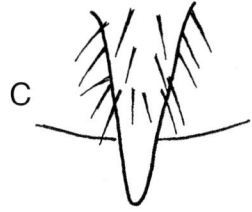

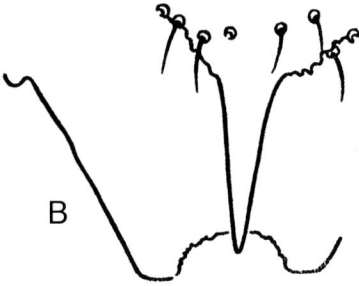

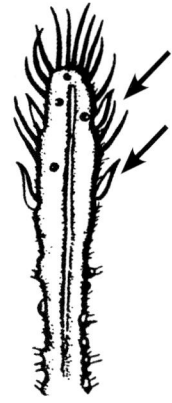

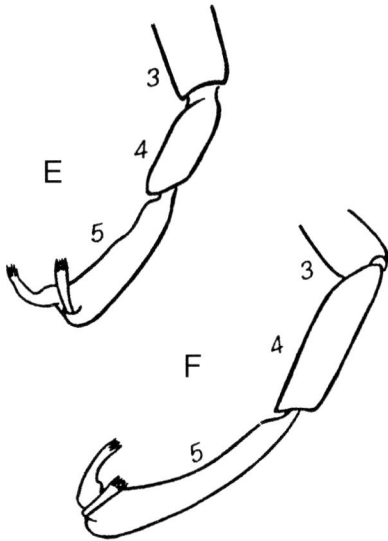

Genus CHAETOCLADIUS Kieffer

1   Outer margin of gonostylus produced into a distinct 'tooth' (arrow, Fig. 46A). Hypopygium Fig. 142A—
             Chaetocladius dentiforceps (Edwards)

—   Gonostylus not as above—   **2**

2   Anal point very slender and delicate in appearance (arrow, Fig. 46B). Hypopygium Fig. 142B—   **Chaetocladius dissipatus** (Edwards)

—   Anal point otherwise—   **3**

3   Anal point short, reaching only about halfway along the gonocoxite lobe (Figs 46C,D)—   **4**

—   Anal point extending to the tip of the gonocoxite lobe or beyond (Figs 46G,H)—   **5**

4   Gonocoxite lobe large, apparently double, occupying about three-quarters of the inner margin of the gonocoxite (arrows, Fig. 46E). Hypopygium Fig. 142C—   **Chaetocladius perennis** (Meigen)

—   Gonocoxite lobe occupying only about half of the inner margin of the gonocoxite and differently shaped (arrows, Fig. 46F). Hypopygium Fig. 142D—   **Chaetocladius melaleucus** (Meigen)

5(3) Anal point triangular (Fig. 46G) and extending well beyond the inner lobe of the gonocoxite. Hypopygium Fig. 143A—
             Chaetocladius piger (Goetghebuer)

—   Anal point roughly parallel-sided and distally rounded (Fig. 46H), hardly reaching beyond the gonocoxite lobe. Hypopygium Fig. 143B—
             Chaetocladius suecicus (Kieffer)

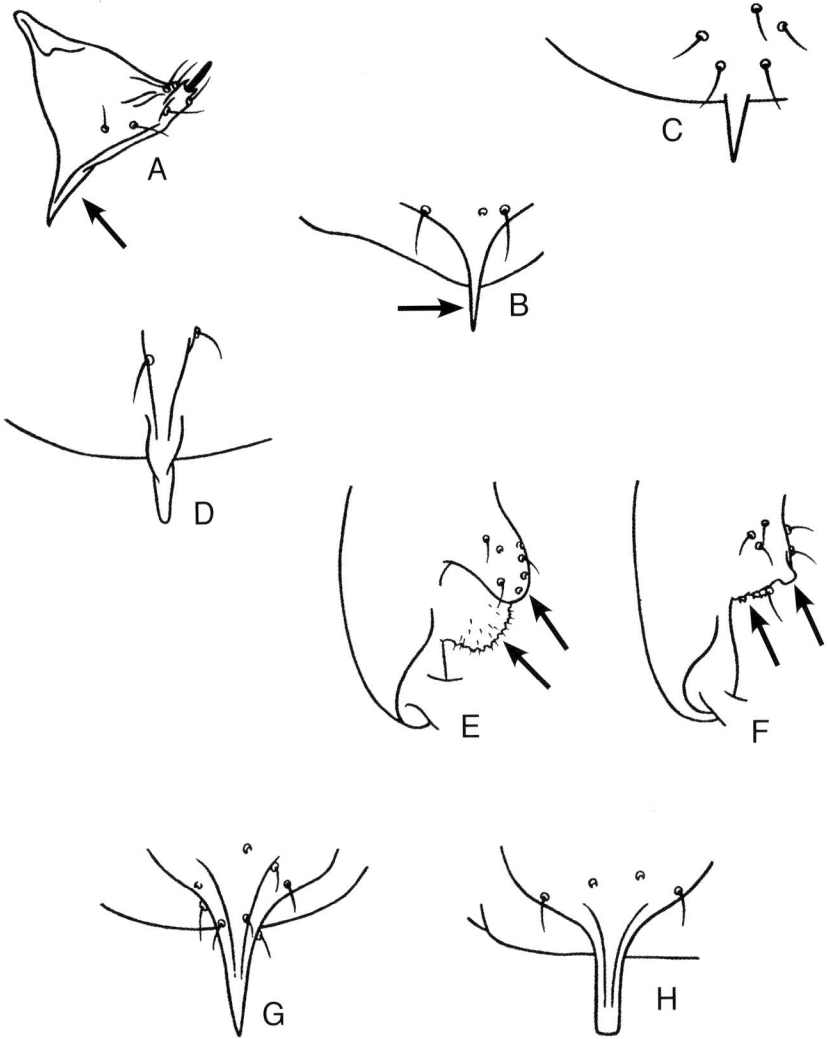

Fig. 46. **A:** gonostylus of *Chaetocladius dentiforceps*. **B–D:** anal points of: B, *C. dissipatus*; C, *C. melaleucus*; D, *C. perennis*. **E, F:** gonocoxites of: E, *C. perennis*; F, *C. melaleucus*. **G, H:** anal points of: G, *C. piger*; H, *C. suecicus*.

Genus CLUNIO Haliday

A marine genus of which only one species has been recorded for Britain and Ireland. The hypopygium (Fig. 143C) is distinctive —

Clunio marinus Haliday

Genus CORYNONEURA Winnertz

1 Tip of antenna bare (Fig. 47B). Hypopygium Fig. 144A —
   Corynoneura carriana Edwards

— Tip of antenna with a group of setae (e.g. arrow, Fig. 47A) —   **2**

2 Gonocoxite without an inner lobe, or with only a very slight lobe (arrows, Figs 47C,D) —   **3**

— Gonocoxite with a prominent lobe (arrows, Fig. 47G–J) —   **7**

3 Apical antennal flagellomere only as long as the preceding two or three combined. Hypopygium Fig. 144B —   **Corynoneura celtica** Edwards

— Apical antennal flagellomere at least as long as the preceding six flagellomeres combined —   **4**

4 Gonostylus without a projecting thumb-shaped crista dorsalis (p. 17), strongly curved and tapered to a finely pointed apex (arrow, Fig. 47E). Hypopygium Fig. 144C —   **Corynoneura edwardsi** Brundin

— Gonostylus with a projecting thumb-shaped crista dorsalis, not so tapered distally (arrow, Fig. 47F) —   **5**

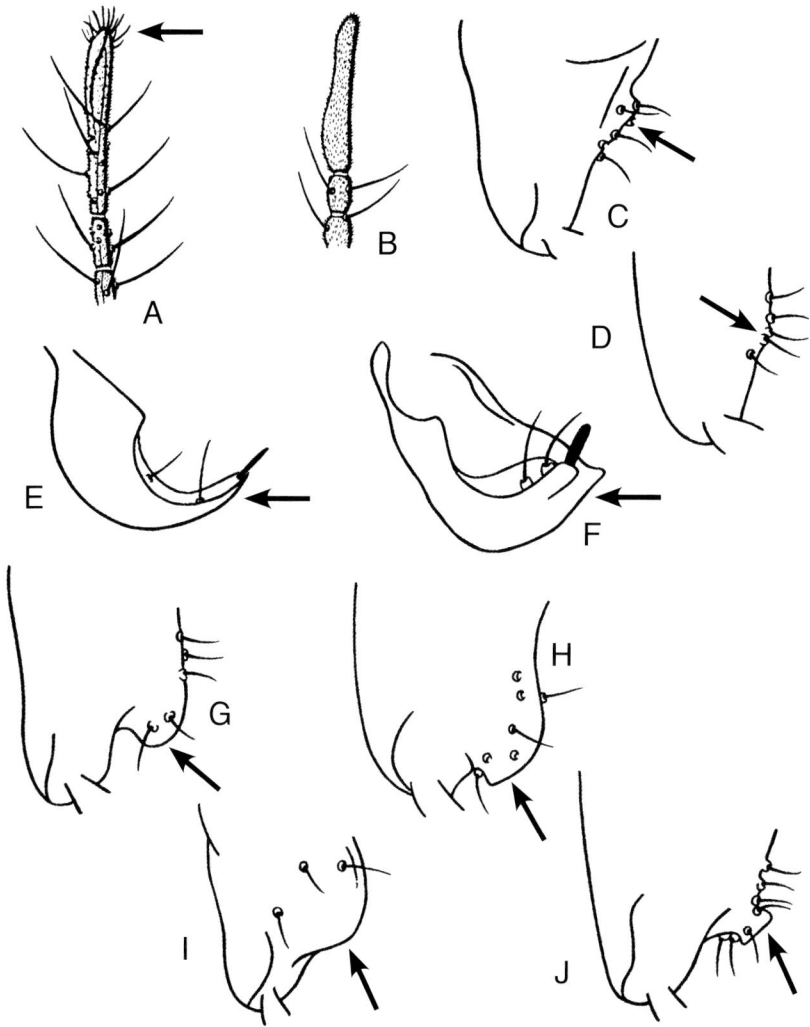

Fig. 47. **A, B:** apices of antennal flagellum of: A, *Corynoneura celtica*; B, *C. carriana*. **C, D:** gonocoxites of: C, *C. celtica*; D, *C. scutellata*. **E, F:** gonostyli of: E, *C. edwardsi*; F, *C. scutellata*. **G–J:** gonocoxites of: G, *C. celeripes*; H, *C. lacustris*; I, *C. coronata*; J, *C. lobata*.

5   Hypopygium with a hinge *h* for the phallapodeme *ph* (p. 17) situated ventrally on the posterior curve of the sternapodeme *st* (Fig. 48C). Penultimate segment of maxillary palp little longer than the first free, spherical segment. Hypopygium Fig. 144D—
Corynoneura gratias Schlee

—   Hinge *h* for phallapodeme *ph* situated laterally on the inner arm of the sternapodeme *st* before its posterior curve (Fig. 48D). Penultimate segment of maxillary palp twice as long as broad—   **6**

6   Short apical seta of posterior tibia strongly bent outwards at the base so that it projects at right angles to the long axis of the tibia (arrow, Fig. 48A). Gonocoxite with a minute subapical projecting lobe (arrow, Fig. 48G). Hypopygium Fig. 145A—   **Corynoneura scutellata** Winnertz

—   Short apical seta of posterior tibia weakly sinuous, projecting in the direction of the long axis of the tibia (arrow, Fig. 48B). Gonocoxite without a lobe. Hypopygium Fig. 145B—**Corynoneura arctica** Kieffer

7(2) Phallapodeme *ph* very long and semicircularly arched (cf. Fig. 48D)— **8**

—   Phallapodeme *ph* short and nearly straight (Fig. 48E)—   **10**

8   Hypopygium with a hinge *h* for the phallapodeme *ph* situated ventrally on the posterior curve of the sternapodeme *st* (Fig. 48F). Hypopygium Fig. 145C—   **Corynoneura coronata** Edwards

—   Hinge *h* for phallapodeme *ph* situated laterally on the inner arm of the sternapodeme *st* (cf. Fig. 48D)—   **9**

9   Lobe of gonocoxite small (arrow, Fig. 47J, p. 89). Hypopygium Fig. 145D—   **Corynoneura lobata** Edwards

—   Lobe of gonocoxite large (arrow, Fig. 47G, p. 89). Hypopygium Fig. 146B—   **Corynoneura celeripes** Winnertz

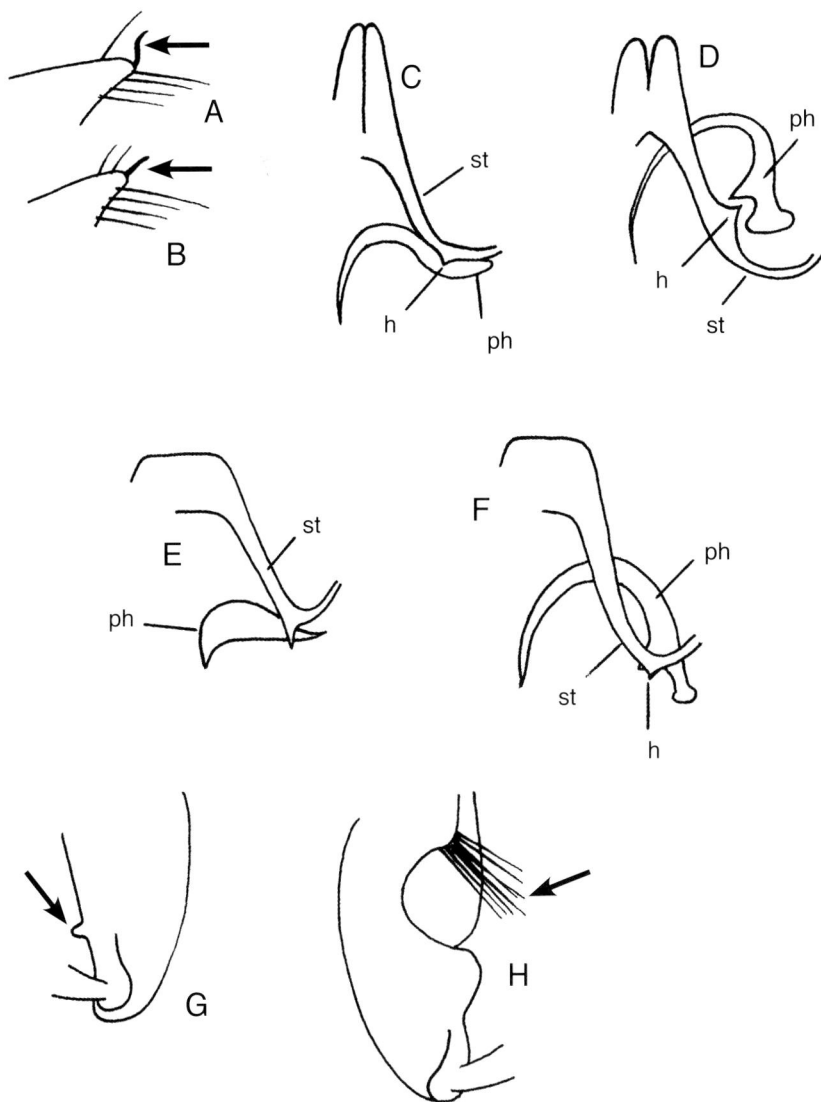

Fig. 48. **A, B:** apex of posterior tibia of: A, *Corynoneura scutellata*; B, *C. arctica*. **C–F:** phallapodemes and sternapodemes of: C, *C. gratias*; D, *C. arctica*; E, *C. lacustris*; F, *C. coronata*. **G, H:** gonocoxites of: G, *C. scutellata*; H, *C. fittkaui*.

10(7) Inner margin of gonocoxite basally with several long setae, about as long as the coxite is wide (arrow, Fig. 48H). Hypopygium Fig. 146A—
Corynoneura fittkaui Schlee

— Base of gonocoxite without long setae on the inner margin; inner lobe extending almost to the tip of the gonocoxite (arrow, Fig. 47H). Hypopygium Fig. 146C—   **Corynoneura lacustris** Edwards

Genus CORYNONEURELLA Brundin

The only representative of this genus described so far is very similar to *Thienemanniella* and *Corynoneura*, but can be distinguished by the apical lobe of the gonocoxite (Fig. 35D, p. 67). Hypopygium Fig. 146D—
Corynoneurella paludosa Brundin

Genus CRICOTOPUS van der Wulp

1 Hypopygium with a long anal point exceeding the posterior margin of tergite IX (Fig. 49A). Hypopygium Fig. 147A—
Cricotopus (Nostococladius) lygropis Edwards

— Hypopygium at most with a minute anal point, set dorsally on tergite IX—   **2**

2 Gonocoxite without an inner lobe—   **3**

— Gonocoxite with a projecting inner lobe which may be double (arrows, Figs 49B–F)—   **4**

3 Antennal ratio 1.5–1.8 (p. 9). Anal vein *An* on wing (Fig. 5, p. 13) extending about half-way along vein Cu_1. Hypopygium Fig. 147B—
Cricotopus (Cricotopus) trifascia Edwards

— Antennal ratio 1.0-1.3. Anal vein on wing scarcely reaching beyond cross-vein FCu. Hypopygium Fig. 147C—
Cricotopus (C.) similis Goetghebuer

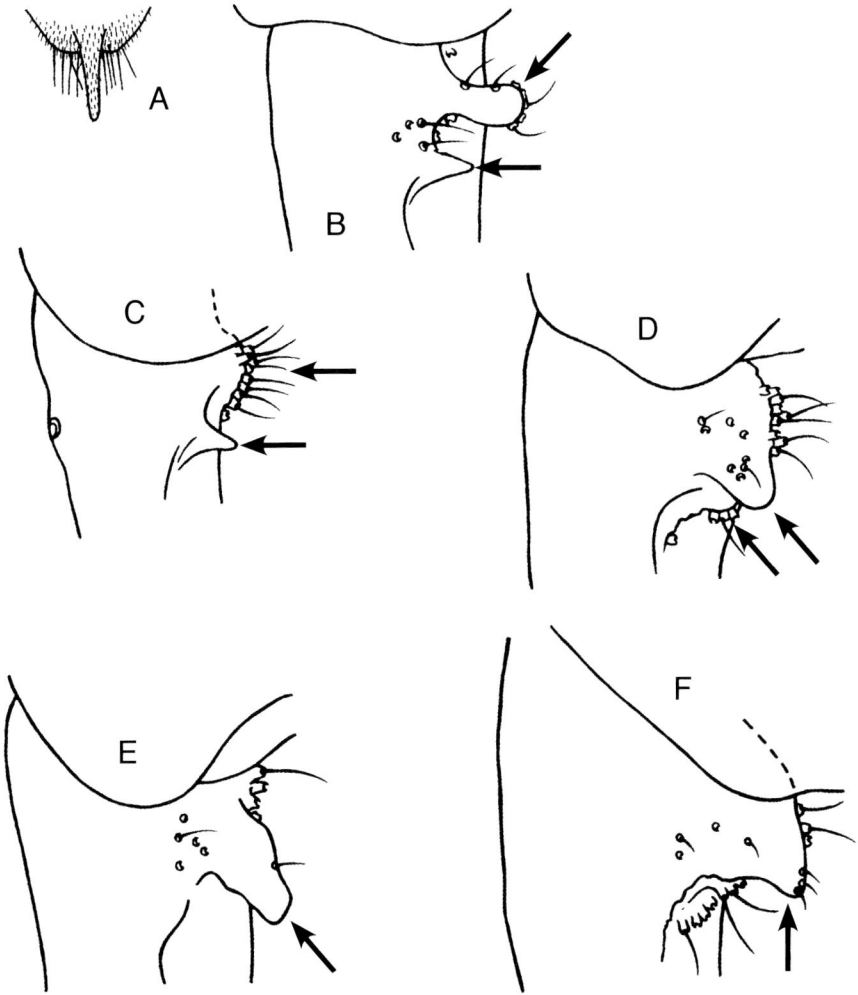

Fig. 49. **A:** anal point of *Cricotopus lygropis*. **B–F:** Gonocoxite lobes of: B, *C. annulator*; C, *C. fuscus*; D, *C. pulchripes*; E, *C. tremulus*; F, *C. festivellis*.

4(2) Lobe of gonocoxite distinctly double (arrows, Figs 49B,C) or broadly rectangular—   **5**

—   Lobe of gonocoxite usually single and relatively slender (arrows, Figs 49E,F), but occasionally a second very small lobe is discernible (lower arrow, Fig. 49D)—   **14**

5   Abdominal tergite III uniformly covered with setae (Fig. 50A)—   **6**

—   Median and lateral setae of tergite III clearly separated (Figs 50B,C)—
                                                                              9

6   Anterior prealar setae *ap* present, continuous with the posterior prealars
     pp (Fig. 50D); scutellar setae *sc* numerous (130–150); dorsocentral setae
     dc dense (120–180 on each side), extending to the scutellum *sc* (Fig.
     50D). Hypopygium Fig. 147D—   **Cricotopus (C.) pilosellus** Brundin

—   Anterior prealar setae absent; scutellar setae fewer; dorsocentral setae
     less numerous, with the prescutellar area bare (e.g. Fig. 50E)—   **7**

7   Megaseta at apex of gonostylus very long, nearly half the length of the
     gonostylus (arrow, Fig. 50F). Hypopygium Fig. 148A—
                                                   Cricotopus (C.) polaris Kieffer

—   Megaseta short—   **8**

8   Antennal ratio 1.0 or less (p. 9). Inner lobe of gonocoxite broadly
     rectangular (arrow, Fig. 50G), rarely with indication of a second lobe.
     Hypopygium Fig. 148B—   **Cricotopus (C.) ephippium** (Zetterstedt)

—   Antennal ratio 1.3 or more. Inner lobe of gonocoxite distinctly two-lobed
     (arrows, Fig. 50H). Hypopygium Fig. 148C—
                                                   Cricotopus (C.) tibialis (Meigen)

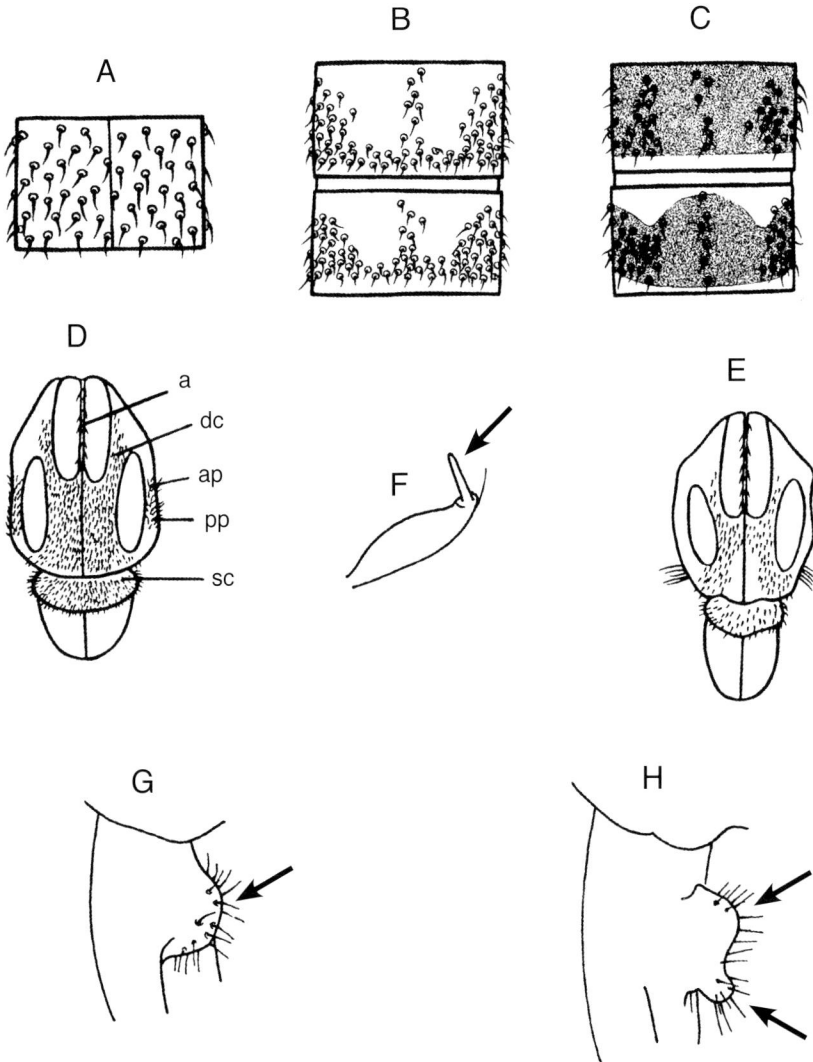

Fig. 50. **A–C:** third and fourth abdominal tergites of: A, *Cricotopus reversus*; B, *C. fuscus*; C, *C. pilitarsis*. **D, E:** dorsal views of the thorax of: D, *C. pilosellus* (a = acrostichal setae, dc = dorsocentral setae, ap = anterior prealar setae, pp = posterior prealar setae, sc = scutellar setae); E, *C. polaris*. **F:** gonostylus of *C. polaris*. **G, H:** gonocoxite lobes of: G, *C. ephippium*; H, *C. tibialis*.

9(5) Tibiae not distinctly ringed. Abdomen without pale markings. The two arms of the gonocoxite lobe are roughly equal in length (arrows, Fig. 51A). Hypopygium Fig. 148D—   **Cricotopus (C.) fuscus** (Kieffer)

—   At least the fore-tibia with a distinct pale median ring. Abdomen usually with conspicuous pale markings. Anterior arm of gonocoxite lobe much longer than the posterior arm (arrows, Figs 51B,C)—   **10**

10   Abdominal tergites with narrow pale bands along the anterior and posterior margins; tergite I sometimes pale. Hypopygium Fig. 149A—
          Cricotopus (C.) cylindraceus (Kieffer)

—   Abdomen coloured otherwise—   **11**

11   Small anal point present on tergite IX. Crista dorsalis of gonostylus (p. 17) extremely narrow (arrow, Fig. 51D). Hypopygium Fig. 149B—
          Cricotopus (C.) tristis Hirvenoja

—   Anal point absent. Crista dorsalis distinct, broadening to the tip of the gonostylus (arrow, Fig. 51E)—   **12**

12   Anterior arm of gonocoxite lobe tapered, pointed distally (arrow, Fig. 51B). Bulk of tergites IV and V pale. Hypopygium Fig. 149C—
          Cricotopus (C.) triannulatus (Macquart)

—   Anterior arm of gonocoxite lobe roughly parallel-sided and broadly rounded distally (arrow, Fig. 51C). Tergites IV and V mainly or all dark—   **13**

13   Tergites I and II pale, the margins between tergites III and IV, IV and V narrowly pale; distal part of hypopygium pale. Anterior arm of gonocoxite lobe relatively weak. Hypopygium Fig. 149D—
          Cricotopus (C.) curtus Hirvenoja

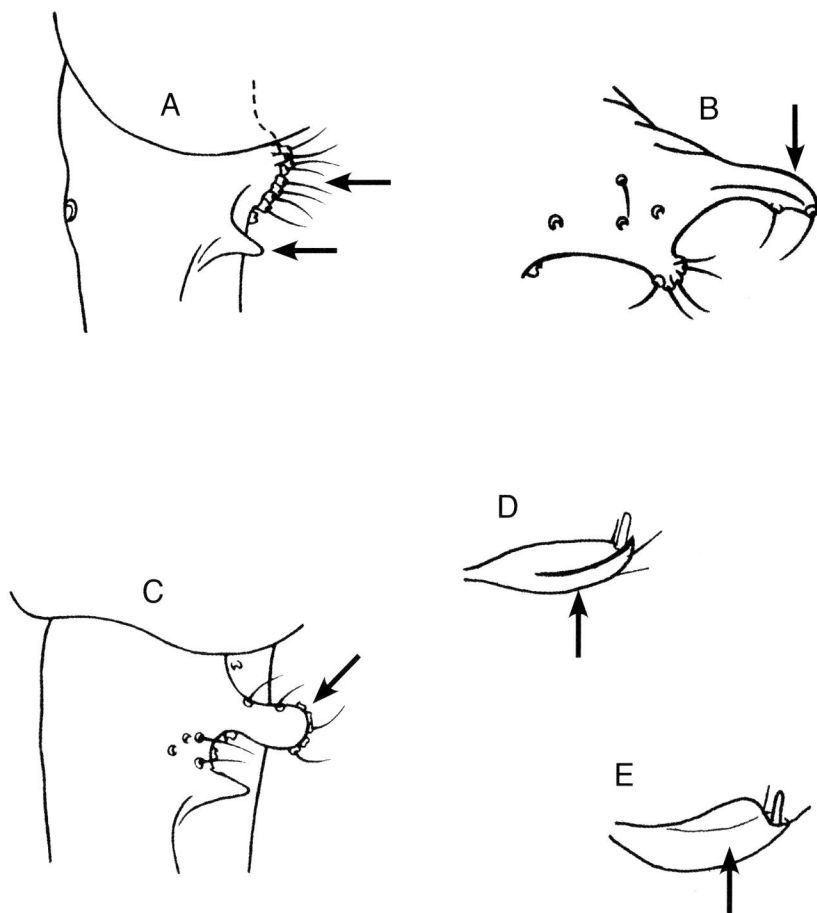

Fig. 51. **A–C:** gonocoxite lobes of: A, *Cricotopus fuscus*; B, *C. triannulatus*; C, *C. annulator*. **D, E:** gonostyli of: D, *C. tristis*; E, *C. triannulatus*.

—(13) Abdomen all dark except distal part of hypopygium, or with tergites I or I and II pale, and the margins between tergites III and IV, IV and V broadly pale. Anterior arm of gonocoxite lobe relatively large (arrow, Fig. 51C). Hypopygium Fig. 150A—

Cricotopus (C.) annulator Goetghebuer

14(4) Inner margin of gonocoxite anterior to the lobe flattened or slightly
       rounded (arrows, Fig. 52A)—   **15**

—   Inner margin of gonocoxite anterior to the lobe either produced to form a
       distinct hump just before the base (arrows, Fig. 52B) or strongly rounded
       (arrows, Figs 52C,D)—   **23**

15   Lobe of gonocoxite directed backwards, very long, nearly reaching the
       insertion of the gonostylus (arrow, Fig. 52E). Hypopygium Fig. 150B—
                                    Cricotopus (C.) vierriensis Goetghebuer

—   Lobe of gonocoxite much shorter—   **16**

16   Fore-*tarsi* partly whitish—   **17**

—   Fore-*tarsi* uniformly dark or legs unicolorous pale—   **18**

17   Second tarsomere of fore-leg mostly white, remaining tarsomeres dark.
       Antennal ratio 1.2–1.4 (p. 9). Anterior leg ratio 0.57–0.69 (p. 14).
       Hypopygium Fig. 150C—   **Cricotopus (C.) pulchripes** Verrall

—   Proximal half of tarsomere 3 and whole of tarsomere 2 of fore-leg white.
       Antennal ratio 1.4–1.6. Anterior leg ratio 0.57–0.64. Hypopygium Fig.
       150D—   **Cricotopus (C.) tremulus** (Linnaeus)

18(16) Fore-*tibiae* indistinctly pale medially or legs all pale—   **19**

—   *All* tibiae with conspicuous pale, median rings—   **20**

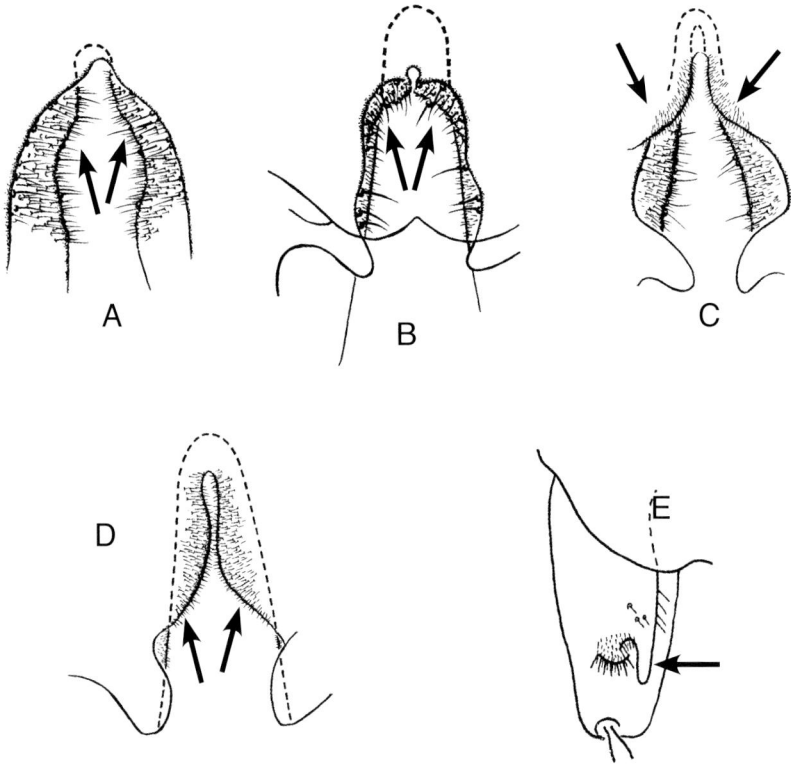

Fig. 52.   **A–D:** ventro-basal area of the hypopygium of: A, *Cricotopus vierriensis*; B, *C. sylvestris*; C, *C. intersectus*; D, *C. brevipalpis*. **E:** gonocoxite lobe of *C. vierriensis*.

19   Gonocoxite lobe strongly bent backwards (arrow, Fig. 53A). Hypopygium
      Fig. 151A—   **Cricotopus (C.) caducus** Hirvenoja

—   Gonocoxite lobe projecting, not strongly curved (arrow, Fig. 53B).
      Hypopygium Fig. 151B—   **Cricotopus (C.) pallidipes** Edwards

20(18) Abdominal tergite IV at least partly dark—   **21**

—   Tergite IV yellow—   **22**

21   Tergite I pale, remainder of abdomen mostly or entirely dark. Gonocoxite
      lobe slender and strongly curved backwards (arrow, Fig. 53C).
      Hypopygium Fig. 151C—   **Cricotopus (C.) flavocinctus** (Kieffer)

—   At least the posterior quarter of tergite IV and the anterior quarter of
      tergite V are pale, tergites I and II sometimes pale, remaining tergites
      sometimes with pale posterior margins. Gonocoxite lobe rather broad
      (arrow, Fig. 53D). Hypopygium Fig. 151D—
                                  Cricotopus (C.) festivellus (Kieffer)

22(20) Tergites I and IV pale, remainder dark. Hypopygium Fig. 152A—
                                  Cricotopus (C.) bicinctus (Meigen)

—   Tergites I, II and IV pale. Hypopygium Fig. 152B—
                                  Cricotopus (C.) albiforceps (Kieffer)

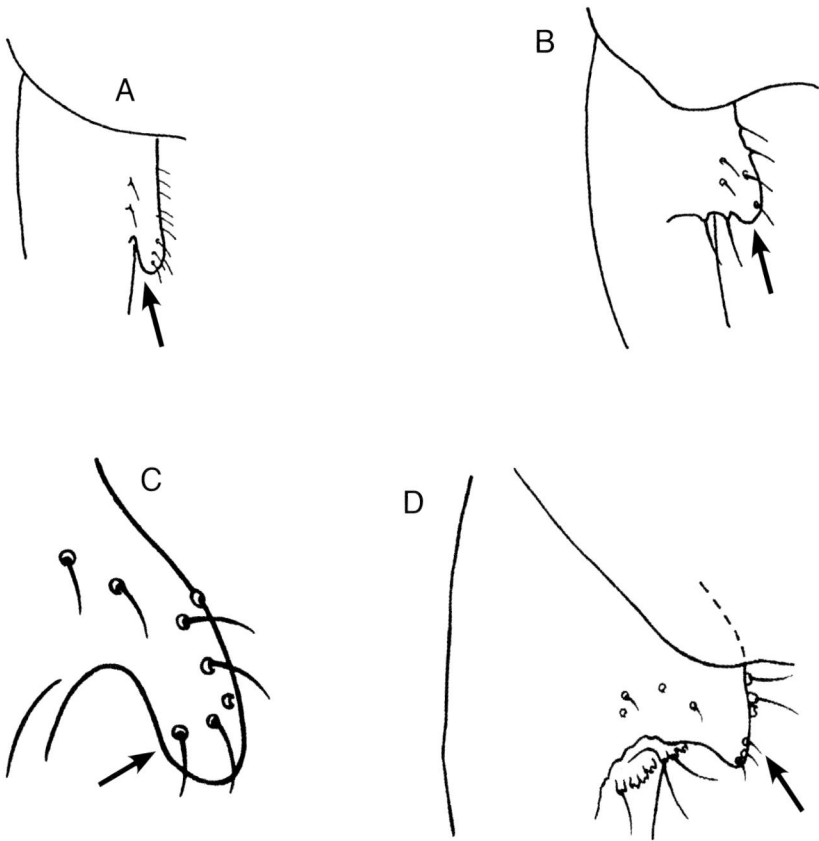

Fig. 53. **A–G:** gonocoxite lobes of: A, *C. caducus*; B, *C. pallidipes*; C, *C. flavocinctus*; D, *C. festivellus*.

23(14)   Inner margin of gonocoxite basally rounded, not produced (e.g. as in Figs 52C,D, p. 99)— **24**

—   Inner margin of gonocoxite produced into a definite hump basally (as in Fig. 52B)— **27**

24   Abdominal tergite III uniformly covered with setae (Fig. 54A).
     Hypopygium Fig. 152C— **Cricotopus (Isocladius) reversus** Hirvenoja

—   Median and lateral setae of tergite III separated by a bare intermediate
     area—   **25**

25   Maxillary palps very short, CP ratio (maximum width of head to length
     of palp excluding basal segment) 2.1–2.6. Hypopygium Fig. 152D—
                                      Cricotopus (I.) brevipalpis Kieffer

—   Maxillary palps normal, CP ratio 1.7 or less—   **26**

26   Legs and abdomen, including the hypopygium, uniformly dark.
     Hypopygium Fig. 153A—   **Cricotopus (I.) obnixus** (Walker)

—   Hypopygium pale distally. Abdominal tergites I and IV sometimes
     pale. Fore-tibia sometimes with a pale median ring. Hypopygium Fig.
     153B—   **Cricotopus (I.) intersectus** (Staeger)

27(23) Abdominal tergite III with an incomplete transverse band of setae
     posteriorly (Fig. 54B). Abdomen mainly dark, at most with posterior
     margins of tergites VIII narrowly pale. Tibiae with or without pale
     median rings—   **28**

—   Abdominal tergite III without a transverse band of setae posteriorly.
     Abdomen usually distinctly banded. Tibiae always with distinct pale
     rings—   **29**

28   Pulvilli absent. Inner dorsal margin of gonocoxite between the lobe and
     apex deeply arcuate (arrow, Fig. 54C). Hypopygium Fig. 153C—
                                       Cricotopus (I.) arcuatus Hirvenoja

—   Small pulvilli present on the apex of the tarsus. Gonocoxite not so deeply
     excavated dorsally (arrow, Fig. 54D). Hypopygium Fig. 153D—
                                      Cricotopus (I.) laricomalis Edwards

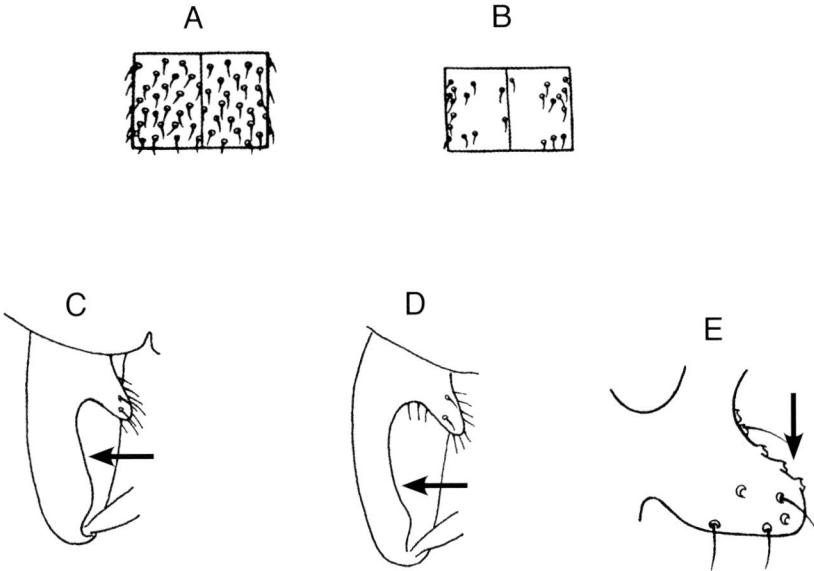

Fig. 54. **A:** setation on third abdominal tergites of *Cricotopus reversus*. **B:** setation on fourth abdominal tergite of *C. laricomalis*. **C–E:** gonocoxite lobes of: C, *Cricotopus arcuatus*; D, *C. laricomalis*; E, *C. pilitarsis*.

29(27) Inner lobe of gonocoxite about 40 μm in breadth, roughly parallel-sided, broadly rounded distally (arrow, Fig. 54E). Hypopygium Fig. 154A — **Cricotopus (I.) pilitarsis** (Zetterstedt)

— Gonocoxite lobe much narrower (measured half-way along), usually distinctly conical in shape — **30**

30 Setal beard ratio (p. 14) 3.0 to 6.0 for the third tarsomere of the fore-leg. Fore-tibiae normally dark, mid- and hind-tibiae usually with distinct pale rings. In dark specimens only the posterior margin of tergite VIII is pale, whereas in pale specimens all tergites have pale borders. Hypopygium Fig. 154B — **Cricotopus (I.) ornatus** (Meigen)

— Setal beard ratio <3.0, usually much less. Fore-tibiae with pale rings. Coloration otherwise — **31**

31   Pale *fore*-tibial rings narrow, occupying one-third the length of the tibia, which is much more broadly darkened basally than distally. Dorsocentral setae numbering between 37 and 43, scutellar setae between 26 and 28. Abdomen with tergite I yellow, IV darkened at least anterolaterally, VII pale posteriorly and the remainder with more or less distinctly pale margins. Hypopygium Fig. 154C—
Cricotopus (I.) speciosus Goetghebuer

—   Rings on *fore*-tibia broader, occupying about half the tibiae. Dorsocentral setae fewer than 30, scutellar setae numbering between 8 and 15—   **32**

32   Tergites I, IV and VII mainly or entirely yellow, remainder dark—   **33**

—   Coloration variable. Sometimes only the posterior margin of tergites VI and VII are pale, but pale markings may be more extensive; however, if tergites I, IV and VII are predominantly pale, then tergite V is also pale. Hypopygium Fig. 154D—   **Cricotopus (I.) sylvestris** (Fabricius)

33   Prescutellar area of scutum darkened. Femora dark. Anterior corners of tergite IV sometimes darkened. Hypopygium Fig. 155A—
Cricotopus (I.) tricinctus (Meigen)

—   Prescutellar area pale. Femora pale proximally, darkened distally. Any darkening of tergite IV is confined to a central triangle. Hypopygium Fig. 155B—   **Cricotopus (I.) trifasciatus** (Meigen)

Genus DIPLOCLADIUS Kieffer

The single European species is readily identified by the characteristic hypopygium (Fig. 155C)—   **Diplocladius cultriger** Kieffer

Genus EPOICOCLADIUS Sulc & Zavrel

Only one species is recorded for Britain and Ireland, which should be readily identified from the characters given in the key to genera (p. 68). The hypopygium is shown in Fig. 155D—   **Epoicocladius ephemerae** (Kieffer)

Genus EUKIEFFERIELLA Thienemann

1   Eyes hairy (pp. 9–10). Squama at base of wing bare. Hypopygium Fig.
     156A—   **Eukiefferiella coerulescens** (Kieffer)

—   Eyes pubescent. Squama at base of wing fringed with setae—   **2**

2   Inner lobe of gonocoxite more or less rectangular (Fig. 55A)—   **3**

—   Inner lobe of gonocoxite elongate (Figs 55B–D)—   **4**

3   Antennal ratio (p. 9) about 0.6 or less. Hypopygium Fig. 156B—
                                              Eukiefferiella devonica (Edwards)

—   Antennal ratio about 0.9. Hypopygium Fig. 156C—
                                              Eukiefferiella ilkleyensis (Edwards)

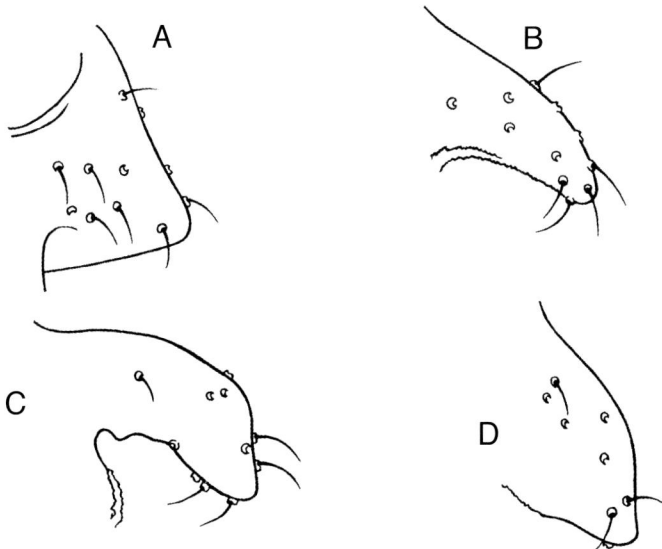

Fig. 55.   **A–D:** gonocoxite lobes of: A, *Eukiefferiella ilkleyensis*; B, *E. clypeata*; C, *E. claripennis*; D, *E. brevicalcar*.

4(2) Gonostylus of unusual shape, strongly expanded proximally (arrow, Fig. 56A). Hypopygium Fig. 156D—   **Eukiefferiella gracei** (Edwards)

—   Gonostylus not expanded proximally—   **5**

5   Gonostylus rather short, not reaching back to the gonocoxite lobe, its inner margin produced into a subapical tooth (arrow, Fig. 56B). Hypopygium Fig. 157A—   **Eukiefferiella minor** (Edwards)

—   Gonostylus elongate, extending to the gonocoxite lobe, without a subapical tooth—   **6**

6   Inner lobe of gonocoxite very slender (Fig. 55B, p. 105). Hypopygium Fig. 157B—   **Eukiefferiella clypeata** (Kieffer)

—   Gonocoxite lobe broader (Figs 55C,D)—   **7**

7   Wing vein R_{2+3} present (see Fig. 5, p. 13)—   **8**

—   Wing vein R_{2+3} absent (Figs 56D,E)—   **10**

8   Gonostylus boat-shaped, widest at about the middle and tapered to a bluntly pointed tip; megaseta sited subapically (arrow, Fig. 56C). Hypopygium Fig. 157C—   **Eukiefferiella ancyla** Svensson

—   Gonostylus narrower, more parallel-sided; megaseta situated near the apex—   **9**

9   Anal lobe of wing weak. Squama at base of wing fringed with more than 10 setae. Mid- and hind-tibia with only one apical spur. Hypopygium Fig. 157D—   **Eukiefferiella dittmari** Lehmann

—   Anal lobe of wing normal. Squama fringed with very few setae (about 4). Mid- and hind-tibia with two apical spurs. Hypopygium Fig. 158A—
                                            Eukiefferiella fittkaui Lehmann

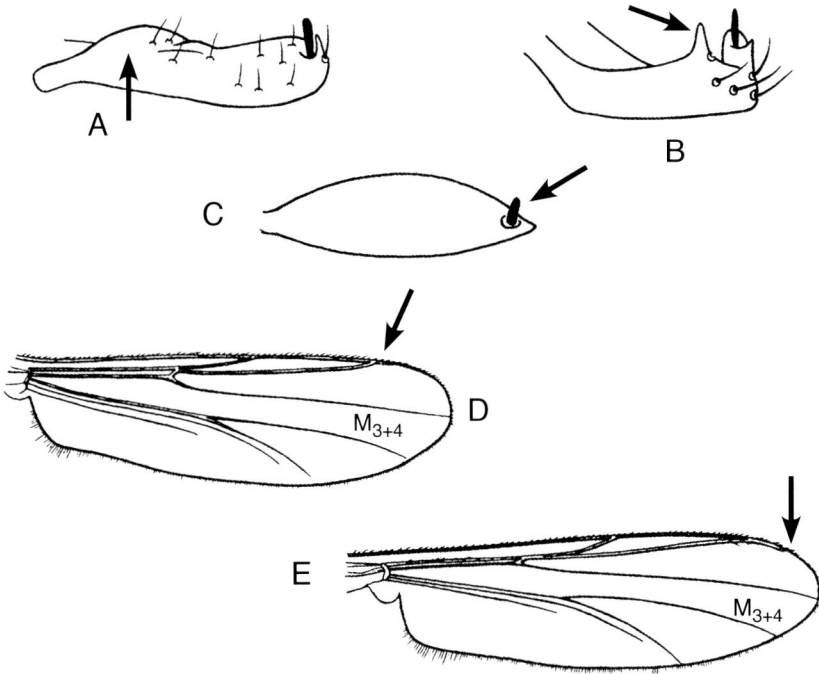

Fig. 56. **A–C:** gonostyli of: A, *Eukiefferiella gracei*; B, *E. minor*; C, *E. ancyla*. **D, E:** wings of: D, *E. claripennis*; F, *E. brevicalcar*.

10(7) Costa of wing ending well proximal to the tip of vein M_{3+4} (arrow, Fig. 56D). Hypopygium Fig. 158B —

Eukiefferiella claripennis (Lundbeck)

— Costa of wing ending above or only slightly proximal to the tip of vein M_{3+4} (arrow, Fig. 56E) — **11**

11 Antennal ratio (p. 9) <0.6. Hypopygium Fig. 158C —

Eukiefferiella tirolensis Goetghebuer

— Antennal ratio >0.6. Hypopygium Fig. 158D —

Eukiefferiella brevicalcar (Kieffer)

Genus EURYCNEMUS van der Wulp

A monospecific genus in which the hypopygium (Fig. 159A) is highly characteristic— **Eurycnemus crassipes** (Meigen)

Genus EURYHAPSIS

Pupal exuviae of a very distinctive species of *Euryhapsis* have been collected in England but the adult remains unknown. Any adult male that keys out to this genus should be referred to a specialist for identification.

Genus GEORTHOCLADIUS Strenzke

The only species that has been described from Europe is easily recognisable by its characteristic hypopygium (Fig. 159B). The anal point is similar to that of *Pseudorthocladius* spp., in that it is covered in microtrichia and bears long setae, but the form of the gonostylus, which is strongly expanded towards the apex, is distinctive—
Georthocladius luteicornis (Goetghebuer)

Genus GYMNOMETRIOCNEMUS Edwards

1   Dark species, thorax black with scutal stripes fused. Inner margin of the gonostylus is expanded medially (arrow, Fig. 57A). Hypopygium Fig. 159C— **Gymnometriocnemus brumalis** (Edwards)

—   Paler species, ground colour of thorax yellowish, scutal stripes separate. Gonostylus not expanded medially (arrow, Fig. 57B). Hypopygium Fig. 159D— **Gymnometriocnemus subnudus** (Edwards)

Genus HALOCLADIUS Hirvenoja

1   Gonocoxite lobe of two flanges, the upper flange *uf* a little more proximal, pale in colour, mostly overlapping the lower flange *lf*, which is concolorous with the rest of the hypopygium (Fig. 57C). Hypopygium Fig. 160A— **Halocladius (Psammocladius) braunsi** (Goetghebuer)

—   Gonocoxite lobe single—   **2**

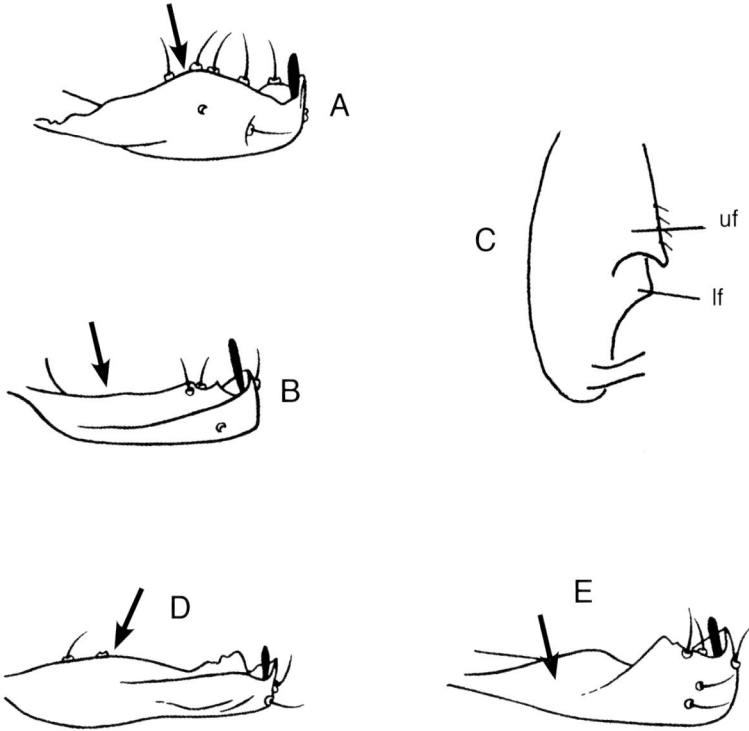

Fig. 57. **A, B:** gonostyli of: A, *Gymnometriocnemus brumalis*; B, *G. subnudus*. **C:** gonocoxite of *Halocladius braunsi*. **D, E:** gonostyli of: D, *H. variabilis*; E, *H. varians*.

2   Antennal ratio 0.6–0.7 (p. 9). Hypopygium Fig. 160B —
          Halocladius (Halocladius) fucicola (Edwards)

—   Antennal ratio >1.0 —   **3**

3   Inner margin of gonostylus somewhat expanded on the basal half to two-thirds (arrow, Fig. 57D). Hypopygium Fig. 160C —
          Halocladius (H.) variabilis (Staeger)

—   Gonostylus narrow basally (arrow, Fig. 57E). Hypopygium Fig. 160D —
          Halocladius (H.) varians (Staeger)

Genus HELENIELLA Gowin

The single species recorded from Britain and Ireland is easily identified from the characters given in the key to genera (p. 66) and from the distinctive hypopygium (Fig. 161A). (Note: some specimens have a small anal point)—
Heleniella ornaticollis (Edwards)

Genus HETEROTANYTARSUS Spärck

The one representative of this genus recorded from Britain and Ireland has a characteristic hypopygium (Fig. 161B)—
Heterotanytarsus apicalis (Kieffer)

Genus HETEROTRISSOCLADIUS Spärck

1   Larger species: wing length >3 mm. Wing membrane with macrotrichia over the entire surface. Hypopygium Fig. 161C—
Heterotrissocladius marcidus (Walker)

—   Smaller species: wing length <3 mm. Wing membrane with macrotrichia restricted to the apical half or less—   **2**

2   Wing length about 2.5 mm. Antennal ratio (p. 9) >1.0 (1.4–1.6). Wing membrane with macrotrichia on approximately the apical half. Hypopygium Fig. 161D—   **Heterotrissocladius grimshawi** (Edwards)

—   Wing length 2.1–2.2 mm. Antennal ratio <1.0 (0.68). Wing membrane with a few macrotrichia near the apex. Hypopygium Fig. 162A—
Heterotrissocladius brundini Sæther & Schnell

Genus KRENOSMITTIA Thienemann & Krüger

1   Smaller: wing length only about 1 mm. Antennal ratio (p. 9) about 0.2; last flagellomere without long plume setae. Hypopygium Fig. 162B —
     Krenosmittia boreoalpina (Goetghebuer)

—   Slightly larger: wing length about 1.2 mm. Antennal ratio about 0.35; last flagellomere with long plume setae. Hypopygium Fig. 162C —
     Krenosmittia camptophleps (Edwards)

Genus LIMNOPHYES Eaton

1   Hypopygium with an elongate projecting ventral lobe between the bases of the gonocoxites (arrow, Fig. 58A). Hypopygium as in Fig. 162D —   **Limnophyes pumilio** (Holmgren)

—   Hypopygium without such a lobe —   **2**

2   Megaseta absent or setaceous; gonostylus narrowed to a long point (arrow, Fig. 59B) —   **3**

—   Gonostylus not narrowed to a long point; megaseta spinous, setaceous or absent —   **5**

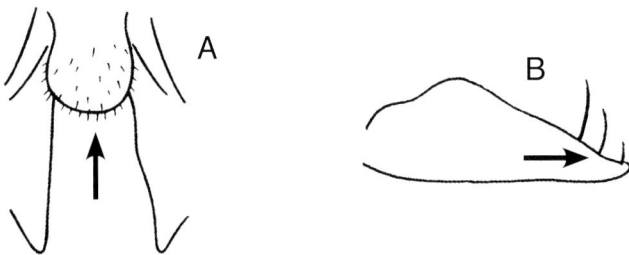

Fig. 58. **A:** globular ventrobasal appendage of the hypopygium of *Limnophyes pumilio*. **B:** gonostylus of *L. paludis*.

Note: thoracic structures referred to in the following part of the key are illustrated in Fig. 59A. For general locations, see Fig. 4, p. 12.

3   Pre-episternum with only an anterior row of setae *as* (Fig. 59B). Hypopygium Fig. 163A —   **Limnophyes paludis** Armitage

—   Pre-episternum with additional posterodorsal setae *ps* (Figs 59C,D) — **4**

4   Anal point not notched. Antennal ratio (p. 9) 0.1–0.3. Thorax as in Fig. 59C. Hypopygium Fig. 163B —   **Limnophyes gurgicola** (Edwards)

—   Anal point usually notched. Antennal ratio 0.5–0.7. Thorax as in Fig. 59D. Hypopygium Fig. 163C —   **Limnophyes pentaplastus** (Kieffer)

5(2) Humeral pit *hp* wide and deep, with lanceolate setae projecting from it or lying within it (e.g. Fig. 59G) —   **6**

—   Humeral pit *hp* small, with lanceolate setae, if present, inserted around its rim —   **7**

6   Anal point *ap* broad, strongly projecting, somewhat parallel-sided (Fig. 59H). Antennal ratio 0.8–1.0. Thorax as in Fig. 59F. Hypopygium Fig. 163D —   **Limnophyes habilis** (Walker)

—   Anal point rounded or broad-conical. Antennal ratio <0.8. Thorax as in Fig. 59E. Hypopygium Fig. 164A —   **Limnophyes difficilis** Brundin

---

Fig. 59. **A:** thorax, lateral view, of *Limnophyes*.
hls = humeral lanceolate setae; hp = humeral pit; as = anterior row of setae on the pre-episternum; ps = posterodorsal setae on the pre-episternum; pls = prescutellar lanceolate setae.

B–F: pre-episternum (left) and humeral area (right) of: B, *Limnophyes paludis*; C, *L. gurgicola*; D, *L. pentaplastus*; E, *L. difficilis*; F, *L. habilis*. **G:** humeral pit of *L. difficilis*. **H:** anal point of *L. habilis*.

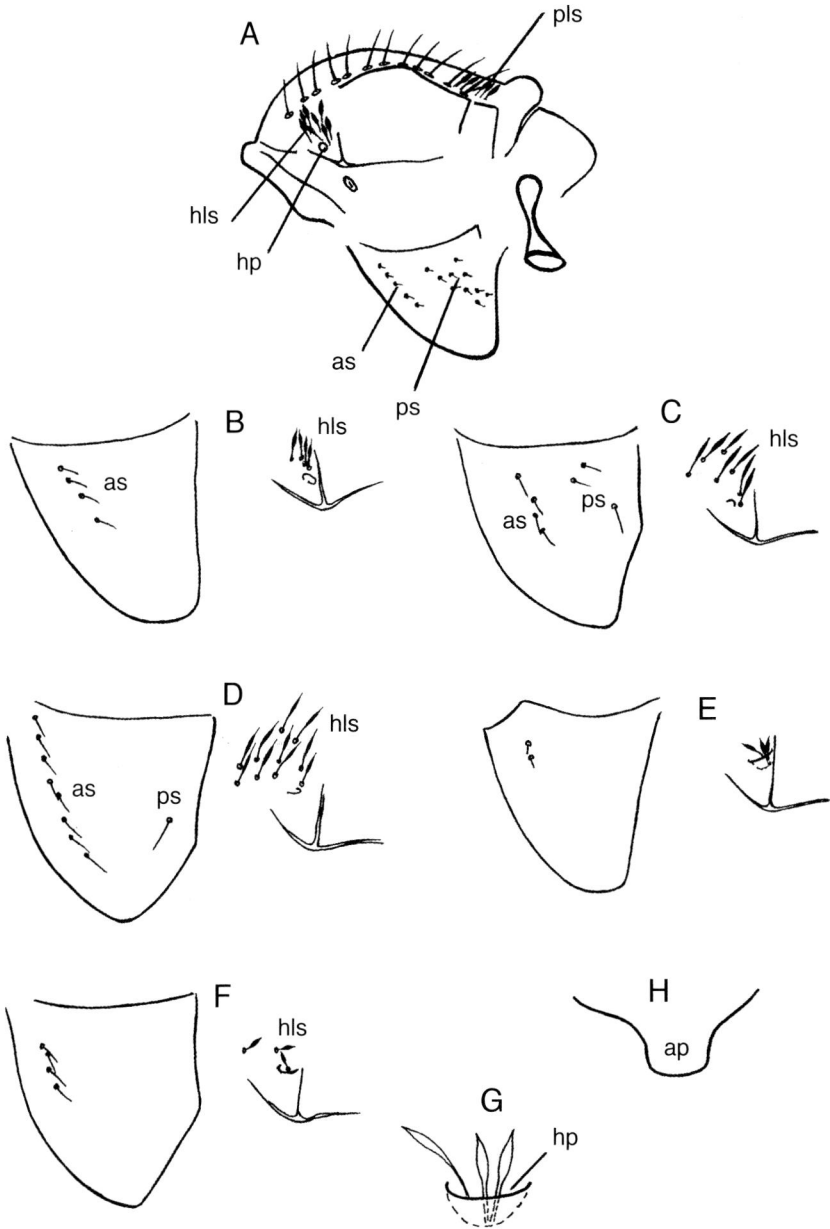

7(5) Pre-episternum without anterior setae, but posterodorsal setae *ps* may be present (e.g. Fig. 60A)—   **8**

—   Pre-episternum with at least one anterior seta *as* (usually an oblique row of setae are present), with or without posterodorsal setae *ps*—   **10**

8   Prescutellar lanceolate setae *pls* (see Fig. 59A, p. 113) numerous (12–36); humeral lanceolate setae *hls* also numerous (Fig. 60B). Hypopygium Fig. 164B—   **Limnophyes brachytomus** (Kieffer)

—   Prescutellar lanceolate setae *pls* less numerous (2–8)—   **9**

9   Humeral lanceolate setae *hls* numerous (10–35) (Fig. 60C). Hypopygium Fig.164C—   **Limnophyes edwardsi** Sæther

—   Humeral lanceolate setae *hls* few (0–8) (Fig. 60A). Hypopygium Fig. 164D—   **Limnophyes asquamatus** Andersen

10(7) Pre-episternum with additional posterodorsal setae *ps* (Fig. 60D). Hypopygium Fig. 165A—   **Limnophyes ninae** Sæther

—   Pre-episternum with at most an anterior row of setae—   **11**

11   Humeral lanceolate setae absent (Fig. 60E). Hypopygium Fig. 165B—
                                    Limnophyes minimus (Meigen)

—   Humeral lanceolate setae present—   **12**

12   Less than 10 humeral lanceolate setae *hls* (Fig. 60F). Virga (p. 17) consisting of 2–4 more or less equally strong spines. Hypopygium Fig. 165C—   **Limnophyes natalensis** (Kieffer)
                and **Limnophyes spinigus** Sæther [see p. 156, Vol. 2]

—   Ten or more humeral lanceolate setae *hls* (Fig. 60G). Virga with a single broad spine. Hypopygium Fig. 165D—   **Limnophyes angelicae** Sæther

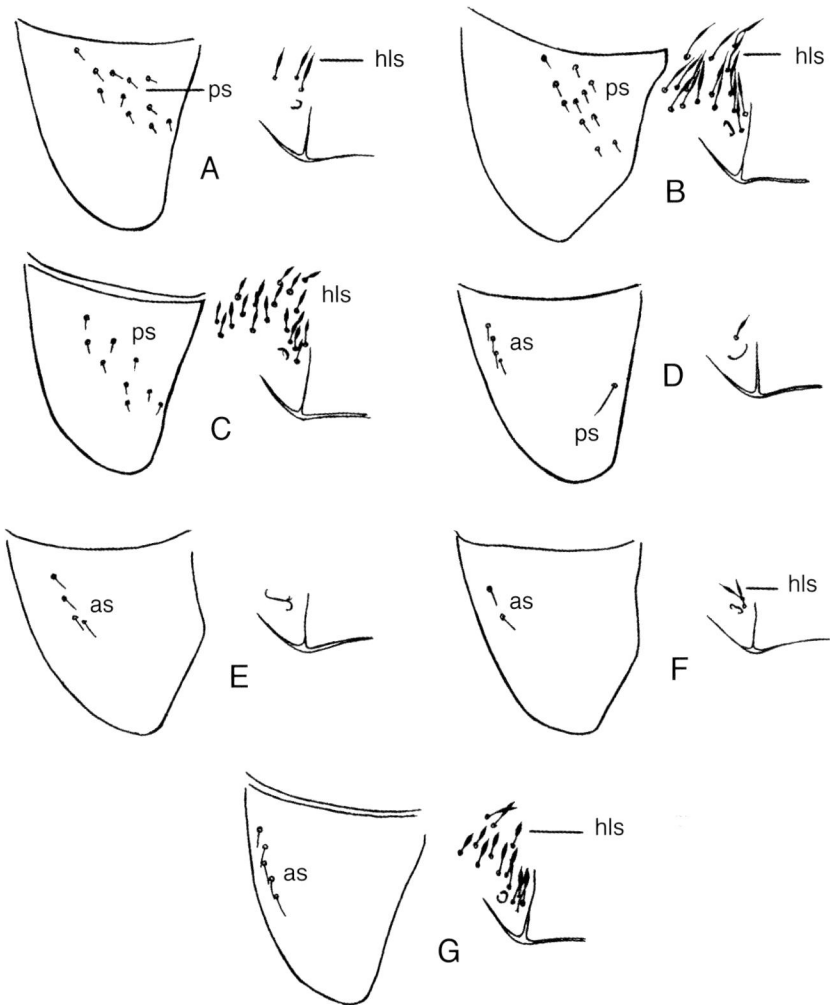

Fig. 60. **A–G:** pre-episternum (left) and humeral area (right) of: A, *Limnophyes asquamatus*; B, *L. brachytomus*; C, *L. edwardsi*; D, *L. ninae*; E, *L. minimus*; F, *L. natalensis*; G, *L. angelicae*.

Genus MESOSMITTIA Brundin

There is one known European species. Hypopygium as in Fig. 166A—

Mesosmittia flexuella (Edwards)

Genus METRIOCNEMUS van der Wulp

1   Entire wing membrane rather densely clothed with macrotrichia (base of cell m (see Fig. 5, p. 13) proximal to cross-vein RM may be bare or nearly so)—   **2**

—   Basal half of wing bare or with a few scattered macrotrichia, apical half more densely covered—   **9**

2   Gonocoxite with a pronounced lobe in the basal half (e.g. arrows, Figs 61A,B)—   **3**

—   Gonocoxite lobe less pronounced (e.g. arrow, Fig. 61C)—   **5**

3   Antennal ratio (p. 9) about 1.0. Hypopygium Fig. 166B—
                                                Metriocnemus cavicola Kieffer

—   Antennal ratio at least 1.5—   **4**

4   Halteres blackened. Hypopygium Fig. 166C—
                                              Metriocnemus eurynotus (Holmgren)

—   Halteres pale. Hypopygium Fig. 166D—   **Metriocnemus sp**.
                              (*hirticollis* sensu Edwards 1929 nec (Staeger 1839))

5(2) Antennal ratio 2.5–3.0. Hypopygium Fig. 167A—
                                                Metriocnemus picipes (Meigen)

—   Antennal ratio 2.0 or less—   **6**

6   Antennal ratio approaching 1.5–2.0. Hypopygium Fig. 167B—
                                                Metriocnemus atriclavus Kieffer

—   Antennal ratio only about 1.0–1.5—   **7**

7   Anal tergite without an anal point or with a very small point ($<15\mu$m long). Hypopygium Fig. 167C—
                                  Metriocnemus beringiensis Cranston & Oliver

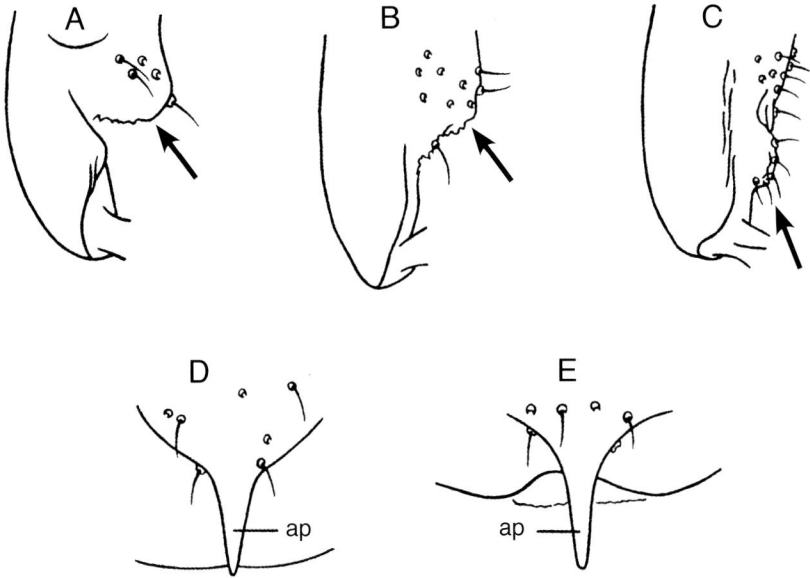

Fig. 61. **A–C:** gonocoxites of: A, *Metriocnemus cavicola*; B, *M. eurynotus*; C, *M. picipes*. **D, E:** anal points of: D, *M. tristellus*; E, *M. ursinus*.

—(7) Anal point well-developed— **8**

8 First tarsomere of hind-leg about half as long as the tibia. Hypopygium Fig. 167D— **Metriocnemus albolineatus** (Meigen)

— First tarsomere of hind-leg about one-third as long as the tibia. Hypopygium Fig. 168A— **Metriocnemus fuscipes** (Meigen)

9(1) Anal point *ap* rather slender, tapering to a point distally (Fig. 61D). Gonostylus without a preapical 'tooth'. Hypopygium Fig. 168B— **Metriocnemus tristellus** Edwards

— Anal point *ap* more robust, bluntly rounded distally (Fig. 61E). Gonostylus with a preapical 'tooth'. Hypopygium Fig. 168C— **Metriocnemus ursinus** (Holmgren)

Genus NANOCLADIUS Kieffer

1   Inner lobe of gonocoxite roughly rectangular (Fig. 62A). Hypopygium
Fig. 169A—   **Nanocladius dichromus** (Kieffer)

—   Inner lobe of gonocoxite conical in shape (Fig. 62B)—   **2**

3   Ground colour of thorax and abdomen golden-brown. Abdominal tergite
setae not arising from sharply demarcated pale spots. Hypopygium Fig.
169B—   **Nanocladius balticus** (Palmén)

—   Ground colour of thorax and abdomen brown to blackish. Tergite setae
arising from distinct pale spots. Hypopygium Fig. 169C—
Nanocladius rectinervis (Kieffer)

Genus ORTHOCLADIUS van der Wulp

1   Anal point *ap* long (Fig. 62C). Lobe of gonocoxite slender, finger-like
(Fig. 62D). Antennal ratio 2.2–2.5 (p. 9). Anal lobe of wing strongly
produced (arrow, Fig. 62J). Fore-tarsus with a beard of long setae.
Hypopygium Fig. 170A—
Orthocladius (Pogonocladius) consobrinus (Holmgren)

—   Without the above combination of characters—   **2**

2   Inner margin of gonocoxite produced into two separate lobes (arrows,
Fig. 62E)—   **3**

—   Gonocoxite not as above—   **4**

3   Anal point *ap* robust (Fig. 62F). Lobes of gonocoxite adjacent, as in Fig.
62E. Hypopygium Fig. 170B—
Orthocladius (Eudactylocladius) gelidus Kieffer

—   Anal point *ap* slender (Fig. 62G). Gonocoxite lobes well separated
(arrows, Fig. 62H). Hypopygium Fig. 170C—
Orthocladius (Eudact.) fuscimanus (Kieffer)*

*N.B. *O. (Eudact.)* sp. a of Pinder (1978) may be no more than an extreme *fuscimanus*; it
differs in possessing a more rounded anterior lobe of the gonocoxite (arrow, Fig. 62I); the
posterior lobe is prominent. The hypopygium is illustrated in Fig. 170D.

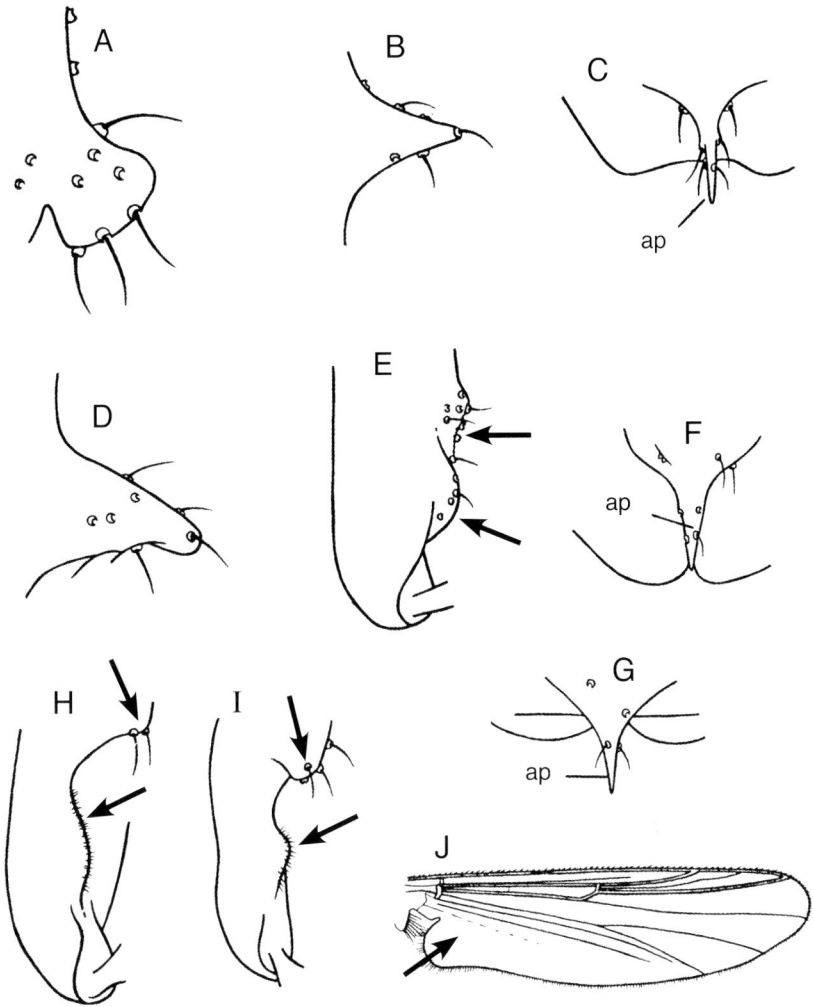

Fig. 62. **A, B:** gonocoxite lobes of: A, *Nanocladius dichromus*; B, *N. rectinervis*. **C, D:** *Orthocladius consobrinus*: C, anal point; D, gonocoxite lobe. **E:** gonocoxite of *O. gelidus*. **F, G:** anal points of: F, *O. gelidus*; G, *O. fuscimanus*. **H, I:** gonocoxites of: H, *O. fuscimanus*; I, *O.* sp. a of Pinder (1978). **J:** wing of *O. consobrinus*.

4(2) Gonocoxite without a projecting lobe. Hypopygium Fig. 171A—
Orthocladius (Eudact.) olivaceus (Kieffer)

—   Gonocoxite with a projecting lobe—   **5**

5   Anal point tapering to an acute point (e.g. Figs 63A,B). Scutellar setae
(Fig. 4, p. 12) usually in a single transverse row—   **6**

—   Anal point more or less parallel-sided with a blunt apex (Figs 63C,D),
or the apex suddenly narrows to a point. Scutellar setae irregularly
distributed (except in some *O. rivicola*)—   **17**

6   Mid-antennal flagellomeres elongate or quadrate; antennal ratio (p. 9)
2.0 or less—   **7**

—   Mid-antennal flagellomeres elongate; antennal ratio about 2.0 or more— **10**

7   Dorsocentral setae (Fig. 4, p. 12) inconspicuous, short, narrow, not
inserted on pale spots. Gonocoxite near base on inner side expanded as a
rectangular lobe (e.g. as in Fig. 63E). Hypopygium Fig. 171B—
Orthocladius (Orthocladius) rubicundus (Meigen)

—   Dorsocentral setae strong, inserted on conspicuous pale spots. Gonocoxite
as above or smoothly curved to base on inner side—   **8**

8   Gonocoxite near its base on the inner side with an angular lobe (arrows,
Fig. 63E). Hypopygium Fig. 171C—
Orthocladius (O.) maius Goetghebuer

—   Gonocoxite smoothly curved to its base on the inner side (e.g. as
indicated by arrows in Fig. 63G)—   **9**

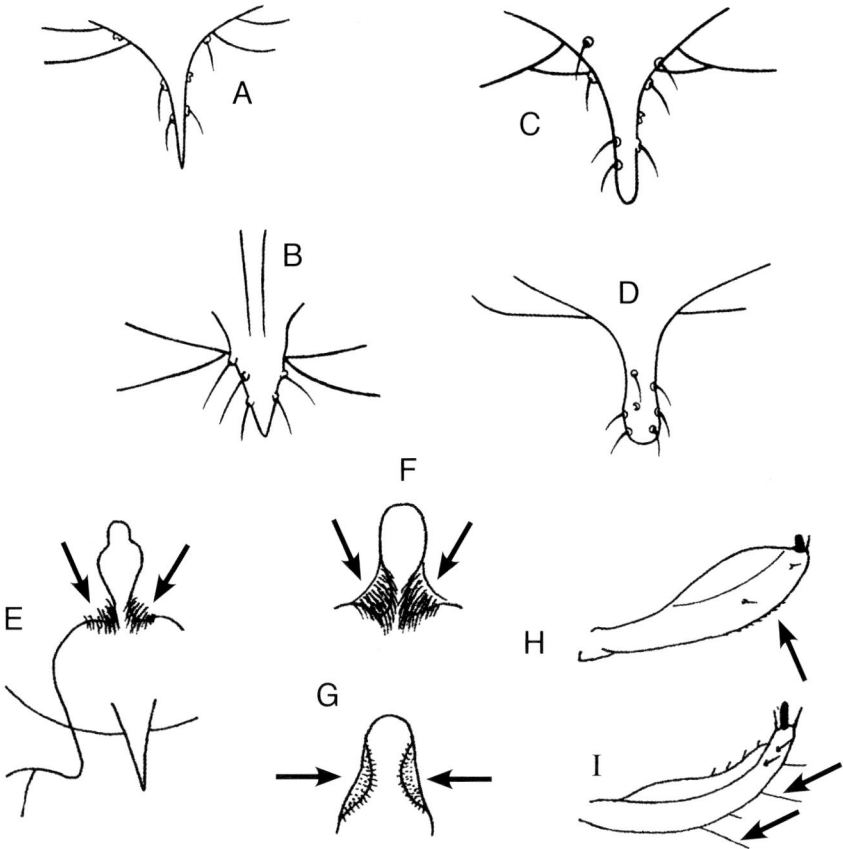

Fig. 63. **A–D:** anal points of: A and B, *Orthocladius oblidens*; C, *O. rivulorum*; D, *O. frigidus.* **E:** gonocoxite lobes and anal point of *O. maius.* **F, G:** ventrobasal contour of gonocoxites of: F, *O. pedestris*; G, *O. oblidens.* **H, I:** gonostyli of: H, *O. ruffoi*; I, *O. lignicola.*

9 Setae on outer surface of gonostylus short (arrow, Fig. 63H). Hypopygium Fig. 171D—   **Orthocladius (O.) ruffoi** Rossaro & Prato

— Setae on outer surface of gonostylus long (arrows, Fig. 63I). Hypopygium Fig. 172A—   **Orthocladius (Symposiocladius) lignicola** Kieffer

10(6) Gonostylus with microtrichia to the tip. Hypopygium Fig. 172B—
Orthocladius (O.) wetterensis Brundin

— Gonostylus bare of microtrichia at the tip—   **11**

11   Dorsocentral setae multiserial and numerous. Hypopygium Fig. 172C—
Orthocladius (O.) holsatus Goetghebuer

— Dorsocentral setae uniserial, few in number—   **12**

12   Gonostylus near megaseta projecting as a tooth-like process supporting the end of the crista dorsalis (arrow, Fig. 64A). Hypopygium Fig. 172D—   **Orthocladius (O.) dentifer** Brundin

— Gonostylus without a projecting 'tooth' near the apex—   **13**

13   Gonocoxite near its base on the inner side with an angular lobe (arrow, Fig. 63F, p. 121). Hypopygium Fig. 173A—
Orthocladius (O.) pedestris Kieffer

— Gonocoxite near its base with a rounded projection (arrow, Fig. 63G) or none—   **14**

14   Gonostylus with a square end (arrow, Fig. 64B). Hypopygium Fig. 173B—   **Orthocladius (O.) glabripennis** (Goetghebuer)

— Gonostylus more boat-shaped, tapering to the apex (arrow, Fig. 64C)—   **15**

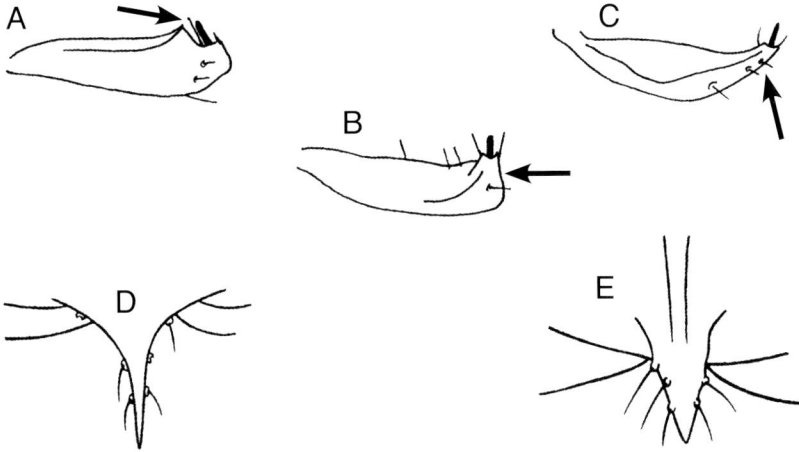

Fig. 64. **A–C:** gonostyli of: A, *Orthocladius dentifer*; B, *O. glabripennis*; C, *O. obumbratus*. **D, E:** variation in anal points of *O. oblidens*.

15 Setal beard ratio on fore-tarsus >3 (p. 14). Hypopygium Fig. 174A—
Orthocladius (O.) rivinus Kieffer

— Setal beard ratio on fore-tarsus <3— **16**

16 Setae of the lower inner margin of the gonostylus very fine, much thinner than the lateral setae of the anal point. (Anal point variable in breadth, Figs 64D,E). Hypopygia Figs 173C and 173D—
Orthocladius (O.) oblidens (Walker)

— Setae of the lower margin of the gonostylus stronger, approaching the diameter of the lateral setae of the anal point. Hypopygium Fig. 174B— **Orthocladius (O.) obumbratus** Johannsen

17(5) Anal point very broad (Fig. 65A). Crista dorsalis of gonostylus (p. 17) absent except near the megaseta, where it is tooth-like or semicircular (arrow, Fig. 65C). Hypopygium Fig. 174C—
Orthocladius (O.) frigidus (Zetterstedt)

—   Anal point narrower (Fig. 65B). Crista dorsalis forming a band along the edge of the gonostylus, but may project further near the megaseta (arrows, Figs 65D–F)—   **18**

18   Antennal ratio <1.7 (p. 9)—   **19**

—   Antennal ratio >1.7—   **21**

19   Lobe of gonocoxite broader, approximately evenly narrowed from its base to the rounded tip (Fig. 65G). Hypopygium Fig. 174D—
Orthocladius (Euorthocladius) rivulorum Kieffer

—   Lobe of gonocoxite contracted quite strongly from the base, thereafter more parallel-sided to the rounded tip (arrow, Fig. 65H)—   **20**

20   Crista dorsalis of gonostylus in dorsal view (i.e. gonostylus edge-on) usually visible as a subapical triangular projection (arrow, Fig. 65E). Hypopygium Fig. 175A—   **Orthocladius (Euorth.) rivicola** Kieffer

—   Crista dorsalis in dorsal view rounded towards the apex of the gonostylus, usually visible as a broad strip along edge of gonostylus (arrows, Fig. 65F), or collapsed. Hypopygium Fig. 175B—
Orthocladius (Euorth.) ashei Soponis

21(18) Maxillary palp segment 3 equal in length to segment 4. Hypopygium Fig. 175C—   **Orthocladius (Euorth.) thienemanni** Kieffer

—   Maxillary palp segment 3 longer than segment 4. Hypopygium Fig. 175D—   **Orthocladius (Euorth.) calvus** Pinder

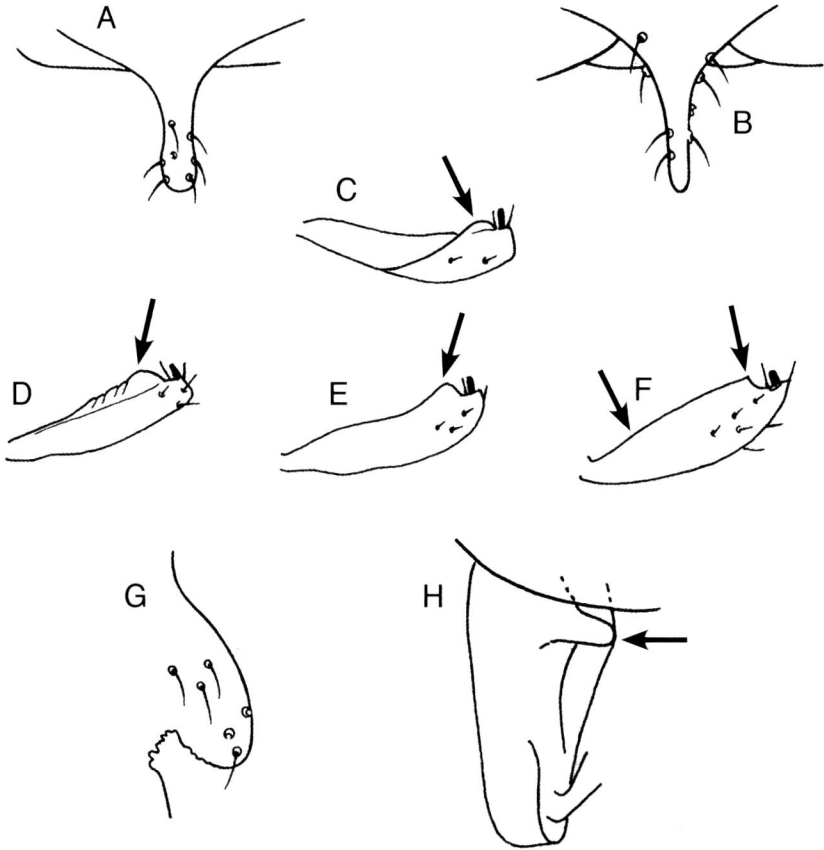

Fig. 65. **A, B:** anal points of: A, *Orthocladius frigidus*; B, *O. thienemanni*. **C–F:** gonostyli of: C, *O. frigidus*; D, *O. thienemanni*; E, *O. rivicola*; F, *O. ashei*. **G:** gonocoxite lobe of *O. rivulorum*. **H:** gonocoxite and lobe of *O. ashei*.

Genus PARACLADIUS Hirvenoja

Only one species belonging to this genus has been recorded for Britain and Ireland. Hypopygium (Fig. 176A) with a minute anal point—

Paracladius conversus (Walker)

Genus PARACRICOTOPUS Thienemann & Harnisch

One species has been recorded for Britain and Ireland; the hairy eyes, well developed pulvilli on the apex of the tarsus and two transverse rows of setae on the tergites are diagnostic. Hypopygium Fig. 176B—

Paracricotopus niger (Kieffer)

Genus PARAKIEFFERIELLA Thienemann*

Parakiefferiella scandica has now been added to the British list [see p. 156, Vol. 2].

1   Thorax black. Wing vein R_{2+3} fused completely with vein R_{4+5} or separate from it only apically. Anal point very broadly rounded (Fig. 66A). Hypopygium Fig. 176C—   **Parakiefferiella coronata** (Edwards)

—   Thorax pale with dark scutal stripes. Wing vein R_{2+3} distinct from R_{4+5}. Anal point more elongate, tip pointed (Fig. 66B) or rounded—   **2**

2   Gonocoxite lobe small, setose and bearing a narrow bare apical projection (arrow, Fig. 66C). Hypopygium Fig. 176D—

Parakiefferiella wuelkeri Moubayed

—   Gonocoxite lobe large, projecting strongly from the lower half of the gonocoxite (Figs 66D,E)—   **3**

3   Anal point flat, triangular, sharply pointed at the apex (Fig. 66B). Hypopygium Fig. 177A—   **Parakiefferiella bathophila** (Kieffer)

—   Anal point with a median ridge, usually with the apex rounded—   **4**

4   Posterior edge of gonocoxite lobe perpendicular to the gonocoxite (arrow, Fig. 66D). Hypopygium Fig. 177B—

Parakiefferiella smolandica (Brundin)

—   Posterior margin of gonocoxite lobe at an acute angle to the gonocoxite (arrow, Fig. 66E). Hypopygium Fig. 177C—

Parakiefferiella fennica Tuiskunen

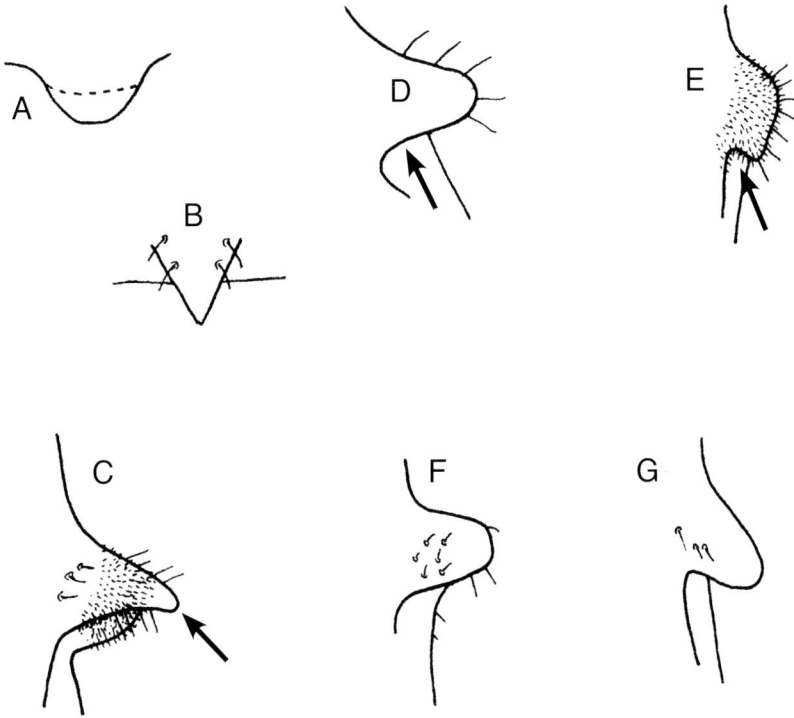

Fig. 66. **A, B:** anal points of: A, *Parakiefferiella coronata*; B, *P. bathophila*. **C–G:** gonocoxite lobes of: C, *P. wuelkeri*; D, *P. smolandica*; E, *P. fennica*; F, *Parametriocnemus stylatus*; G, *P. boreoalpinus*.

Genus PARALIMNOPHYES Brundin

One species has been recorded for Europe and the British Isles. Hypopygium Fig. 177D — **Paralimnophyes longiseta** (Thienemann)

Genus PARAMETRIOCNEMUS Goetghebuer

1   Gonocoxite lobe broadly rounded apically (Fig. 66F). Hypopygium Fig. 178A — **Parametriocnemus stylatus** (Spärck)

—   Gonocoxite lobe narrowed to the rounded apex (Fig. 66G). Hypopygium Fig. 178B — **Parametriocnemus boreoalpinus** Gouin

Genus PARAPHAENOCLADIUS Thienemann

1   Anal point covered with microtrichia to the apex (Fig. 67A)—   **2**

—   Anal point apex bare (Figs 67B–D)—   **3**

2   Wing cell m proximal to cross-vein RM (see Fig. 5, p. 13) without macrotrichia. Hypopygium Fig. 178C—
        Paraphaenocladius pseudirritus Strenzke

—   Wing cell m proximal to RM with at least 4 macrotrichia. Hypopygium Fig. 178D—   **Paraphaenocladius irritus** (Walker)

3(1) Anal point very slender distally (Fig. 67B). Hypopygium Fig. 179A—
        Paraphaenocladius exagitans (Johannsen) ssp. **monticola** Strenzke

—   Anal point broader distally (Figs 67C,D)—   **4**

4   Antennal ratio 0.4–0.6 (p. 9). Hypopygium Fig. 179B—
        Paraphaenocladius penerasus (Edwards)

—   Antennal ratio 0.7–1.1. Hypopygium Fig. 179C—
        Paraphaenocladius impensus (Walker)

Genus PARATRICHOCLADIUS Santos Abreu

1   Gonocoxite lobe broad (arrows, Fig. 67E). Hypopygium Fig. 179D—
        Paratrichocladius skirwithensis (Edwards)

—   Gonocoxite lobe slender, conical (arrow, Fig. 67F)—   **2**

2   Gonostylus broad with crista dorsalis well developed (arrow, Fig. 67G). Hypopygium Fig. 180A—   **Paratrichocladius nigritus** (Goetghebuer)

—   Gonostylus narrower with crista dorsalis projecting near the megaseta (arrow, Fig. 67H). Hypopygium Fig. 180B—
        Paratrichocladius rufiventris (Meigen)

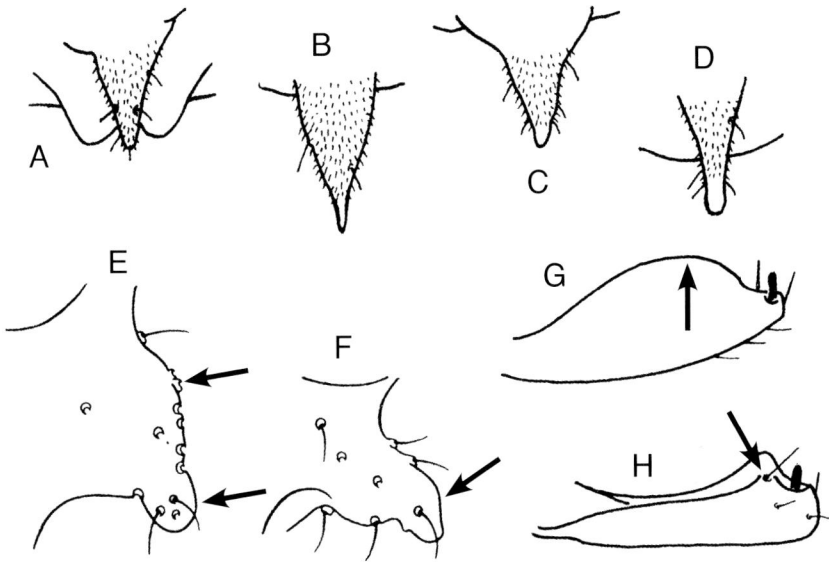

Fig. 67. **A–D:** anal points of: A, *Paraphaenocladius irritus*; B, *P. exagitans monticola*; C, *P. penerasus*; D, *P. impensus*. **E, F:** gonocoxite lobes of: E, *Paratrichocladius skirwithensis*; F, *P. rufiventris*. **G, H:** gonostyli of: G, *P. nigritus*; H, *P. rufiventris*.

Genus PARATRISSOCLADIUS Zavrel

There is only one European representative of this genus. Hypopygium Fig. 180C — **Paratrissocladius excerptus** (Walker)

Genus PARORTHOCLADIUS Thienemann

Only one species belonging to this genus occurs in Britain and Ireland. The hypopygium (Fig. 180D), especially in the form of the anal point, resembles those of *Orthocladius (Euorthocladius)* species (p. 124 and Figs 174C,D, 175A–C) but the absence of acrostichal setae (Fig. 4, p. 12) is distinctive — **Parorthocladius nudipennis** (Kieffer)

Genus PSECTROCLADIUS Kieffer

1   Last tarsomere dorsoventrally flattened (arrow, Fig. 68A)—   **2**

—   Last tarsomere laterally compressed (arrow, Fig. 68B)—   **4**

2   Hypopygium without an anal point, or an anal point is scarcely indicated. Hypopygium Fig. 181A—
    Psectrocladius (Mesopsectrocladius) barbatipes Kieffer

—   Anal point present, but may be small—
                                         (ALLOPSECTROCLADIUS), **3**

3   Mid-tibia with well developed apical spurs. Hypopygium Fig. 181B—
    Psectrocladius (Allopsectrocladius) obvius (Walker)

—   Middle tibia with a single apical spur. Hypopygium Fig. 181C—
    Psectrocladius (A.) platypus (Edwards)

4   Internal margin of the inner lobe of the gonocoxite emarginate *twice* (basally and medially) leaving a pear-shaped space between the opposing lobes. Hypopygium Fig. 181D—
    Psectrocladius (Monopsectrocladius) calcaratus (Edwards)

—   No anterior (basal) emargination of the gonocoxite lobes; median emargination present or absent—   (PSECTROCLADIUS), **5**

5   Fore-tarsus with a beard of short setae (beard ratio >3.5; p. 14)—   **6**

—   Fore-tarsus setae less than 3 times the diameter of tarsomere 1—   **7**

6   Dorsal internal setae *dis* of gonocoxites short (27–55 μm) (see Fig. 68C). Body usually dark in colour: head and scutellum black, scutal bands fused. Hypopygium Fig. 182A—
    Psectrocladius (Psectrocladius) ventricosus Kieffer

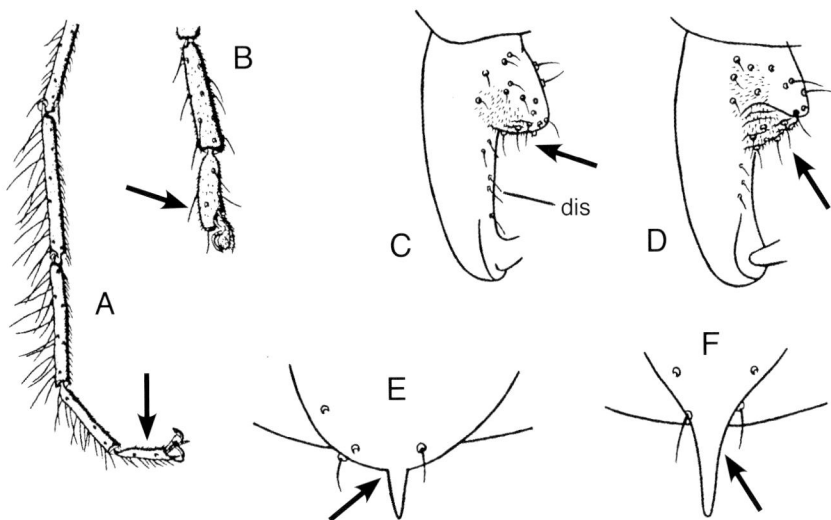

Fig. 68. **A, B:** apical segments of fore-tarsi of: a, *Psectrocladius obvius* (last segment dorsoventrally compressed); B, *P. sordidellus* (last segment cylindrical). **C, D:** gonocoxites of: C, *P. oxyura*; D, *P. fennicus*. **E, F:** anal points of: E, *P. psilopterus*; F, *P. oxyura*.

—(6) Dorsal internal setae of gonocoxite longer (55–95 μm). Body usually pale in colour: head and scutellum yellow, scutal bands separated by yellow ground colour of thorax. Hypopygium Fig. 182B—

Psectrocladius (P.) barbimanus (Edwards)

7(5) Inner lobe of gonocoxite bulging posteriad (arrow, Fig. 68D). Wing length well over 3 mm. Hypopygium Fig. 182C—

Psectrocladius (P.) fennicus Storå

— If as large, gonocoxite inner lobe truncate or obliquely truncate posteriorly (arrow, Fig. 68C)— **8**

8 Anal point abruptly projecting from rounded posterior margin of tergite IX (arrow, Fig. 68E)— **9**

— Anal point elongate, widening anteriad to merge with the posterior margin of tergite IX (e.g. arrow, Fig. 68F)— **10**

9   Antennal ratio <1.5. Small species: wing length about 2 mm. Hypopygium
     Fig. 182D —   **Psectrocladius (P.) bisetus** Goetghebuer

—   Antennal ratio 1.5 or more.   Larger: wing length about 3 mm.
     Hypopygium Fig. 183A —   **Psectrocladius (P.) psilopterus** (Kieffer)

10(8) Dorsocentral setae numerous (13–26), the most anterior situated before
     the lateral scutal band *lsb* (Fig. 69A). Tergite IX gradually narrowed
     towards the anal point, with the junction between the two difficult to
     define (Fig. 69C). Hypopygium Fig.183B —
                             Psectrocladius (P.) oxyura Langton

—   Dorsocentral setae fewer (5–15), the most anterior situated above the
     lateral scutal band *lsb* (Fig. 69B). Tergite IX rounded posteriorly, and the
     base of the anal point is more distinctly defined (e.g. as in Fig. 69D) —
                                                                  11

11   Gonocoxite lobe with internal margin straight, shallowly emarginate or
     indented (arrow, Fig. 69E) —   **12**

—   Gonocoxite lobe deeply and broadly excavated (arrow, Fig. 69F) —   **15**

12   Gonocoxite dorsal internal setae *dis* shorter, 27–33 μm (see Fig. 68C, p.
     131). Hypopygium Fig. 183C —
                             Psectrocladius (P.) sordidellus (Zetterstedt)

—   Dorsal internal setae of gonocoxites longer, >35 μm —   **13**

13   Longest setae of hind-tarsus shorter than the length of the last tarsomere.
     Mid-tibia with 2 apical spurs, one small and conical. Antennal ratio about
     2.0 or less (p. 9). Megaseta of gonostylus 16 μm or less. Smaller, paler
     species, wing length about 2 mm or less. Hypopygium Fig. 183D —
                             Psectrocladius (P.) schlienzi Wülker

—   Longest setae of hind-tarsus about as long as the last tarsomere. Megaseta
     longer. Mid-tibia with or without an additional small spur. Larger, darker
     species, wing length >2.0 mm —   **14**

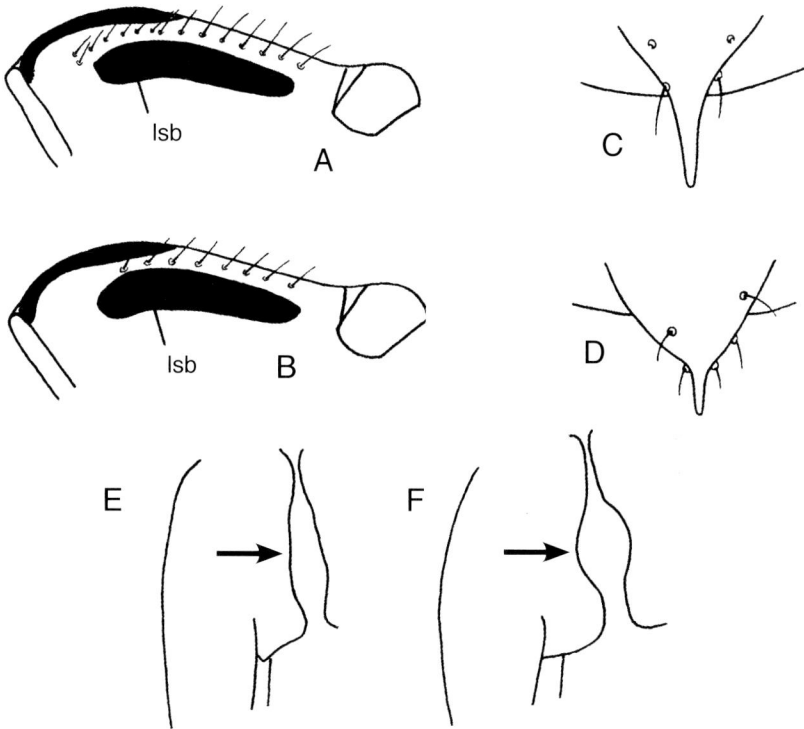

Fig. 69. **A, B:** dorsal part of thorax of: A, *Psectrocladius oxyura*; B, *P. sordidellus*; **C, D:** anal points of C, *P. oxyura*; D, *P. barbimanus*. **E, F:** basal lobes of gonocoxites of: E, *P. octomaculatus*; F, *P. limbatellus.*

14　Antennal ratio >2.0 (p. 9). Mid-tibia usually with 2 apical spurs, one small and conical. Hypopygium Fig. 184A—

Psectrocladius (P.) sp. A*

*This is sp. A of Langton (1980, 1984, 1991).

—　Antennal ratio <2.0. Mid-tibia rarely with an additional small spur. Hypopygium Fig. 184B— **Psectrocladius (P.) limbatellus** (Holmgren)

15(11) Antennal ratio <1.5 (p. 9). Mid-tibia with 1 apical spur. Wing length about 2 mm. Hypopygium Fig. 184C—
                    Psectrocladius (P.) oligosetus Wülker

—   Antennal ratio >1.5. Mid-tibia usually with 2 apical spurs. Wing length >>2.0mm. Hypopygium Fig. 184D—
                    Psectrocladius (P.) octomaculatus Wülker

Genus PSEUDORTHOCLADIUS Goetghebuer

1   Antennal ratio <0.7 (p. 9). Ground colour of thorax yellowish. Hypopygium Fig. 185A—
                    Pseudorthocladius curtistylus (Goetghebuer)

—   Antennal ratio >0.7. Thorax mainly black or dark brown—   **2**

2   Spines on the virga (p. 17) robust and long, about 1.5 times as long as the gonostylus. Hypopygium Fig. 185B—
                    Pseudorthocladius cranstoni Sæther & Sublette

—   Spines on the virga narrower and much shorter, about 0.5 times as long as the gonostylus—   **3**

3   Wings densely 'hairy' with macrotrichia. Lobe of gonocoxite rounded (arrow, Fig. 70A). Hypopygium Fig. 185C—
                    Pseudorthocladius pilosipennis Brundin

—   Wings without macrotrichia. Lobe of gonocoxite not as above (arrows, Figs 70B,C)—   **4**

4   Lobe of gonocoxite somewhat triangular (arrow, Fig. 70B). Hypopygium Fig. 185D—   **Pseudorthocladius filiformis** (Kieffer)

—   Lobe of gonocoxite rectangular (Fig. 70C). Hypopygium Fig. 186A—
                    Pseudorthocladius rectangilobus Caspers & Siebert

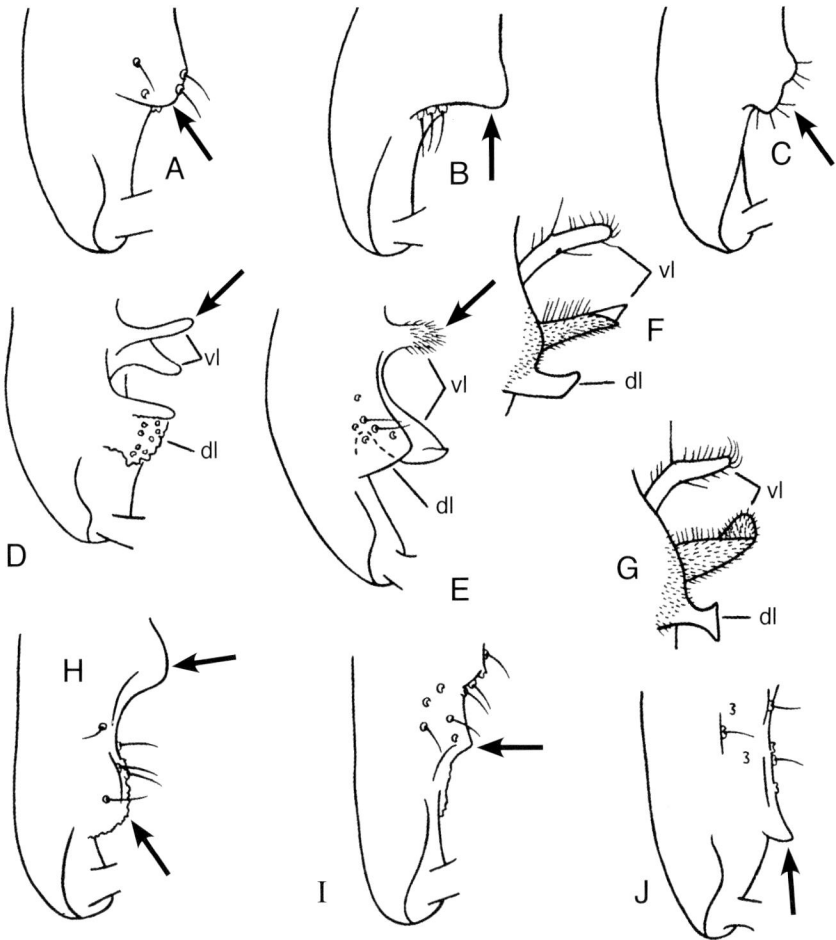

Fig. 70. **A–E:** gonocoxites of: A, *Pseudorthocladius pilosipennis*; B, *P. filiformis*; C, *P. rectangilobus*; D, *Pseudosmittia forcipata*; E, *P. angusta*. **F, G:** gonocoxite lobes of: F, *Pseudosmittia trilobata*; G, *P. obtusa*. **H–J:** gonocoxites of: H, *Pseudosmittia gracilis*; I, *P. oxoniana*; J, *P. albipennis*.

Genus PSEUDOSMITTIA Edwards

1   Gonocoxite with three lobes, two ventral lobes *vl* and one dorsal lobe *dl* (Figs 70D–G)—   **2**

—   Gonocoxite with one or two lobes only (arrows, Figs 70H–J)—   **5**

2   Dorsal lobe *dl* of gonocoxite narrow, fishtail- or foot-shaped apically Fig. 70G, p. 135); posterior ventral lobe *vl* pubescent to the tip (Fig. 70G). Hypopygium Fig. 186B —   **Pseudosmittia obtusa** Strenzke

—   *IF* the dorsal lobe *dl* of the gonocoxite is narrow, it is weakly club-shaped (Fig. 70F) and the tip of the posterior ventral lobe *vl* is not pubescent (Fig. 70F)—   **3**

3   Dorsal lobe *dl* of gonocoxite slender, weakly club-shaped; posterior ventral lobe *vl* with a bare apical triangular projection (Fig. 70F); hypopygium otherwise as in *P. obtusa* above—
          Pseudosmittia trilobata (Edwards)

—   Dorsal lobe *dl* broader (Figs 70D,E); posterior ventral lobe *vl* pubescent to its tip (as in Figs 186C,D)—   **4**

4   Anterior ventral lobe *vl* of gonocoxite about six times as long as broad (arrow, Fig. 70D). Hypopygium Fig. 186C—
          Pseudosmittia forcipata (Goetghebuer)

—   Anterior ventral lobe *vl* about twice as long as broad (arrow, Fig. 70E). Hypopygium Fig. 186D—   **Pseudosmittia angusta** (Edwards)

5(1) Antennal ratio (p. 9) very low, about 0.3 or less—   **6**

—   Antennal ratio at least 0.6—   **7**

6   Virga (p. 17) with a single spine. Antennal ratio 0.21–0.27—
          Pseudosmittia holsata Thienemann & Strenzke*

—   Virga with a median spine and additional rows of lateral spinules. Antennal ratio 0.3–0.4. Hypopygium Fig. 187A—
          Pseudosmittia gracilis (Goetghebuer)*

*Separation of these two species was kindly provided by O. A. Sæther.

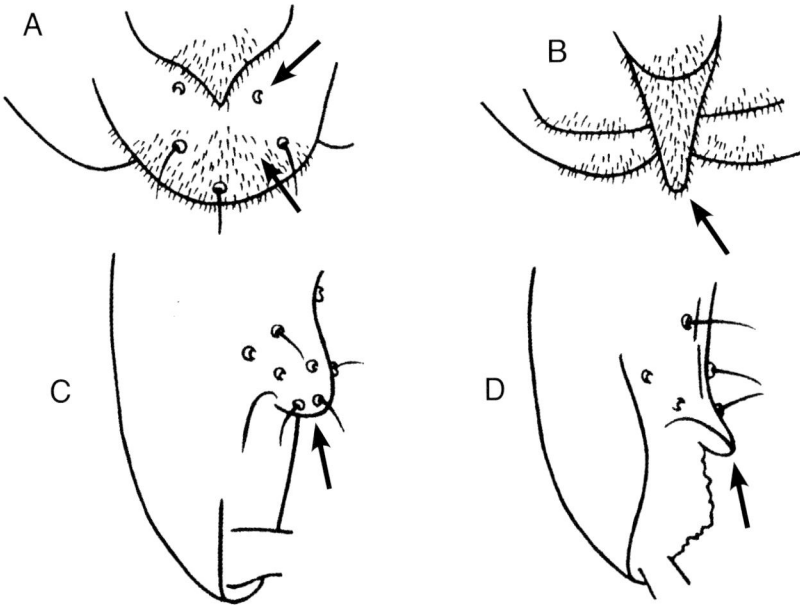

Fig. 71. **A, B:** anal points of: A, *Pseudosmittia oxoniana*; B, *P. albipennis*. **C, D:** gonocoxites of: C, *P. brevifurcata*; D, *P. albipennis*.

7(5) Anal point very short (arrow, Fig. 71A). Hypopygium Fig. 187B —
      Pseudosmittia oxoniana (Edwards)

—   Anal point well developed (arrow, Fig. 71B).

8   Wing costa is not or scarcely produced. Lobe of gonocoxite is large, rounded and bearing several long setae (arrow, Fig. 71C). Hypopygium Fig. 187C. (Occurs on rocky coasts:) —
       Pseudosmittia brevifurcata (Edwards)

—   Wing costa rather strongly produced. Gonocoxite lobe smaller, slender and bare at the apex (arrow, Fig. 71D) (depending on the position (aspect) of the mount on the slide, it can look rather different). Hypopygium Figs 188A,B —   **Pseudosmittia albipennis** (Goetghebuer)*

*Formerly recognised as two distinct species: *Orthosmittia albipennis* (Goetghebuer) and *Pseudosmittia curticosta* (Edwards).

Genus RHEOCRICOTOPUS Brundin

1   Gonostylus curved sharply upwards at the tip (Fig. 72A). Hypopygium
     Fig. 188C— **Rheocricotopus (Psilocricotopus) chalybeatus** (Edwards)

—   Gonostylus not as above—   **2**

2   Crista dorsalis (p. 17) projecting strongly near the megaseta of the
     gonostylus (arrows, Figs 72B,C)—   **3**

—   Crista dorsalis forming a low band along the edge of the gonostylus
     (arrows, Fig. 72D,E)—   **5**

3   Anal lobe of wing (Fig. 5, p. 13) hardly expressed. Hypopygium Fig.
     188D—   **Rheocricotopus (P.) atripes** (Kieffer)

—   Anal lobe of wing projecting—   **4**

4   Antennal ratio (p. 9) about 1.0. Hypopygium Fig. 189A—
                              Rheocricotopus (P.) tirolus Lehmann

—   Antennal ratio >1.4. Hypopygium Fig. 189B—
                              Rheocricotopus (P.) glabricollis (Meigen)

5(2) Humeral pits (Fig. 4, p. 12) large and conspicuous. Basal lobe of
     the gonocoxite projecting backwards as a 'tooth' (arrow, Fig. 72F).
     Hypopygium Fig. 189C—   **Rheocricotopus (R.) effusus** (Walker)

—   Humeral pits small and indistinct. Basal lobe of the gonocoxite rounded
     (arrow, Fig. 72G). Hypopygium Fig. 189D—
                              Rheocricotopus (Rheocricotopus) fuscipes (Kieffer)

Genus RHEOSMITTIA Ashe & Cranston

The one species recorded for Britain and Ireland is readily distinguished by the
characters used in the key to genera (p. 69) and the form of the hypopygium
(Fig. 190A)—   **Rheosmittia spinicornis** (Brundin)

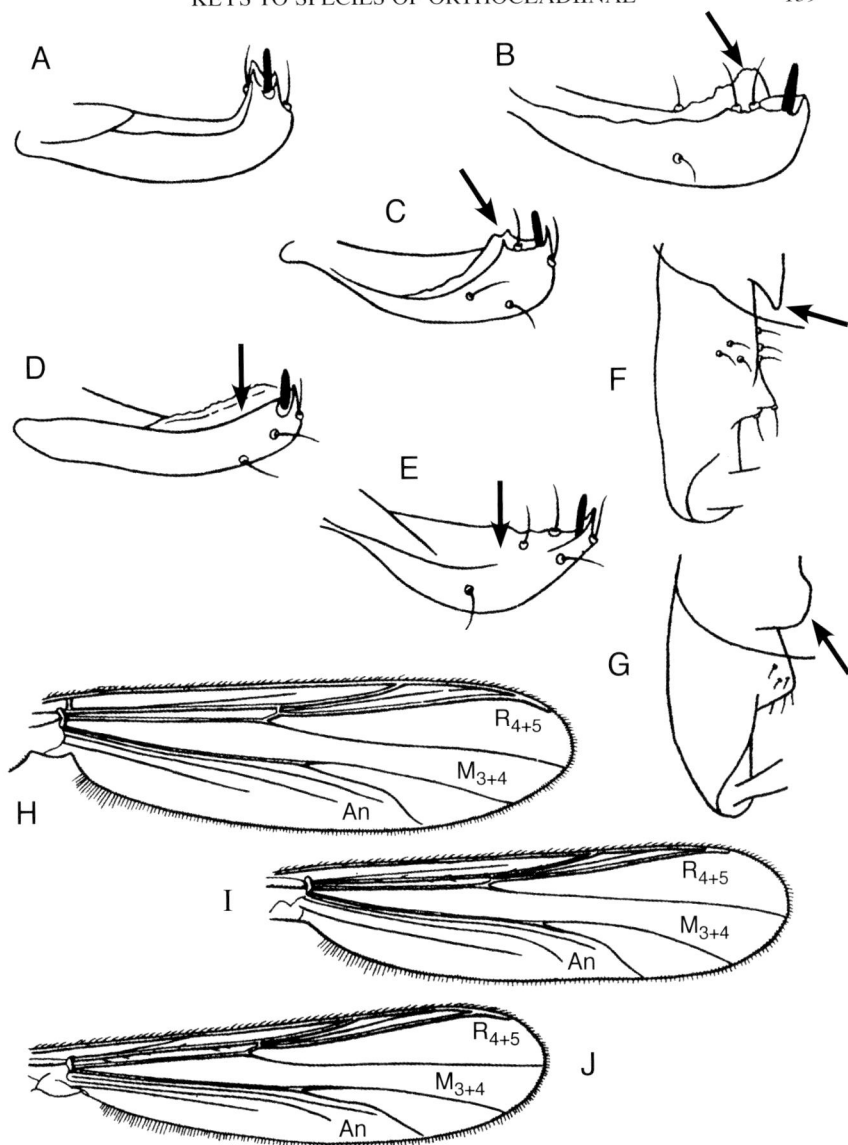

Fig. 72. **A–E:** gonostyli of: A, *Rheocricotopus chalybeatus*; B, *R. atripes*; C, *R. glabricollis*; D, *R. effusus*; E, *R. fuscipes*. **F, G:** gonocoxites of: F, *R.effusus*; G, *R. fuscipes*. **H–J:** wings of: H, *Smittia pratorum*; I, *S. edwardsi*; J, *S. nudipennis*.

Genus SMITTIA Holmgren

1   Inner expansion of gonostylus weak (arrow, Fig. 73A). Gonocoxite lobe characteristically shaped (Fig. 73B). Hypopygium Fig. 190B —
Smittia contingens (Walker)

—   Inner margin of gonostylus strongly expanded subapically (arrows, Figs 73C–F). Gonocoxite lobe not as in Fig. 73B —   **2**

2   Antennal ratio 2.3 or more (p. 9). Hypopygium Fig. 190C —
Smittia foliacea (Kieffer)

—   Antennal ratio <2.3 —   **3**

3   Anal point short, microtrichia extending almost to apex (Fig. 73G)—   **4**

—   Anal point longer, distal half bare (Fig. 73H) —   **5**

4   Inner margin of gonostylus expanded distally, for less than a quarter of its total length (arrow, Fig. 73D). Antennal ratio 1.0–1.8. Hypopygium Fig. 191A—   **Smittia leucopogon** (Meigen)

—   Inner expansion of gonostylus more extensive, occupying roughly half the total length of the gonostylus (arrow, Fig. 73E). Antennal ratio 1.5–2.2. Hypopygium Fig. 191B—   **Smittia aterrima** (Meigen)

5(3) Wing vein R_{4+5} ending above or beyond the tip of vein M_{3+4} (Fig. 72H, p. 139)—   **6**

—   Wing vein R_{4+5} ending proximal to the tip of vein M_{3+4} (Figs 72I,J)—   **8**

6   Gonostylus very broad, apical breadth nearly half or more than half the gonostylus length (Figs 73I,J). Gonocoxite lobe triangular, sharply pointed (arrow, Fig. 73K). Hypopygium Fig. 191C—
Smittia amoena Caspers

—   Gonostylus normal. Gonocoxite lobe with a hooked tip (arrow, Fig. 73L)—   **7**

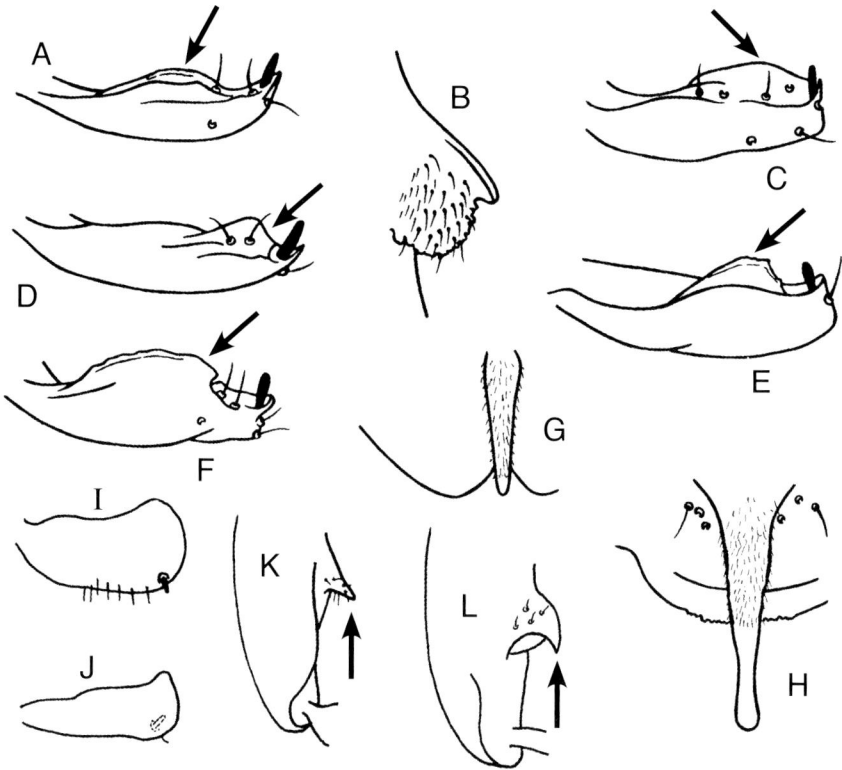

Fig. 73. **A, B:** *Smittia contingens*: A, gonostylus; B, gonocoxite lobe. **C–F:** gonostyli of: C, *S. foliacea*; D, *S. leucopogon*; E, *S. aterrima*, F, *S. pratorum*. **G, H:** anal points of: G, *S. leucopogon*; H, *S. pratorum*. **I, J:** two views of the broad gonostylus of *S. amoena*. **K, L:** gonocoxites of: K, *S. amoena*; L, *S. pratorum*.

7   Antennal ratio about 1.0. Hypopygium Fig. 191D —
                        Smittia superata Goetghebuer

—   Antennal ratio about 1.5. Hypopygium Fig. 192A —
                        Smittia pratorum (Goetghebuer)

8(5) Antennal ratio 1.2–1.6. Anal lobe of wing obtuse (Fig. 72D, p. 139). Hypopygium Fig. 192B —   **Smittia edwardsi** Goetghebuer

—   Antennal ratio 1.0–1.2. Anal lobe absent or weak (Fig. 72E). Hypopygium Fig. 192C —   **Smittia nudipennis** (Goetghebuer)

Genus SYNORTHOCLADIUS Thienemann

The single European species has a distinctive hypopygium (Fig. 192D)—
Synorthocladius semivirens (Kieffer)

Genus THALASSOSMITTIA Strenzke & Remmert

The single West Palaearctic species is easily recognisable from the hypopygium (Fig. 193A). A coastal species—
Thalassosmittia thalassophila (Bequaert & Goetghebuer)

Genus THIENEMANNIA Kieffer

1   Eyes hairy (p. 9). Gonocoxite lobe well developed (arrow, Fig. 74A). Hypopygium Fig. 193B—   **Thienemannia gracilis** Kieffer

—   Eyes pubescent (p. 9). Gonocoxite lobe weak—   **2**

2   Antepronotal lobes distinctly narrowed dorsally (arrow, Fig. 74B). Last antennal flagellomere clubbed, about six times as long as wide. Hypopygium Fig. 193C—   **Thienemannia gracei** (Edwards)

—   Antepronotal lobes not or slightly narrowed dorsally (arrow, Fig. 74C). Apical flagellomere not clubbed, eight to ten times as long as wide. Hypopygium Fig. 193D—   **Thienemannia fulvofasciata** (Kieffer)

Genus THIENEMANNIELLA Kieffer

1   Gonocoxite without a distinct lobe (arrow, Fig. 74D). Hypopygium Fig. 194A—   **Thienemanniella flavescens** (Edwards)

—   Gonocoxite with a well developed inner lobe (Figs 74E–I)—   **2**

2   Last antennal flagellomere only as long as the preceding 2–3 flagellomeres combined—   **3**

—   Last flagellomere at least as long as the preceding 5 combined—   **4**

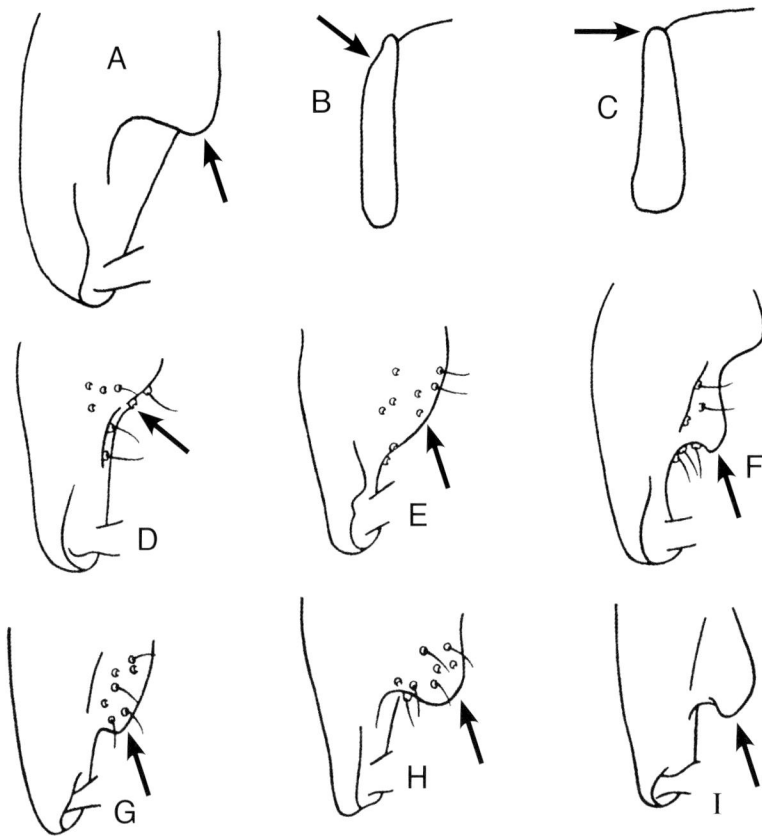

Fig. 74. **A:** gonocoxite of *Thienemannia gracilis*. **B, C:** lateral views of antepronota of: B, *T. gracei*; C, *T. fulvofasciata*. **D–I:** gonocoxites of: D, *Thienemanniella flavescens*; E, *T. clavicornis*; F. *T. acuticornis*; G, *T. vittata*; H, *T. majuscula*; I, *T. lutea*.

3   Gonocoxite lobe gently rounded, tapered distally and extending almost to the end of gonocoxite (arrow, Fig. 74E). Hypopygium Fig. 194B —
Thienemanniella clavicornis (Kieffer)

—   Gonocoxite lobe ending rather abruptly, about halfway along the gonocoxite (arrow, Fig. 74F). Hypopygium Fig. 194C —
Thienemanniella acuticornis (Kieffer)

4(2)   Gonocoxite lobe more or less rectangular (arrow, Fig. 74G, p. 143).
Hypopygium Fig. 194D—   **Thienemanniella vittata** (Edwards)

—   Gonocoxite lobe rounded (arrow, Figs 74H,I)—   **5**

5   Gonocoxite lobe bearing microtrichia only (arrow, Fig. 74I). Hypopygium
Fig. 195A—   **Thienemanniella lutea** (Edwards)

Gonocoxite lobe very broad, bearing several long setae dorsally (e.g. arrow, Fig. 74H)—   **6**

6   Antennae with 11 flagellomeres; last flagellomere as long as the previous 5 together. Hypopygium Fig. 195B—
Thienemanniella obscura Brundin

—   Antennae with 12 flagellomeres; last flagellomere as long as the previous 8–10 together. Hypopygium Fig. 195C—
Thienemanniella majuscula (Edwards)

Genus TOKUNAGAIA Sæther

So far, one species has been found in Britain and Ireland. Hypopygium Fig. 196A—   **Tokunagaia tonollii** (Rossaro)

Genus TRISSOCLADIUS Kieffer

Only one member of the genus has so far been recorded for Britain and Ireland. The posterior margin of the gonostylus is strongly produced (arrow, Fig. 75A). Hypopygium Fig. 196B—   **Trissocladius brevipalpis** Kieffer

Genus TVETENIA Kieffer

1   Wing vein R_{2+3} ending roughly mid-way between veins R_1 and R_{4+5} (arrow, Fig. 75B). Inner margin of the gonostylus produced into a tooth-like process subapically (arrow, Fig. 75C). Hypopygium Fig. 196C—
Tvetenia verralli (Edwards)

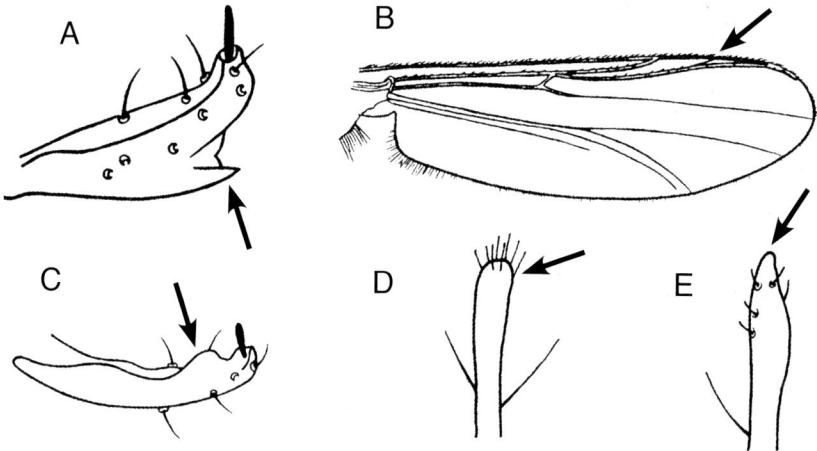

Fig. 75. **A:** gonostylus of *Trissocladius brevipalpis*. **B:** wing of *Tvetenia verralli*. **C:** gonostylus of *T. verralli*. **D, E:** tip of antenna of: D, *T. calvescens*; E, *T. bavarica*.

—(1) Wing vein R_{2+3} not distinguishable. Inner margin of gonostylus not produced—   **2**

2   Antennal ratio 1.0–1.3 (p. 9). Hypopygium Fig. 196D—
         Tvetenia discoloripes Goetghebuer

—   Antennal ratio 0.6–0.8—   **3**

3   Antenna with apical flagellomere rounded at the tip (arrow, Fig. 75D). Hypopygium Fig. 197A—   **Tvetenia calvescens** (Edwards)

—   Antenna with apical flagellomere narrowed into a blunt point at the tip (arrow, Fig. 75E). Hypopygium Fig. 197B—
         Tvetenia bavarica (Goetghebuer)

Genus ZALUTSCHIA Lipina

The one species recorded for Britain and Ireland has a very distinctive hypopygium (Fig. 197C)—   **Zalutschia humphriesiae** Dowling & Murray

SUBFAMILY CHIRONOMINAE

KEY TO FORTY-SEVEN GENERA OF CHIRONOMINAE*

*Including *Fleuria*, recently added to the British list [see p. 163, Vol. 2].

1   Wing membrane usually lacking macrotrichia. If macrotrichia are present then the squama at the base of the wing (Fig. 5, p. 13) is fringed with setae— Tribes CHIRONOMINI and PSEUDOCHIRONOMINI, **2**

—   Wing membrane with macrotrichia, squama bare—
Tribe TANYTARSINI, **36**
(p. 155)

2   Wing membrane bearing macrotrichia at least towards the tip—   **3**

—   Wing membrane bare—   **6**

3   Inferior volsella (pp. 15–16) extremely broad and bulbous apically (Fig. 76A)—   KIEFFERULUS Goetghebuer (p. 175, 1sp.)

—   Inferior volsella more slender, not or scarcely enlarged distally—   **4**

4   Antennal ratio about 3.0 (p. 9). Gonostylus abruptly rounded distally (Fig. 76B)—   SERGENTIA Kieffer (p. 190, 3spp.)

—   Antennal ratio about 2.0 or less. Gonostylus more tapered distally (Fig. 76C)—   **5**

5   Gonostylus with many short setae on the inner side, denser towards the tip (Fig. 76C). Hind-tibiae often with 2 short apical spurs (Fig. 76E)—   PHAENOPSECTRA Kieffer (p. 183, 2spp.)

—   Gonostylus with long setae on the inner side distributed from the tip to the middle or beyond (Fig. 76D). Hind-tibiae with 1 long apical spur—**29**

6(2) All tibiae with long conspicuous spurs (Figs 76G,H). Eyes kidney-shaped, without long dorsal projections—
PSEUDOCHIRONOMUS Malloch (p. 194, 1sp.)

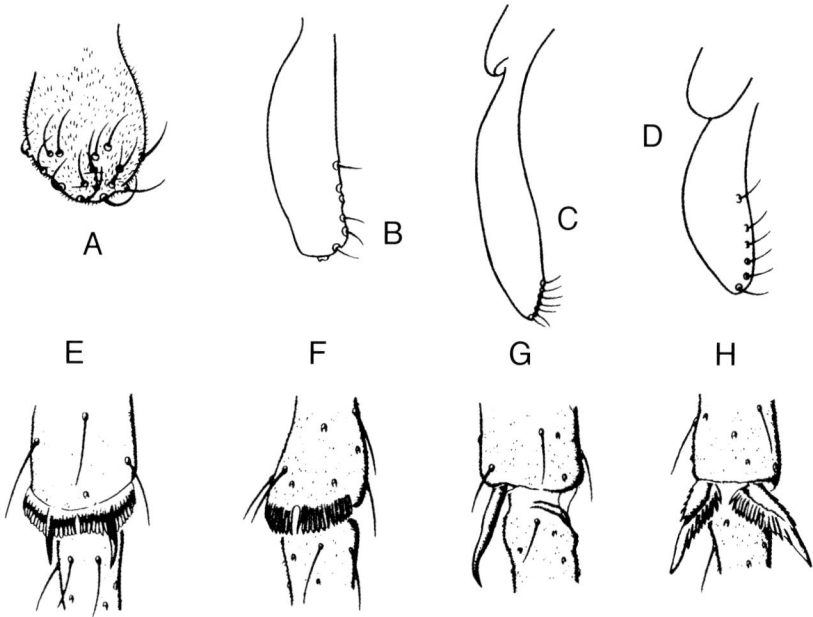

Fig. 76. **A:** inferior volsella of *Kiefferulus tendipediformis*. **B–D:** gonostyli of: B, *Sergentia coracina*; C, *Phaenopsectra flavipes*; D, *Polypedilum sordens*. **E, F:** hind-tibial combs of: E, *Phaenopsectra flavipes*; F, *Graceus ambiguus*. **G, H:** *Pseudochironomus prasinatus*: G, fore-tibial spurs; H, hind-tibial spurs.

—(6) Fore-tibiae with spurs very small or absent. Eyes strongly produced dorsally (cf. Fig. 3A, p. 10)—   **7**

7 Combs of hind-tibiae (see p. 14) composed of very short free spinules, without any indication of a spur (Fig. 76F)—
GRACEUS Goetghebuer (p. 174, 1sp.)

— Combs of hind-tibiae composed of basally fused spinules, and with at least 1 distinct spur (as in Fig. 76E)—   **8**

8 Both combs of posterior tibiae with 1 short or moderate spur—   **9**

— One comb bearing 1 long spur, the other without a spur or, occasionally, with 1 very small spur—   **29**

9   Pulvilli *p* on the apex of the tarsus large and distinct (Fig. 77A)—   **10**

—   Pulvilli very small or absent—   **28**

10 Antepronotum *apr* large (Fig. 4, p. 12), reaching to the anterior margin of the scutum, and not completely separated into two lobes anteriorly (Figs 77B,C)—   **11**

—   Antepronotum reduced, not usually reaching to the anterior margin of the scutum, but if so it is completely divided into two anterior lobes—   **23**

11 Inferior volsella reaching well beyond the tip of the gonocoxite and bearing long curved setae (e.g. arrow, Fig. 77D)—   **12**

—   Inferior volsella not reaching beyond the gonocoxite and without long curved setae (Fig. 78C), or the volsella is absent—   **15**

12 Inferior volsella with a narrow stem, bowed ventrally, the apex clubbed or bifurcate and bearing strong setae (arrow, Fig. 77D)—
                                    DICROTENDIPES Kieffer (p. 170, 6spp.)

—   Inferior volsella broad and almost straight, long setae more extensive—   **13**

13 Anal point very broad (arrow, Fig. 77E). Superior volsella short, broad and pubescent (Fig. 77F)—   XENOCHIRONOMUS Kieffer (p. 193, 1sp.)

—   Anal point usually narrower (e.g. Figs 77G,H). Superior volsella well developed, usually ending in a bare chitinised spur or hook (e.g. Figs 77I,J)—   **14**

14 Bare, narrow part of superior volsella arising from the *dorsal* surface of the large pubescent basal part of the appendage (Fig. 77I)—
                                    EINFELDIA Kieffer (p. 170, 2spp.)

—   *EITHER:* bare, narrow part of superior volsella arising from the *apex* of the basal pubescent part; *OR:* superior volsella strongly chitinised and bare except for a few long setae basally (Fig. 77J)—
                                    CHIRONOMUS Meigen (p. 158, 30spp.)

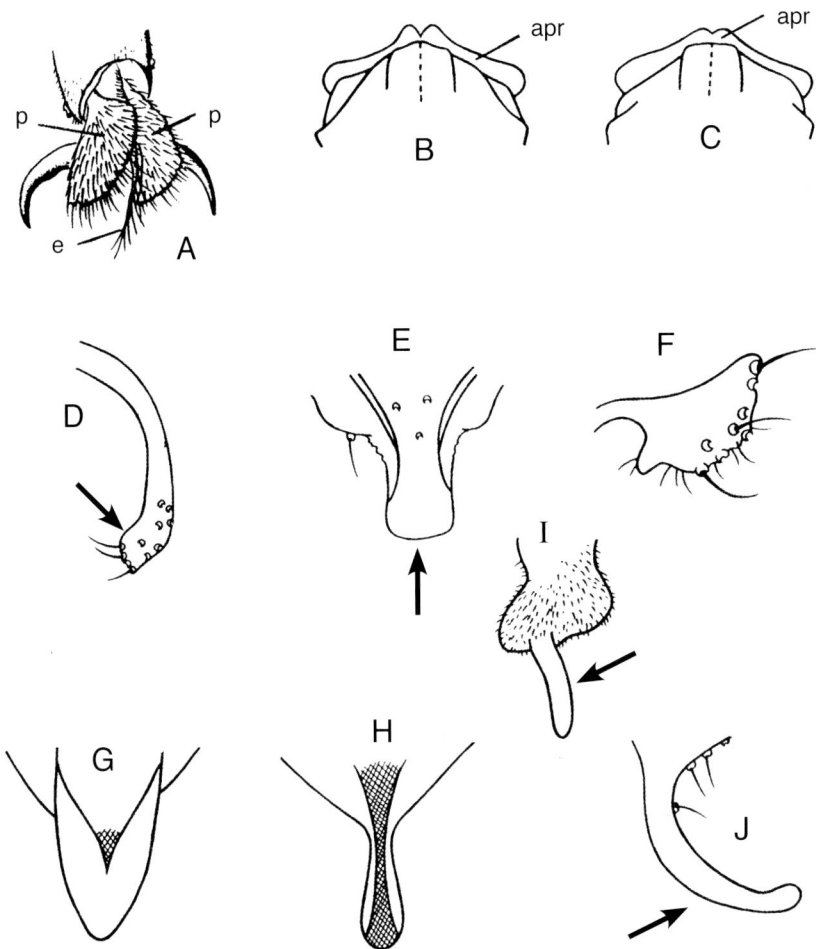

Fig. 77. **A:** foot of *Chironomus salinarius* (e = empodium between the two pulvilli p). **B, C:** anterior thorax, dorsal views, to show the antepronotum of: B, *Chironomus tentans*; C, *C. salinarius*. **D:** lateral view of inferior volsella of *Dicrotendipes pulsus*. **E, F:** *Xenochironomus xenolabis*: E anal point; F superior volsella. **G, H:** anal points of: G, *Chironomus obtusidens*; H, *C. aprilinus*. **I, J:** superior volsellae of: I, *Einfeldia pagana*; J, *Chironomus anthracinus*;

15(11)   Superior volsella *sv* rod-like, of variable length and bearing a few apical setae (e.g. Figs 78A,B)—   **16**

—   Superior volsella *sv* in the form of a short, broad pubescent pad (e.g. Fig. 78F) or sometimes reduced or absent—   **18**

16   Inferior volsella *iv* in the form of a small pubescent pad (e.g. Fig. 78C)—   PARACHIRONOMUS Lenz (p. 178, 13spp.)

—   Inferior volsella absent—   **17**

17   Gonostylus long, strongly incurved and swollen basally with an apical 'tooth' (arrow, Fig. 78A). On each side of the anal point there is a short tubercle *t*, bearing several setae (Fig. 78D)—
     MICROCHIRONOMUS Kieffer (p. 175, 2spp.)

—   Gonostylus long and incurved but not much swollen basally, without an apical 'tooth' (Fig. 78E). Anal tergite without processes next to the anal point—   CRYPTOTENDIPES Beck & Beck (p. 168, 5spp.)

18(15)   Inferior volsella *iv* in the form of a small pubescent pad or flap (Fig. 78F). Superior volsella *sv* short and broad, densely pubescent and with 2 to several long setae (Fig. 78F)—   **19**

—   Appendages not as above—   **20**

19   Anal tergite bands Y-shaped. Superior volsella with 2 setae (arrows, Fig. 78G)—   SAETHERIA Jackson (p. 190, 1sp.)

—   Anal tergite bands not strongly Y-shaped. Superior volsella with more than 2 setae (Fig. 78H)—
     PARACLADOPELMA Harnisch (p. 182, 3spp.)

20(18)   Gonostylus short and broad (Fig. 79A, p. 153). Superior volsella short, broad and pubescent (Fig. 78H)—
     CRYPTOCHIRONOMUS Kieffer (p. 166, 7spp.)

—   Gonostylus longer (e.g. Figs 79B–E). Superior volsella strongly reduced or absent—   **21**

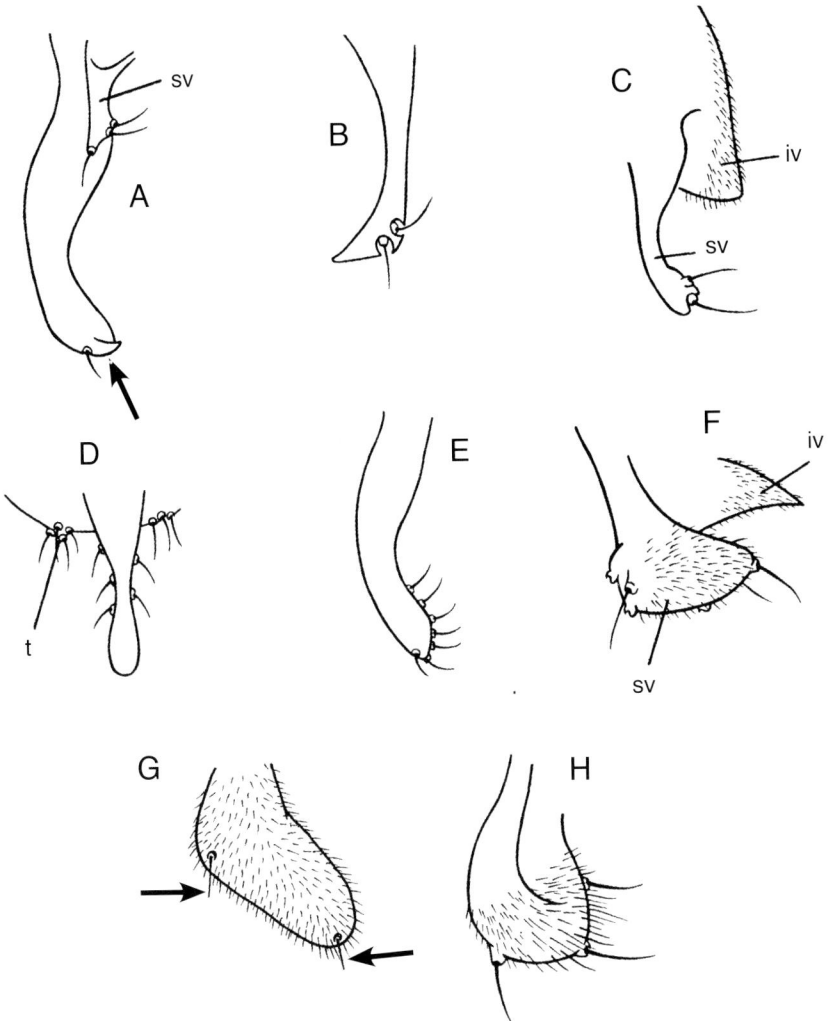

Fig. 78. **A:** gonostylus and superior volsella of *Microchironomus tener*. **B:** superior volsella of *Parachironomus monochromus*; **C:** superior and inferior volsellae of *Parachironomus frequens*. **D:** anal point of *Microchironomus deribae*. **E:** gonostylus of *Cryptotendipes nigronitens*. **F:** superior and inferior volsellae of *Paracladopelma laminatum*. **G, H:** superior volsellae of: G, *Saetheria reissi*; H, *Cryptochironomus rostratus*.

21   Gonostylus with a dorsal keel (arrow, Fig. 79B)—
        DEMICRYPTOCHIRONOMUS Lenz (p. 169, 2spp.)
—   Gonostylus without a keel dorsally—   **22**

22   Gonostylus of uniform thickness or gently tapered from the base to the
     tip (Figs 79C,D)—   HARNISCHIA Kieffer (p. 174, 2spp.)

—   Gonostylus of varying thickness and abruptly curved at about the middle
     (Fig. 79E)—   CLADOPELMA Kieffer (p. 164, 5spp.)

23(10) Antepronotum (Fig. 4, p. 12) extending to the anterior edge of the
        scutum but deeply divided into two anterior lobes—   **24**

—   Antepronotum reduced, not reaching to front edge of the scutum— **27**

24   Wing membrane with a broad, transverse, brown band in the region
     of the median cross-vein MCu (Fig. 5, p. 13). Abdomen with whole
     of segment I and the distal three-quarters of segments III and IV pale,
     remainder of abdomen dark—   DEMEIJEREA Kruseman (p. 168, 1sp.)

—   Wing membrane unmarked. Abdominal segments I, III and IV not paler
     than remainder of abdomen—   **25**

25   Beard of long setae on the fore-tarsus. Both combs on the mid- and
     hind-tibiae (p. 15) with a small to moderate spur (very rarely one is
     missing)—   ENDOCHIRONOMUS Kieffer (p. 172, 2spp.)

—   No beard of setae on the fore-tarsus. Combs of mid- and hind-tibiae with
     variable reduction in the number of spurs—   **26**

26   Superior volsella with basal setiferous part subcylindrical, not demarcated
     from the more apical bare part (Fig. 79F)—
                             SYNENDOTENDIPES Grodhaus (p. 193, 3spp.)

—   Superior volsella with basal setiferous part broad, more or less demarcated
     from the apical bare part (Fig. 79G)—
                             TRIBELOS Townes (p. 193, 1sp.)

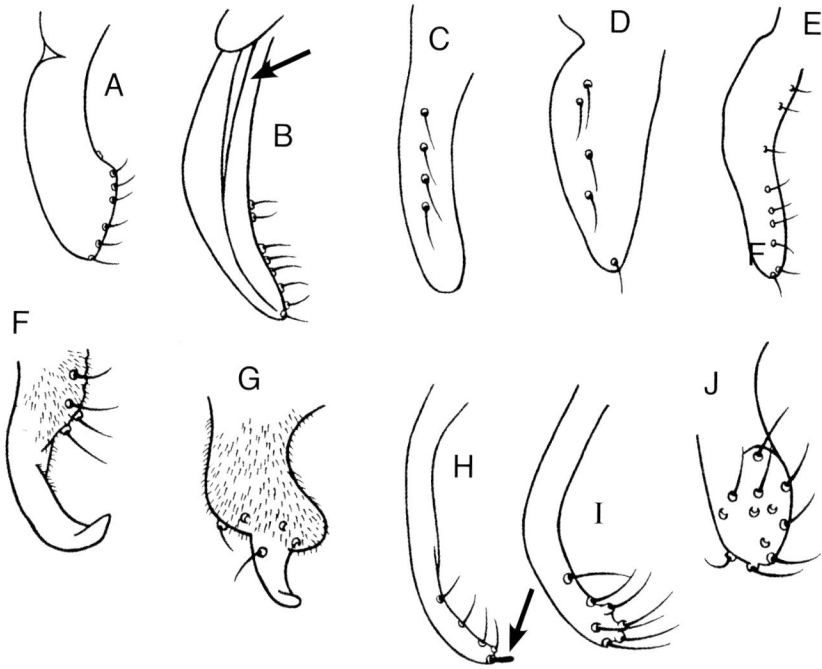

Fig. 79. **A–E:** gonostyli of: A, *Cryptochironomus redekei*; B, *Demicryptochironomus vulneratus*; C, *Harnischia curtilamellata*; D, *H. fuscimana*; E, *Cladopelma viridulum*. **F, G:** superior volsellae of: F, *Synendotendipes dispar*; G, *Tribelos intextus*. **H–J:** inferior volsellae of: H, *Stenochironomus hibernicus*; I, *Nilothauma brayi*; J, *Paratendipes albimanus*.

27(23) Wing membrane with distinct dark markings. Inferior volsella very long with a well differentiated terminal spine (arrow, Fig. 79H)—
        STENOCHIRONOMUS Kieffer (p. 190, 3spp.)

— Wing membrane unmarked. Inferior volsella of normal shape, lacking a terminal spine— GLYPTOTENDIPES Kieffer (p. 172, 10spp.)

28(9) Antennal ratio about 0.3 (p. 9). Inferior volsella slender and strongly curved (Fig. 79I)— NILOTHAUMA Kieffer (p. 178, 1sp.)

— Antennal ratio >1.0. Inferior volsella broad and almost straight (Fig. 79J)— PARATENDIPES Kieffer (p. 182, 3spp.)

29(5,8) Squama at base of wing bare—   **30**

—   Squama at base of wing with a fringe of setae—   **33**

30   Wings covered with greyish spots—
                                    ZAVRELIELLA Kieffer* (p. 193, 1sp.)

*N.B. The single species is possibly always parthenogenetic in Britain and Ireland, as no males have been found.

—   Wings unmarked—   **31**

31   Gonostylus only half as long as the gonocoxite—
                                    PARALAUTERBORNIELLA Lenz (p. 182, 1sp.)

—   Gonostylus twice as long as the gonocoxite—   **32**

32   Anal point short and slender (Fig 80A)—
                        LAUTERBORNIELLA Thienemann & Bause (p. 175, 1sp.)

—   Anal point longer, broadened distally (Fig. 80B)—
                                    PAGASTIELLA Brundin (p. 178, 1sp.)

33(29) Tergite VIII anteriorly narrowed (Fig. 80C)—
                                    POLYPEDILUM Kieffer (p. 184, 18spp.)

—   Tergite VIII quadrate—   **34**

34   Anal tergite conically enlarged medially, terminating in a short, narrow anal point (Fig. 80D). Superior volsella somewhat swollen for the basal two-thirds, tip narrow (Fig. 80E)—   OMISUS Townes (p. 178, 1sp.)

—   Anal tergite not strongly projecting medially. Superior volsella not as above—   **35**

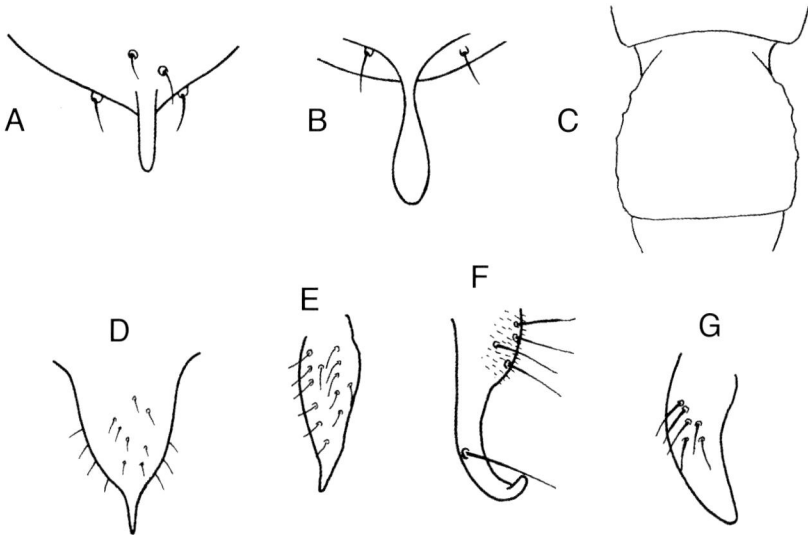

Fig. 80. **A, B:** anal points of: A, *Lauterborniella agrayloides*; B, *Pagastiella orophila*. **C:** abdominal segment VIII of *Polypedilum arundineti*. **D, E:** *Omisus caledonicus*: D, anal point; E, superior volsella. **F, G:** superior volsellae of: F, *Stictochironomus sticticus*; G, *Microtendipes pedellus*.

35   Superior volsella with a broad base bearing a number of setae, and a long, narrow, more or less curved apical projection with a long lateral seta (Fig. 80F). Wings with distinct dark markings but sometimes only a single dark patch is present in the region of cross-vein RM. Legs usually distinctly ringed—   STICTOCHIRONOMUS Kieffer (p. 191, 4spp.)

—   Superior volsella blade-like with setae on the dorsal surface (Fig. 80G). Wings without dark markings. Legs not ringed—
                    MICROTENDIPES Kieffer (p. 176, 9spp.)

36(1)   All maxillary palp segments short. Tibiae without combs, but with 2 robust, thorn-like spurs distally—
                    CORYNOCERA Zetterstedt (p. 195, 1sp.)

—   Maxillary palps longer. Legs with combs on mid- and hind tibiae—   **37**

37   Combs of hind-tibia usually contiguous, with or without spurs; if combs
     are clearly separated, spurs are absent—   **38**

—   Combs of hind-tibia well separated, at least 1 comb bearing a longish
     spur—   **40**

38   Combs of hind-tibia with 2 spurs—
     PARATANYTARSUS Thienemann & Bause (p. 200, 13spp.)

—   Combs of hind-tibia usually without spurs, occasionally with 1 spur— **39**

39   Small species (wing length 1.0–2.4 mm), with antennal ratio <1.0 (p. 9)
     and median volsella (p. 15) short (<40 μm), with a brush of leaf-like or
     spoon-shaped setae at the tip—   PARAPSECTRA Reiss (p. 199, 2spp.)

—   Usually larger; when as small as above and antennal ratio <1.0, the
     median volsella is long, extending beyond the base of the gonostylus
     (e.g. Fig. 81A)—   MICROPSECTRA Kieffer (p. 196, 15spp.)

40(37) Wing membrane densely covered with macrotrichia distally, elsewhere
     almost or completely bare. Inferior volsella not strongly curved—   **41**

—   Entire wing usually densely clothed with macrotrichia; if not, then the
     inferior volsella is bent into a right-angle (Fig. 81B)—   **45**

41   Median volsella of hypopygium with long, branched, flattened setae
     (Fig. 81C)—   CLADOTANYTARSUS Kieffer (p. 194, 9spp.)

—   Median volsella with setae unbranched—   **42**

42   Superior volsella with a long digitus, usually exceeding the inner
     margin of the volsella (arrow, Fig. 81D). Anal point broadly rounded
     (Fig. 81E)—   NEOZAVRELIA Goetghebuer (p. 198, 3spp.)

—   Digitus absent from superior volsella. Anal point elongate—   **43**

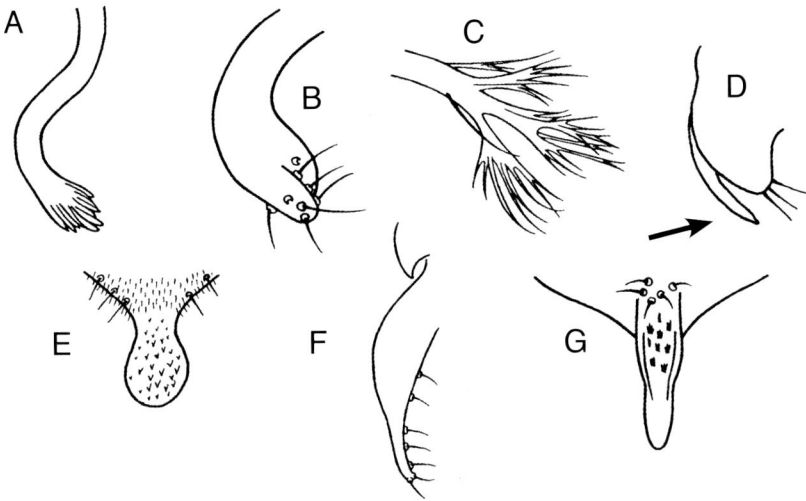

Fig. 81. **A:** median volsella of *Micropsectra attenuata*. **B:** inferior volsella of *Tanytarsus sylvaticus*. **C:** median volsella of *Cladotanytarsus mancus*. **D, E:** *Neozavrelia fuldensis*: D, superior volsella and digitus; E, anal point. **F:** gonostylus of *Rheotanytarsus pentapoda*. **G:** anal point of *Tanytarsus pallidicornis*.

43 Eyes hairy (cf. Fig. 3B, p. 10)—   ZAVRELIA Kieffer (p. 218, 1sp.)

— Eyes bare—   **44**

44 Pulvilli *p* on the apex of the tarsus well developed, about half as long as the claws (see Fig. 77A, p. 149). Wing vein R_{4+5} ending distinctly proximal to vein M_{3+4}—   STEMPELLINA Thienemann & Bause (p. 206, 2spp.)

— Pulvilli absent. Wing vein R_{4+5} ending above or slightly proximal to the tip of vein M_{3+4}—   STEMPELLINELLA Brundin (p. 206, 3spp.)

45(40) Gonostylus usually abruptly narrowed distally (Fig. 81F). If not, the antennal flagellum is composed of 12 flagellomeres only. Anal point without groups of spines—
RHEOTANYTARSUS Thienemann & Bause (p. 204, 9spp.)

— Gonostylus not abruptly narrowed distally. Antennal flagellum composed of 13 flagellomeres. Anal point frequently with groups of short spines dorsally (e.g. Fig. 81G)—   **46**

46 Anal point with 2 orally-directed rods (arrows, Fig. 82A)—
    VIRGATANYTARSUS Pinder (p. 218, 2spp.)

—   Anal point without such processes—
    TANYTARSUS van der Wulp (p. 206, 38spp.)

KEYS TO 256 SPECIES IN 47 GENERA OF CHIRONOMINAE

Tribe CHIRONOMINI

Genus CHIRONOMUS Meigen

Note: in cross-section, the anal point of *Chironomus* is roughly T-shaped, since the dorsal keels are expanded into broad lamellae. In the illustrations of the hypopygia of *Chironomus* species (Volume 2, pp. 89–96), the ventral contours are cross-hatched in order to distinguish the dorsal lamellae from the more ventral parts.

1   Anal tergite with a pair of prominent lobes flanking the anal point (arrows, Fig. 82B,C)—   (CAMPTOCHIRONOMUS), 2

—   Anal tergite without lobes on either side of the anal point—   3

2   Lobes flanking the anal point relatively short (arrows, Fig. 82B). Gonostylus relatively slender (Fig. 82D). Hypopygium Fig. 198A—
    Chironomus (Camptochironomus) tentans Fabricius

—   Lobes flanking the anal point longer (arrows, Fig. 82C). Gonostylus more robust (Fig. 82E). Hypopygium Fig. 198B—
    Chironomus (Campt.) pallidivittatus auctt.

3(1) Superior volsella (Fig. 8, p. 16) broad, somewhat rectangular, pubescent, with setae above and beneath, and with a short darkened projection on the medial margin (Fig. 82F). Hypopygium Fig. 198C—
    Chironomus (Chaetolabis) macani Freeman

—   Superior volsella not as above—   4

4   Superior volsella broad for about two-thirds of its length, pubescent and setose, more so beneath than above, with a narrow, bare apical projection directed obliquely backwards (Fig. 82G). Hypopygium Fig. 199A—
    Chironomus (Lobochironomus) dissidens Walker
    and **Chironomus (L.) carbonarius** Meigen [see p. 158, Vol. 2]

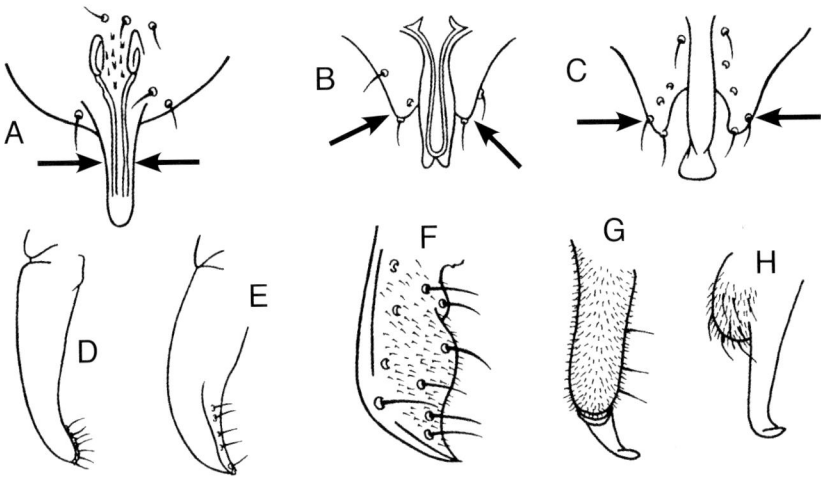

Fig. 82. **A:** anal point of *Virgatanytarsus triangularis*. **B, C:** anal tergites of: B, *Chironomus tentans*; C, *C. pallidivittatus*. **D, E:** gonostyli of: D, *C. tentans*; E, *C. pallidivittatus*. **F:** superior volsella of *C. macani*. **G, H:** superior volsellae of: G, *C. dissidens*; H, *C. dorsalis*.

—(4) Superior volsella only swollen towards the base, either externally (Fig. 82H) or internally (e.g. Figs 84A–G, p. 163)—   **5**

5   Superior volsella with a pubescent swelling externally at the base (Fig. 82H), Hypopygium Fig. 199B—   **Chironomus (L.) dorsalis** Meigen
and **Chironomus (L.) crassimanus** Strenzke [see p. 159, Vol. 2]

—   Superior volsella not swollen externally at the base—
(CHIRONOMUS), **6**

6   Wings less than 2.5 mm long, with dark spots, two between veins R_{4+5} and M_{1+2}, and one between M_{1+2} and M_{3+4}, posterior veins broadly darkened. Hypopygium Fig. 199C—
Chironomus (Chironomus) strenzkei Fittkau*

*This is a South American species, imported on aquarium plants, sometimes becoming established for a while in commercial and, occasionally, home aquaria.

—   Wings longer and without spots on the membrane—   **7**

7   Anal point parallel-sided or tapered from base to tip (e.g. Figs 83A–C)— **8**

—   Anal point constricted basally and expanded in distal half (Fig. 83D)—**21**

8   Anal point very broad (Figs 83A,B)—   **9**

—   Anal point more slender (e.g. Fig. 83C)—   **10**

9   Inferior volsella very broad. Hypopygium Fig. 199D—
                                              Chironomus (C.) sp. a

—   Inferior volsella normal, more slender. Hypopygium Fig. 200A—
                                     Chironomus (C.) obtusidens Goetghebuer

10(8) Frontal tubercles (Fig. 3A, p. 10) minute (<10 μm long) or absent. A dark
      species with a reticulate pattern on abdominal tergite IX. Hypopygium
      Fig. 200B—   **Chironomus (C.) inermifrons** Goetghebuer

—   Frontal tubercles well developed (>30 μm long). (Dark or light species,
    with or without a reticulate pattern on abdominal tergite IX)—   **11**

11 Fore-tarsus with a beard of long setae; beard ratio >4.5 (see p. 14)
    (arrows, Fig. 83E)—   **12**

—   Fore-tarsus with a beard of short setae (beard ratio <4.0) or absent
    (arrows, Fig. 83F)—   **15**

12 Entirely black. Beard ratio 4.5–5.7. Hypopygium Fig. 200C—
                                    Chironomus (C.) anthracinus Zetterstedt

—   Not entirely black, abdominal tergites with pale posterior borders, or
    more extensively pale. Beard ratio >6.0—   **13**

13 Abdomen mainly dark brown but tergites with narrowly pale posterior
    borders. Hypopygium Fig. 200D— **Chironomus (C.) annularius** auctt.
      and **Chironomus (C.) entis** Schobanov [see p. 160, Vol. 2]

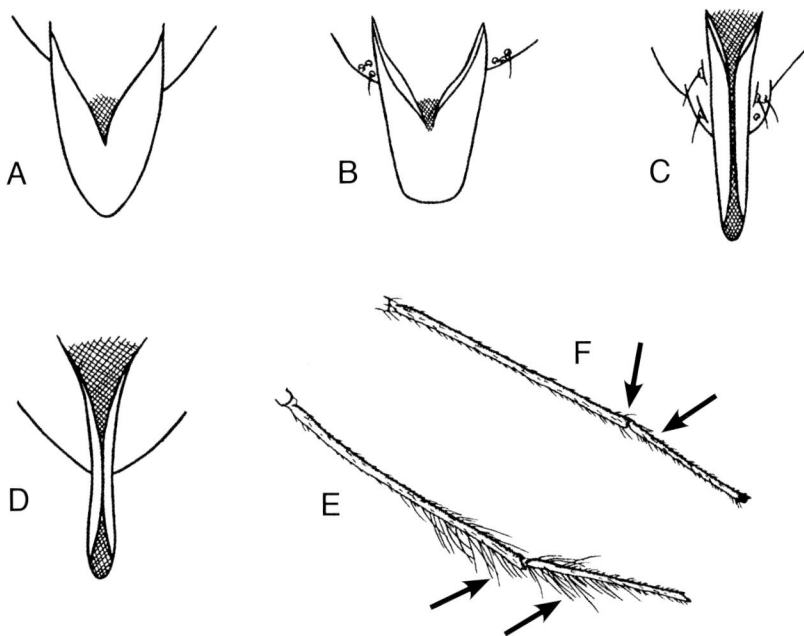

Fig. 83. **A–D:** anal points of: A, *Chironomus obtusidens*; B, *Chironomus* sp. *a.*; C, *Chironomus prasinus*; D, *C. plumosus*. **E, F:** setal beards on fore-tarsi of: E, *C. anthracinus*; F, *C. venustus.*

—(13)   Abdomen greenish—   **14**

14   Anal point narrow (Fig. 83C). Hypopygium Fig. 201A—
                    Chironomus (C.) prasinus Meigen
             and **Chironomus (C.) entis** Schobanov [see p. 160, Vol. 2]

—   Anal point broader. Hypopygium Fig. 201B—
                    Chironomus (C.) nudiventris Ryser, Scholl & Wülker

15(11) Dark species: black, or brown with abdominal tergites pale posteriorly—   **16**

—   Ground colour pale: yellowish or greenish—   **19**

16 Brown, with posterior margins of abdominal segments pale. Hypopygium
    Fig. 201C—   **Chironomus (C.) commutatus** Keyl

—   Black—   **17**

17 Abdominal tergite IX with reticulation. Hypopygium Fig. 201D—
                            Chironomus (C.) lacunarius Wülker

—   Abdominal tergite IX without reticulation—   **18**

18 Superior volsella slightly curved (Fig. 84B), not darker than the rest of
    the hypopygium. Hypopygium Fig. 202A—
                            Chironomus (C.) venustus sensu Pinder 1978

—   Superior volsella strongly curved (Fig. 84C) and distinctly darker than
    the rest of the hypopygium. Hypopygium Fig. 202B—
                            Chironomus (C.) longistylus Goetghebuer

19(15) Superior volsella tapered to a pointed apex (Fig. 84A). Hypopygium
    Fig. 202C—   **Chironomus (C.) cingulatus** Meigen

—   Superior volsella roughly parallel-sided, or medially swollen, blunt
    apically (Figs 84B,C)—   **20**

20 Larger: wing length >4.0 mm. Antennal ratio >4.0 (p. 9). Hypopygium
    Fig. 202D—   **Chironomus (C.) nuditarsis** Keyl

—   Smaller: wing length <4.0 mm. Antennal ratio <4.0. Hypopygium Fig.
    203A—   **Chironomus (C.) bernensis** Klötzli

21(7)   Superior volsella slender, not strongly expanded distally (Figs
    84D,E)—   **22**

—   Superior volsella broadened distally into a club- or foot-shape (Figs
    84F,G)—   **25**

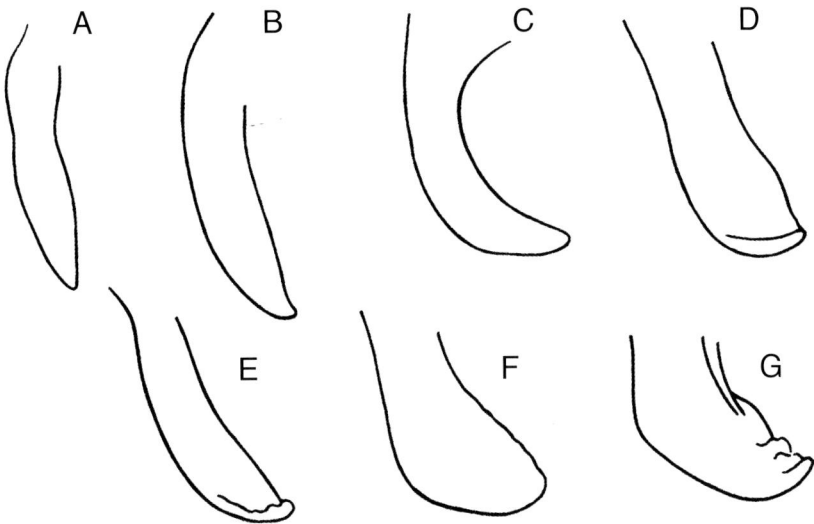

Fig. 84. **A–G:** superior volsellae of: A, *Chironomus cingulatus*; B, *C. venustus*; C, *C. longistylus*; D, *C. dorsalis*; E, *C. plumosus*; F, *C. riparius*; G, *C. luridus*.

22   Fore-tarsus without a distinct beard of setae. Fore-leg ratio at least 1.5 (p. 14). Hypopygium Fig. 203B—   **Chironomus (C.) dorsalis** auctt.

—   Fore-tarsus with a distinct beard of setae. Fore-leg ratio <1.4—   **23**

23   Strikingly black, including halteres and abdominal setae. Fore-leg ratio scarcely or not exceeding 1.0. Wing length about 6.0 mm. Hypopygium Fig. 203C—   **Chironomus (C.) pilicornis** (Fabricius)

—   Lighter in colour, halteres and abdominal setae pale. Abdomen often extensively pale. Fore-leg ratio at least 1.2—   **24**

24   Thorax with pale ground colour; abdomen usually with extensive pale markings. Wing length >4.5 mm. Fore-tarsus with a beard of long setae (beard ratio >6.0, see p. 14). Superior volsella pale. Hypopygium Fig. 204A—   **Chironomus (C.) plumosus** (L.)

—(24) Thorax black; abdomen dark brown. Wing length 3–4 mm. Fore-tarsus with a beard usually of shorter setae. Superior volsella strongly chitinised. Hypopygium Fig. 204B—
Chironomus (C.) salinarius Kieffer

25(21) Fore-tarsus with a distinct beard of setae (beard ratio >4.5, see p. 14). Hypopygium Fig. 204C— **Chironomus (C.) aprilinus** Meigen

— Fore-tarsus without a distinct beard of setae (beard ratio <3.0)— **26**

26 Abdominal tergite I entirely pale or occasionally with a small greyish spot centrally. Superior volsella as in Fig. 84G, p. 163. Hypopygium Fig. 205A— **Chironomus (C.) luridus** Strenzke

— Abdominal tergite I with a distinctly darkened anterior band or entirely dark— **27**

27 Entirely blackish brown. Hypopygium Fig. 205B—
Chironomus (C.) lugubris Zetterstedt
and **Chironomus holomelas** Keyl [see p. 161, Vol. 2]

— Abdomen with pale bands— **28**

28 Fore-leg ratio >1.55 (p. 14). Hypopygium as in *C. riparius*—
Chironomus (C.) pseudothummi Strenzke

— Fore-leg ratio <1.5— **29**

29 Postnotum black except for a yellow spot on each side anterolaterally. Hypopygium Fig. 205C— **Chironomus (C.) riparius** Meigen

— Postnotum black with anterior one-quarter to one-third yellow. Hypopygium Fig. 205D— **Chironomus (C.) piger** Strenzke

Genus CLADOPELMA Kieffer

1 Anal tergite with wing-like lateral expansions (arrows, Fig. 85A). Hypopygium Fig. 206A— **Cladopelma goetghebueri** Spies & Sæther

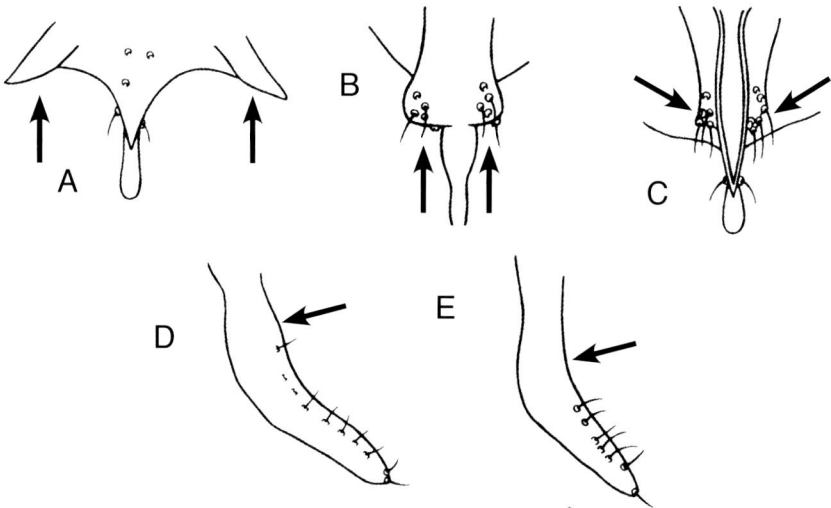

Fig. 85.   **A–C:** anal tergites of: A, *Cladopelma goetghebueri*; B, *C. krusemani*; C, *C. virescens*. **D, E:** gonostyli of: D, *C. viridulum*; E, *C. edwardsi*.

—(1)   Anal tergite not as above—   **2**

2   Base of anal point covered by a large median expansion of the anal tergite (arrows, Fig. 85B). Hypopygium Fig. 206B—
                              Cladopelma krusemani (Goetghebuer)
               and **Cladopelma bicarinata** (Brundin) [see p. 162, Vol. 2]

—   Not as above—   **3**

3   Anal point flanked basally by a pair of swellings bearing numerous strong setae (arrows, Fig. 85C). Hypopygium Fig. 206C—
                              Cladopelma virescens (Meigen)

—   Not as above—   **4**

4   Inner margin of gonostylus somewhat swollen in the basal half (arrow, Fig. 85D). Hypopygium Fig. 206D—   **Cladopelma viridulum** (L.)

—   Inner margin of gonostylus smoothly curved, not swollen basally (arrow, Fig. 85E). Hypopygium Fig. 207A— **Cladopelma edwardsi** (Kruseman)

Genus CRYPTOCHIRONOMUS Kieffer

1   Frontal tubercles (Fig. 3A, p. 10) minute, not longer than broad, or absent—   **2**

—   Frontal tubercles well developed, much longer than broad—   **3**

2   Apical hooks of hind-femora conspicuously darkened (arrow, Fig. 86A). Hypopygium Fig. 207B—
                    Cryptochironomus denticulatus (Goetghebuer)

—   Apical hooks of hind-femora pale and inconspicuous. Hypopygium Fig. 207C—   **Cryptochironomus rostratus** Kieffer

3(1) Gonostylus distinctly broadened distally (Fig. 86B–D)—   **4**

—   Gonostylus not broadened distally (Fig. 86E)—   **6**

4   Anal point somewhat broadened distally (arrow, Fig. 86F). Hypopygium Fig. 207D—   **Cryptochironomus supplicans** (Meigen)

—   Anal point tapered (Fig. 86G)—   **5**

5   Outer margin of superior volsella distinctly notched (arrow, Fig. 86K). Entirely dark brown in colour. Hypopygium Fig. 208A—
                    Cryptochironomus redekei (Kruseman)

—   Outer margin of superior volsella smoothly rounded (Fig. 63J). Abdomen green, ground colour of thorax pale with dark brown scutal stripes. Hypopygium Fig. 208B—   **Cryptochironomus psittacinus** (Meigen)

6(3) Anal point parallel-sided or slightly expanded distally (Fig. 86H). Fore-tarsus with a distinct beard of setae. Hypopygium Fig. 208C—
                    Cryptochironomus albofasciatus (Staeger)

—   Anal point tapered (Fig. 86I). Fore-tarsus without a beard of setae. Hypopygium Fig. 208D—   **Cryptochironomus obreptans** (Walker)

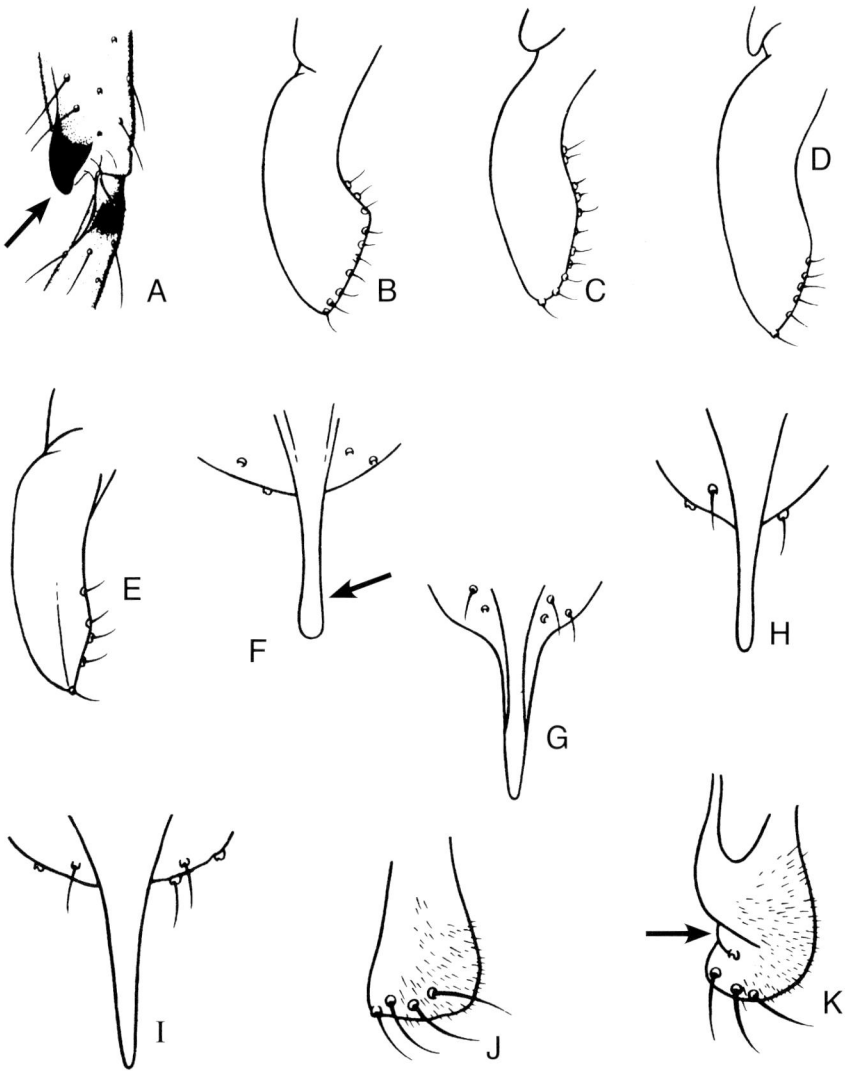

Fig. 86. **A:** tip of posterior femur of *Cryptochironomus denticulatus*. **B–E:** gonostyli of: B, *C. redekei*; C, *C. psittacinus*; D, *C. supplicans*; E, *C. albofasciatus*. **F–I:** anal points of: F, *C. supplicans*; G, *C. redekei*; H, *C. albofasciatus*; I, *C. obreptans*. **J, K:** superior volsellae of: J, *C. psittacinus*; K, *C. redekei*.

Genus CRYPTOTENDIPES Beck & Beck

1   Anal tergite strongly expanded dorsally (arrows, Fig. 87A). Gonostylus becomes narrower just beyond the middle, producing a distinctly swollen apical half (Fig. 87C)—   **2**

—   Anal tergite not swollen dorsally (Fig. 87B). Gonostylus with distinct emargination in the apical half (arrow, Fig. 87D) or at most a narrower mid-section (Figs 87E,F)—   **3**

2   Anal point short, not longer than the superior volsella. Hypopygium Fig. 209A—   **Cryptotendipes nigronitens** (Edwards)

—   Anal point longer than the superior volsella. Hypopygium Fig. 209B—
Cryptotendipes usmaensis (Pagast)

3(1) Gonostylus abruptly contracted just beyond the middle, producing a distinctly emarginate apical half (arrow, Fig. 87D). Anal point short, not longer than the superior volsella. Hypopygium Fig. 209C—
Cryptotendipes pflugfelderi Reiss

—   Gonostylus without distinct emargination in the apical half—   **4**

4   Gonostylus apically pointed (arrow, Fig. 87E). Hypopygium Fig. 209D—   **Cryptotendipes holsatus** Lenz

—   Gonostylus apically rounded (arrow, Fig. 87F). Hypopygium Fig. 210A—   **Cryptotendipes pseudotener** (Goetghebuer)

Genus DEMEIJEREA Kruseman

The single European species is readily identified from the characters mentioned in the key to genera (p. 152). Hypopygium Fig. 210B—
Demeijerea rufipes (L.)

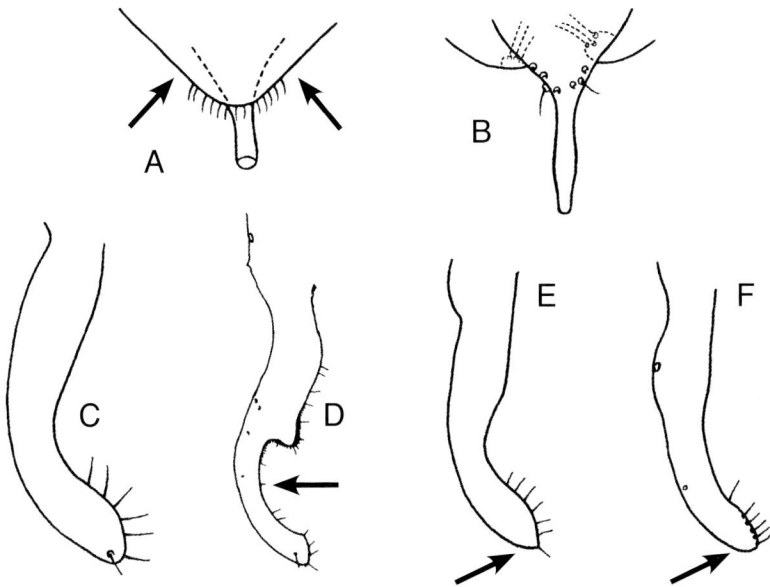

Fig. 87. **A, B:** anal points of: A, *Cryptotendipes nigronitens*; B, *C. pseudotener*.
C–F: gonostyli of: C, *C. nigronitens*; D, *C. pflugfelderi;* E, *C. holsatus*; F,
C. pseudotener.

Genus DEMICRYPTOCHIRONOMUS Lenz

1   Superior volsella of hypopygium pubescent. Hypopygium Fig. 210C—
**Demicryptochironomus (Demicryptochironomus)
vulneratus** (Zetterstedt)

—   Superior volsella bare. Hypopygium Fig. 210D—
Demicryptochironomus (Irmakia) neglectus Reiss

Genus DICROTENDIPES Kieffer

1	Inferior volsella of the hypopygium forked at the tip (arrow, Fig. 88A). Hypopygium Fig. 211A— **Dicrotendipes pallidicornis** (Goetghebuer)

—	Inferior volsella not forked, at most strongly indented at the tip—	**2**

2	Inferior volsella broad, with a membranous dorsal expansion (arrow, Fig. 88B). Hypopygium Fig. 211B— **Dicrotendipes notatus** (Meigen)

—	Inferior volsella slender—	**3**

3	Inferior volsella very long and strongly curved (Figs 88C,D) (in life, the curve of the appendage is vertical and in an unsquashed mount appears as drawn in Fig. 88E)—	**4**

—	Inferior volsella shorter and less strongly curved (Fig. 88F); superior volsella short, not clubbed, but with a short, beak-like process (arrow, Fig. 88G). Hypopygium Fig. 211C— **Dicrotendipes lobiger** (Kieffer)

4	Gonostylus very long and narrow throughout its length (Fig. 88H). Hypopygium Fig. 211D— **Dicrotendipes nervosus** (Staeger)

—	Gonostylus shorter, broadest in its basal half (arrow, Fig. 88I)—	**5**

5	Inferior volsella symmetrically expanded at the tip, with preapical setae irregularly arranged (arrow, Fig. 88J). Hypopygium Fig. 212A—
Dicrotendipes tritomus (Kieffer)

—	Inferior volsella more strongly expanded externally at the tip, with preapical setae in transverse rows. Hypopygium Fig. 212B—
Dicrotendipes pulsus (Walker)

Genus EINFELDIA Kieffer

1	Anal point very broad (Fig. 88K). Thorax green. Hypopygium Fig. 212C— **Einfeldia pagana** (Meigen)

—	Anal point more slender. Thorax green with black scutal stripes. Hypopygium Fig. 212D— **Einfeldia palaearctica** Ashe

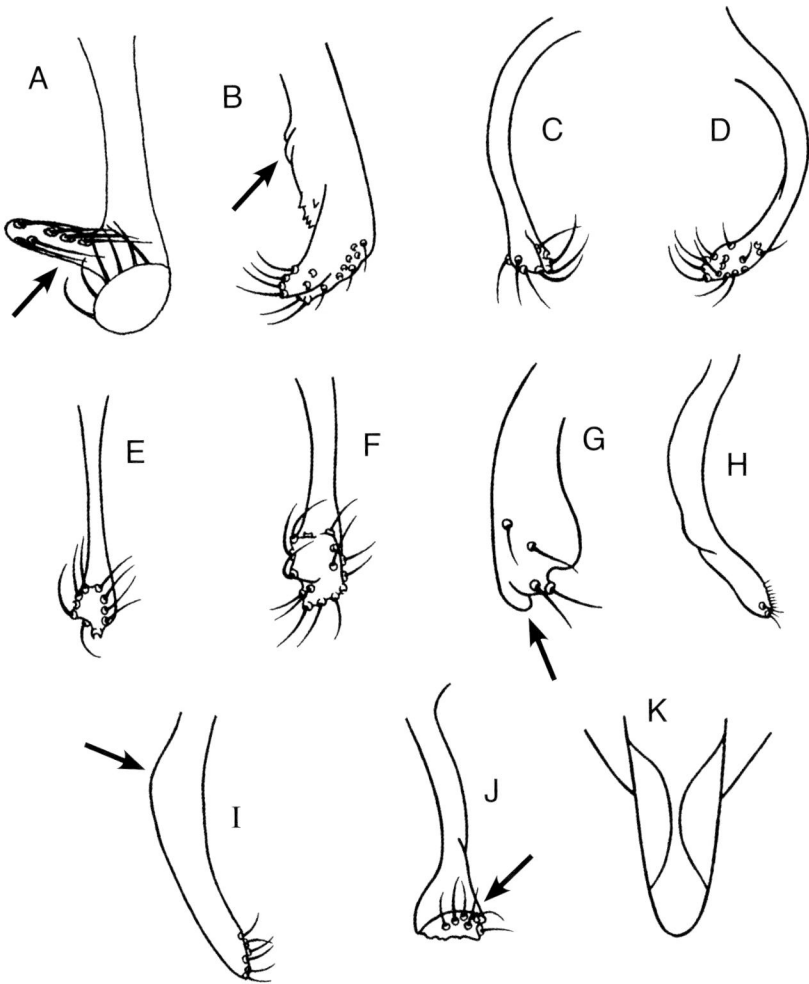

Fig. 88. **A, B:** inferior volsellae of: A, *Dicrotendipes pallidicornis*; B, *D. notatus.* **C, D:** *D. pulsus*: C, gonostylus; D, inferior volsella. **E, F:** inferior volsellae of E, *D. tritomus*; F, *D. lobiger*; **G:** superior volsella of *D. lobiger*. **H, I:** gonostyli of: H, *D. nervosus*; I, *D. pulsus.* **J:** superior volsella of *D. tritomus.* **K:** anal point of *Einfeldia pagana.*

Genus ENDOCHIRONOMUS Kieffer

1   Anal point slender (Fig. 89A), extending two-thirds of the way along the inferior volsella. Hypopygium Fig. 213A—

Endochironomus tendens (Fabricius)

—   Anal point more robust (Fig. 89B), reaching the tip of the inferior volsella. Hypopygium Fig. 213B—

Endochironomus albipennis (Meigen)

Genus FLEURIA Kieffer*

*__Fleuria lacustris__ has now been added to the British list [see p. 163, Vol. 2].

Genus GLYPTOTENDIPES Kieffer

1   Superior volsella straight for most of its length but abruptly hooked at the tip (arrow, Fig. 89C)—   **2**

—   Superior volsella curved over its entire length, not abruptly hooked apically (Fig. 89D)—   **6**

2   Second tarsomere of fore-leg distinctly shorter than the third (Fig. 89E). Hypopygium Fig. 213C—

Glyptotendipes (Glyptotendipes) barbipes (Staeger)
and **Glyptotendipes (G.) salinus** Michailova [see p. 164, Vol. 2]

—   Second tarsomere of fore-leg equal to or longer than the third—   **3**

3   Anal point long and slender (Fig. 89F). Not predominantly black. Hypopygium Fig. 213D—   **Glyptotendipes (G.) cauliginellus** (Kieffer)

—   Anal point shorter and broad, at least apically (Fig. 89G). Mostly black—   **4**

4   Anal point broadest medially, not clubbed (Fig. 89H). Fore-leg ratio about 1.2 (p. 14). Hypopygium Fig. 214A—

Glyptotendipes (G.) paripes (Edwards)

—   Anal point clubbed distally (Fig. 89G). Anterior leg ratio about 1.5—   **5**

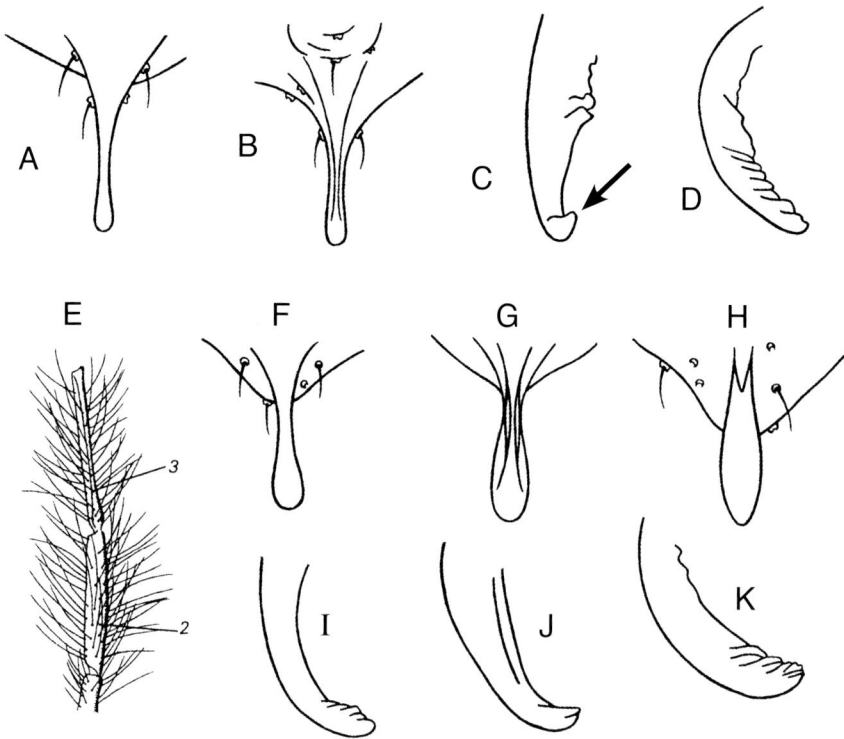

Fig. 89. **A, B:** anal points of: A, *Endochironomus tendens*; B, *E. albipennis*. **C, D:** superior volsellae of: D, *Glyptotendipes barbipes*; E, *G. viridis*. **E:** second and third segments of anterior tarsus of *G. barbipes*. **F–H:** anal points of: F, *G. cauligenellus*; G, *G. pallens*; H, *G. paripes*. **I–K:** superior volsellae of: I, *G. mancunianus*; J, *G. foliicola*; K, *G. imbecilis*.

5   Fore-tarsus with a setal beard. Frontal tubercles usually present (Fig. 3A, p. 10). Hypopygium Fig. 214B — **Glyptotendipes (G.) pallens** (Meigen)

—   Fore-tarsus without a setal beard. Frontal tubercles absent. Hypopygium Fig. 214C — **Glyptotendipes (G.) glaucus** (Meigen)

6(1) Superior volsella broadest basally, tapered (Fig. 89I,J) —   **7**

—   Superior volsella narrow basally, broadened to the middle and scarcely tapered distally (Fig. 89D,K) —   **9**

7   Abdomen mainly pale green. Hypopygium Fig. 214D—
     Glyptotendipes (Heynotendipes) signatus (Kieffer)

—   Abdomen dark brown or dark olive green—   **8**

8   Ground colour of thorax greenish, scutal stripes black. Hypopygium Fig.
     215A— **Glyptotendipes (Caulochironomus) mancunianus** (Edwards)

—   Thorax all black. Hypopygium Fig. 215B—
     Glyptotendipes (C.) foliicola sensu Pinder 1978 ?(Kieffer)

9(6) Anal point short, parallel-sided (Fig. 90A). Abdomen entirely pale green.
     Hypopygium Fig. 215C—
     Glyptotendipes (C.) viridis sensu Pinder 1978? (Macquart)*

—   Anal point longer, narrow basally and broadened towards the apex (Fig.
     90B). Abdomen darkened distally. Hypopygium Fig. 215D—
     Glyptotendipes (C.) imbecilis (Walker)*

     *Contreras Lichtenberg (2001) has recently synonymised *G. viridis* and *g. imbecilis.*

Genus GRACEUS Goetghebuer

The single European member of the genus is readily identified from the
characters given in the key to genera (p. 147). Hypopygium Fig. 216A—
     Graceus ambiguus Goetghebuer

Genus HARNISCHIA Kieffer

1   Gonostylus broad, tapering distally (Fig. 90C). Anal point bare, only
     slightly broadened in the distal half (Fig. 90D). Hypopygium Fig.
     216B—   **Harnischia fuscimana** Kieffer

—   Gonostylus relatively slender, parallel-sided (Fig. 90E). Anal point with
     several lateral setae and with a broad expansion distally (arrow, Fig.
     90F). Hypopygium Fig. 216C— **Harnischia curtilamellata** (Malloch)

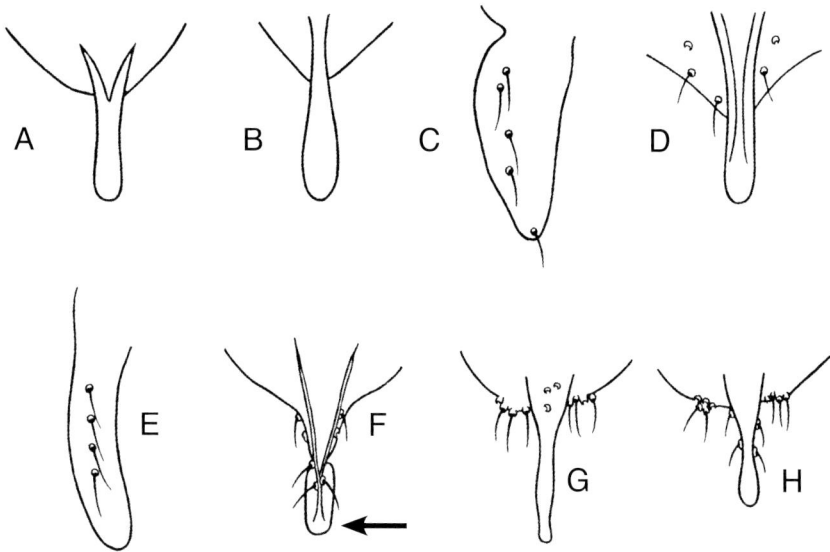

Fig. 90. **A, B:** anal points of: A, *Glyptotendipes viridis*; B, *G. imbecilis*. **C, D:** *Harnischia fuscimana*: C, gonostylus; D, anal point. **E, F:** *H. curtilamellata*: E, gonostylus; F, anal point. **G, H:** anal points of: G, *Microchironomus tener*; H, *M. deribae*.

Genus KIEFFERULUS Goetghebuer

The single European species has a distinctive hypopygium (Fig. 216D)—
Kiefferulus tendipediformis (Goetghebuer)

Genus LAUTERBORNIELLA Thienemann & Bause

The single species referred to this genus may be readily identified from the characters mentioned in the key to genera (p. 154). Hypopygium Fig. 217A— **Lauterborniella agrayloides** (Kieffer)

Genus MICROCHIRONOMUS Kieffer

1   Anal point long, rod-like, bare (Fig. 90G). Hypopygium Fig. 217B—
Microchironomus tener (Kieffer)

—   Anal point shorter, expanded distally with strong lateral setae on the basal half (Fig. 90H). Hypopygium Fig. 217C—
Microchironomus deribae (Freeman)

Genus MICROTENDIPES Kieffer

1   Anal point triangular, pointed apically (Figs 91A,B)—   **2**

—   Anal point rounded distally, parallel-sided or weakly tapered (e.g. Figs 91C,D)—   **4**

2   Superior volsella broad, rounded apically (Fig. 91E). Hypopygium Fig. 217D—   **Microtendipes rydalensis** (Edwards)

—   Superior volsella narrow, tapered towards the apex (Figs 91F,G)—   **3**

3   Abdominal tergites I–V pale green, not darkened basally. Fore-tibia uniformly dark brown. Tarsomeres 1 and 2 yellow. Hypopygium Fig. 218A—   **Microtendipes britteni** (Edwards)

—   Abdominal tergites I–V olive green, extreme bases blackish. Fore-tibia dark brown at each end, paler (sometimes indistinctly so) medially. First tarsomere of fore-tarsus yellow basally, gradually darkened to the apex, tarsomere 2 dark brown. Hypopygium Fig. 218B—
     Microtendipes confinis (Meigen)

4(1) Inferior volsella very short, scarcely reaching beyond tip of the gonocoxite. Hypopygium Fig. 218C—   **Microtendipes tarsalis** (Stephens)

—   Inferior volsella reaching well beyond the tip of the gonocoxite—   **5**

5   Superior volsella with a basal expansion bearing several long setae directed towards the mid-line (arrow, Fig. 91H). Hypopygium Fig. 218D—   **Microtendipes nitidus** (Meigen)

—   Superior volsella not expanded basally, bearing 1 long seta directed towards the mid-line (arrows, Figs 91I,J)—   **6**

6   Superior volsella with 3–4 long setae dorsally (Fig. 91J). Hypopygium Fig. 219A—   **Microtendipes diffinis** (Edwards)

—   Superior volsella with 5–10 long dorsal setae (arrows, Fig. 91F–I)—   **7**

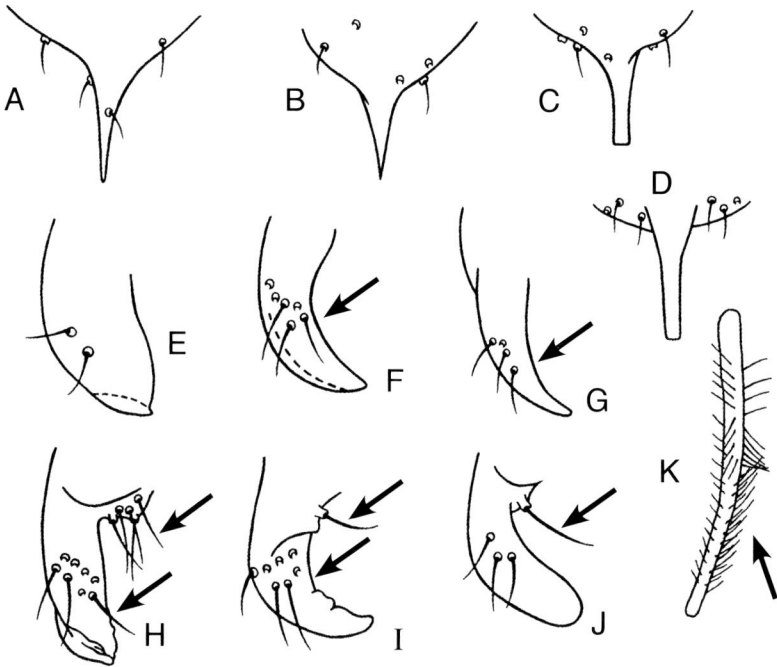

Fig. 91. **A–D:** anal points of: A, *Microtendipes rydalensis*; B, *M. confinis*; C, *M. tarsalis*; D, *M. chloris*. **E–J:** superior volsellae of: E, *M. rydalensis*; F, *M. pedellus*; G, *M. confinis*; H, *M. nitidus*; I, *M. chloris*; J, *M. diffinis*. **K:** fore-leg femur of *M. pedellus*.

7   Fore-femur with all setae directed towards its apex. Dark brown. No setal beard on fore-tarsus. Hypopygium Fig. 219B —   **Microtendipes sp.a**

—   Fore-femur with a group of setae in the apical half reversed, directed towards its base (arrow, Fig. 91K). Abdomen usually with tergites I–V green; when brown, the fore-tarsus has a setal beard —   **8**

8   Fore-tarsus without a setal beard. Abdominal segments I–V pale green, remainder black. Fore-tibiae pale medially, darkened at the base and tip. Hypopygium Fig. 219C —   **Microtendipes pedellus** (De Geer)

—   Fore-tarsus with a setal beard (but longer hairs are easily lost). Abdominal segments I–V dark green or blackish. Fore-tibiae blackish. Hypopygium Fig. 219D —   **Microtendipes chloris** (Meigen)

Genus NILOTHAUMA Kieffer

The one species recorded for Britain and Ireland has a highly characteristic hypopygium (Fig. 220A)— **Nilothauma brayi** (Goetghebuer)

Genus OMISUS Townes

The single European species is readily identifiable from the characters used in the key to genera (p. 154). Hypopygium Fig. 220B—
Omisus caledonicus (Edwards)

Genus PAGASTIELLA Brundin

There is one European representative of this genus, identifiable from the characters given in the key to genera (p. 150). Hypopygium Fig. 220C—
Pagastiella orophila (Edwards)

Genus PARACHIRONOMUS Lenz

1   Gonocoxite appears 'shaggy', with very long sinuous setae (Fig. 92A). Hypopygium Fig. 221A— **Parachironomus danicus** Lehman

—   Gonocoxite with short stiff setae—   **2**

2   At least one of the distal setae of superior volsella arising from a large distinct pit (arrows, Figs 92B,C)—   **3**

—   Neither of the distal setae of superior volsella arising from a distinct pit (Figs 92D,E)—   **11**

3   Inner margin of gonostylus swollen in distal half before tapering to apex (arrows, Figs 92F,G)   **4**

—   Gonostylus not as above, roughly parallel-sided or with outer margin somewhat expanded (Figs 92H–J)—   **5**

4   Superior volsella very long, distally produced into a beak-like process (Fig. 92B). Hypopygium Fig. 221B—
Parachironomus tenuicaudatus (Malloch)

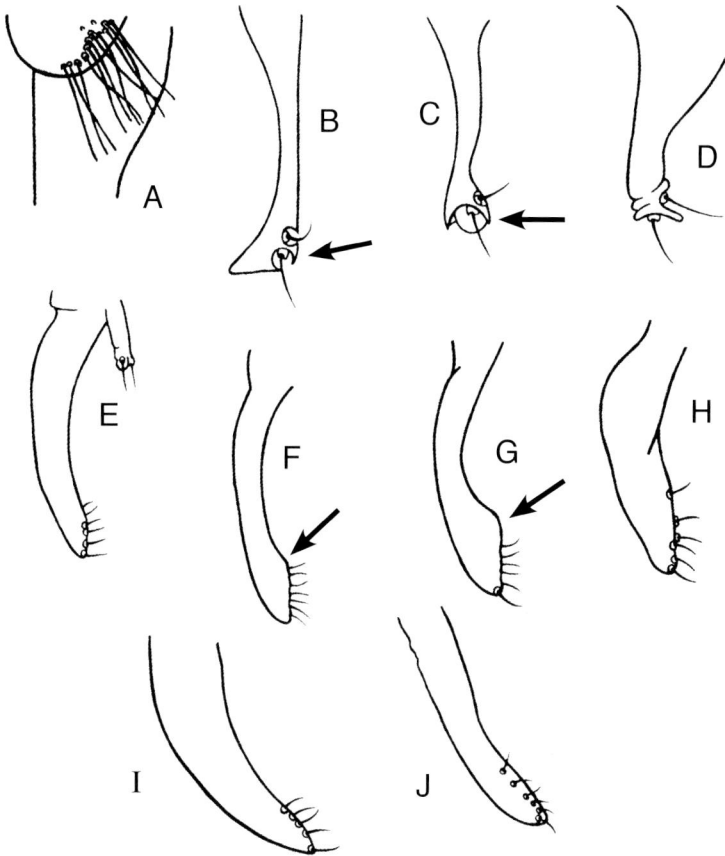

Fig. 92. **A:** gonocoxite apex of *Parachironomus danicus*. **B–D:** superior volsellae of: B, *P. tenuicaudatus*; C, *P. monochromus*; D, *P. vitiosus*. **E:** gonostylus and superior volsella of *P. arcuatus*. **F–J:** gonostyli of: F, *P. tenuicaudatus*; G, *P. monochromus*; H, *P. varus*; I, *P. parilis*; J, *P. digitalis*.

—(4) Superior volsella shorter and differently shaped (Fig. 92C). Hypopygium
Fig. 221C—   **Parachironomus monochromus** van der Wulp

5(3) Superior volsella with a distal lateral process (arrows, Figs 93A,B)— **6**

—   Superior volsella lacking such a process (Figs 93C,D)—   **10**

6   Thorax brown. Hypopygium Fig. 221D—
    Parachironomus subalpinus (Goetghebuer)

—   Ground colour of thorax green—   **7**

7   Gonostylus with a basal 'neck', swollen medially, giving it a humped appearance (Fig. 92H, p. 179). Hypopygium Fig. 222A—
    Parachironomus varus (Goetghebuer)

—   Gonostylus distinctly tapered from near the base to its apex, or more or less parallel-sided for much of its length—   **8**

8   Gonostylus distinctly tapered from near the base to its tip (Fig. 92I, p. 179). Hypopygium Fig. 222B—   **Parachironomus parilis** (Walker)

—   Gonostylus long and narrow, more or less parallel-sided for much of its length—   **9**

9   Setae on anal tergite above the anal point small, few and not set on pale spots. Microtrichia on dorsal surface of gonostylus towards its tip evenly distributed. Hypopygium Fig. 222C—
    Parachironomus swammerdami (Kruseman)

—   Setae on anal tergite above the anal point longer, denser and set on pale oval spots. Microtrichia on dorsal surface of gonostylus towards its tip forming a quilted pattern (arrow, Fig. 93E). Hypopygium Fig. 222D—
    Parachironomus mauricii (Kruseman)

10(5) Distal seta of the superior volsella arises from a large pit, whereas the more proximal seta arises from a smaller pit (arrows, Fig. 93C). Hypopygium Fig. 223A—   **Parachironomus digitalis** (Edwards)

—   The two setae of the superior volsella arise from pits of similar size (arrows, Fig. 93D). Hypopygium Fig. 223B—
    Parachironomus biannulatus (Staeger)

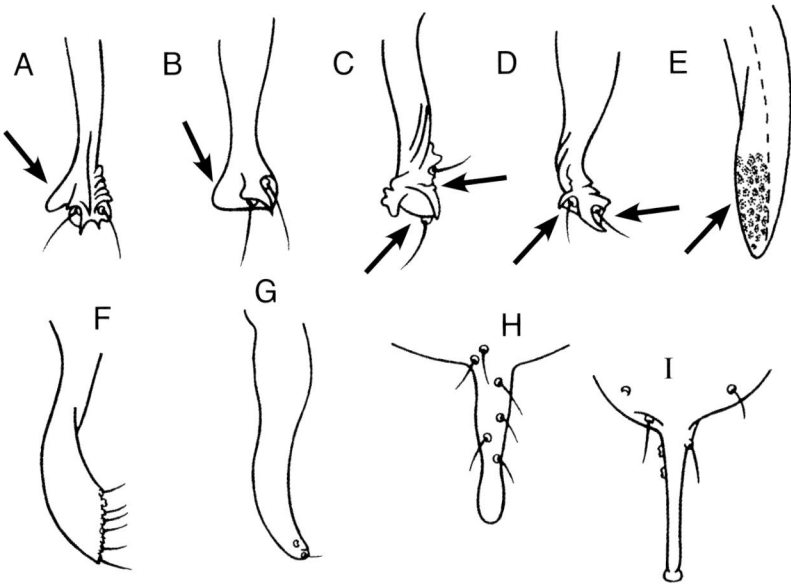

Fig. 93. **A–D:** superior volsellae of: A, *Parachironomus varus*; B, *P. parilis*; C, *P. digitalis*; D, *P. biannulatus*. **E:** apex of gonostylus of *P. mauricii*. **F, G:** gonostyli of: F, *P. vitiosus*; G, *P. frequens*. **H, I:** anal points of: H, *P. frequens*; I, *P. arcuatus*.

11(2)   Gonostylus short and plump (Fig. 93F). Hypopygium Fig. 223C—
Parachironomus vitiosus (Goetghebuer)

—   Gonostylus long and slender (Fig. 93G)—   **12**

12   Anal point broad, expanded distally (Fig. 93H). Hypopygium Fig. 223D—   **Parachironomus frequens** (Johannsen)

—   Anal point slender, not expanded distally (Fig. 93I). Hypopygium Fig. 224A—   **Parachironomus arcuatus** (Goetghebuer)

Genus PARACLADOPELMA Harnisch

1   Superior volsella not expanded distally (Fig. 94A). Gonostylus slightly constricted subapically (arrow, Fig. 94D). Hypopygium Fig. 224B—
Paracladopelma nigritulum (Goetghebuer)

—   Superior volsella *sv* strongly expanded distally (Figs 94B,C). Gonostylus not constricted subapically (Figs 94E,F)—   **2**

2   Posterior median corner of inferior volsella *iv* produced into a fine point (arrow, Fig. 94B). Hypopygium Fig. 224C—
Paracladopelma laminatum (Kieffer)

—   Inferior volsella *iv* broadly rounded posteriorly (arrow, Fig. 94C). Hypopygium Fig. 224D—   **Paracladopelma camptolabis** (Kieffer)

Genus PARALAUTERBORNIELLA Lenz

Only one species is known, which is easily identified from its distinctive hypopygium (Fig. 225A)—   **Paralauterborniella nigrohalteralis** (Malloch)

Genus PARATENDIPES Kieffer

1   Gonostylus slender, not broadened medially (Fig. 94G). Anal point parallel-sided or tapered towards the apex (Fig. 94I). Hypopygium Fig. 225B—   **Paratendipes nudisquama** (Edwards)

—   Gonostylus broadened medially (arrow, Fig. 94H). Anal point somewhat expanded distally (arrow, Fig. 94J)—   **2**

2   First tarsomere of fore-leg all white. Hypopygium Fig. 225C—
Paratendipes albimanus (Meigen)

—   First tarsomere of fore-leg yellowish-white on the basal one-third to one-half. Hypopygium as in *albimanus*—   **Paratendipes plebeius** (Meigen)

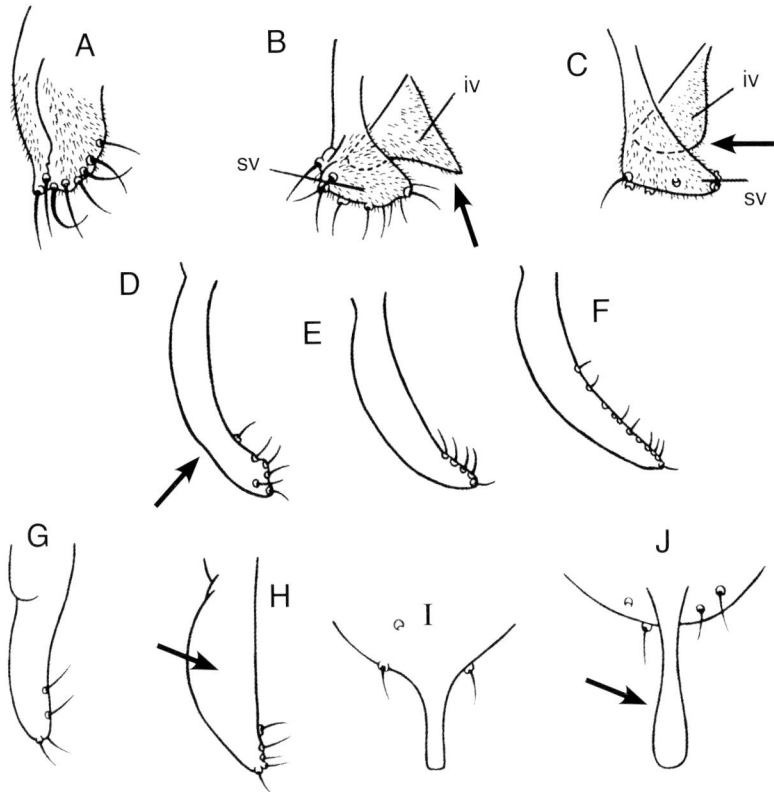

Fig. 94 **A:** superior volsella of *Paracladopelma nigritulum*. **B, C:** superior and inferior volsellae of: B, *P. laminatum*; C, *P. camptolabis*. **D–H:** gonostyli of: D, *P. nigritulum*; E, *P. laminatum*; F, *P. camptolabis*; G, *Paratendipes nudisquama*; H, *P. albimanus*. **I, J:** anal points of: I, *P. nudisquama*; J, *P. albimanus*.

Genus PHAENOPSECTRA Kieffer

1   Abdomen dark brown to black. Hypopygium Fig. 226A —

Phaenopsectra flavipes (Meigen)

—   Abdomen green. Hypopygium Fig. 226B —

Phaenopsectra punctipes (Wiedemann)

Genus POLYPEDILUM Kieffer

1   Wing membrane with macrotrichia—   (PENTAPEDILUM), **2**

—   Wing membrane without macrotrichia—   **5**

2   Superior volsella of hypopygium sickle-shaped, without a long lateral seta (Fig. 95A). Hypopygium Fig. 226C—
Polypedilum (Pentapedilum) nubens (Edwards)

—   Superior volsella not as above, bearing 1 long lateral seta (arrows, Figs 95B–D)—   **3**

3   Gonostylus short and broad (Fig. 95E). Superior volsella with the lateral seta inserted about one-third of the way along (Fig. 95B). Hypopygium Fig. 226D—   **Polypedilum (Pent.) sordens** (van der Wulp)

—   Gonostylus longer (Figs 95F,G). Superior volsella with the lateral seta inserted at least half-way along (Fig. 95C,D)—   **4**

4   Superior volsella with the lateral seta inserted half-way along (Fig. 95C) (occasionally with 2 setae, the distal of which is beyond half-way). Anal point slightly expanded distally and broadly rounded at the apex (Fig. 95H). Hypopygium Fig. 227A—   **Polypedilum (Pent.) tritum** (Walker)

—   Superior volsella with the lateral seta inserted about two-thirds of the way along (Fig. 95D). Anal point not expanded distally, more pointed at the tip (Fig. 95I). Hypopygium Fig. 227B—
Polypedilum (Pent.) uncinatum Goetghebuer

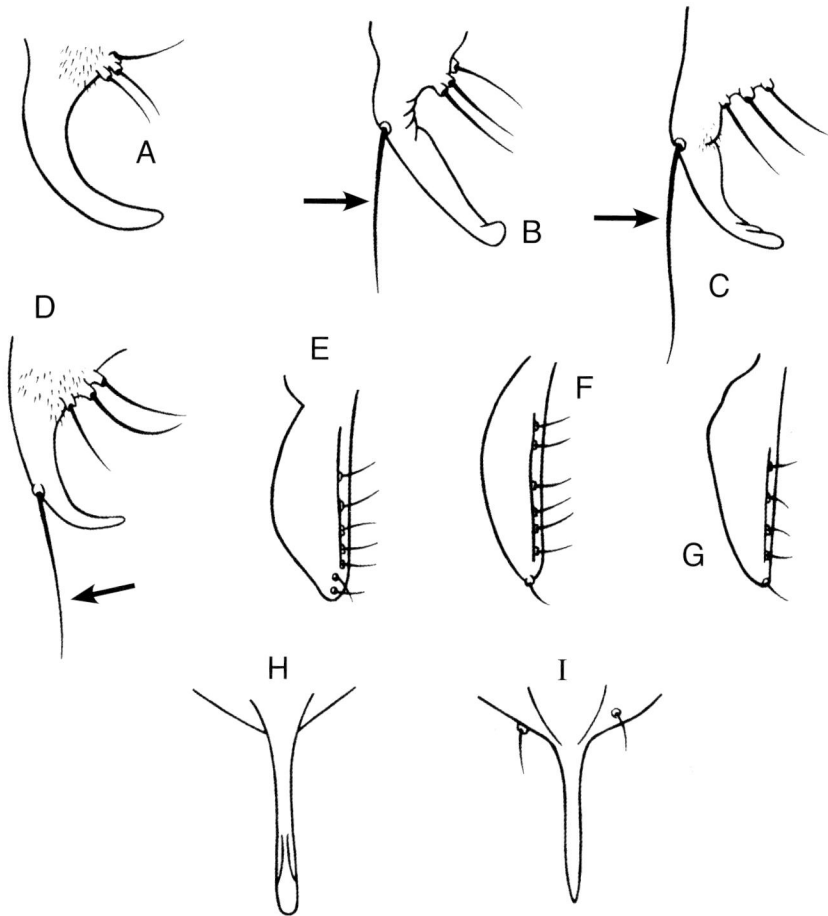

Fig. 95. **A–D:** superior volsellae of: A, *Polypedilum nubens*; B, *P. sordens*; C, *P. tritum*; D, *P. uncinatum*. **E–G:** gonostyli of: E, *P. sordens*; F, *P. tritum*; G, *P. uncinatum*. **H, I:** anal points of: H, *P. tritum*; I, *P. uncinatum*.

5(1) Anal tergite usually with a lobe on each side of the anal point (arrows, Figs 96A–F). Superior volsella broad, pad-like (arrow, Fig. 96I)—
(TRIPODURA), **6**

— Anal tergite without such lobes (Figs 96G,H). Superior volsella in the form of a hook (arrow, Fig. 96J)—   **11**

6   Anal point slender (Fig. 96A). Hypopygium Fig. 227C—
Polypedilum (Tripodura) apfelbecki (Strobl)

— Anal point rather broad, at least at the tip (Figs 96B–F)—   **7**

7   Wing membrane unmarked—   **8**

— Wing membrane with spots—   **10**

8   Anal point with the dorsal lamella on each side not connected to the expanded apex (Fig. 96F). Hypopygium Fig. 227D—
Polypedilum (T.) tetracrenatum Hirvenoja

— Dorsal lamellae of the anal point extending to the expanded apex (Figs 96B,C)—   **9**

9   Anal point broadest subapically (Fig 96B). Hypopygium Fig. 228A—
Polypedilum (T.) bicrenatum Kieffer

— Anal point broadest medially (Fig. 96C). Hypopygium Fig. 228B—
Polypedilum (T.) pullum (Zetterstedt)

10(7) Wings with 4 spots (in pale specimens obscure). Femora with a pale band towards the tips. Lateral lobes of anal tergite rather broad (arrows, Fig. 96D). Hypopygium Fig. 228C—
Polypedilum (T.) quadriguttatum Kieffer

— Wings with 3 spots (usually dark). Femora in dark individuals with narrow apical and basal dark bands. Lateral lobes of anal tergite more slender (arrows, Fig. 96E) or absent. Hypopygium Fig. 228D—
Polypedilum (T.) scalaenum (Schrank)

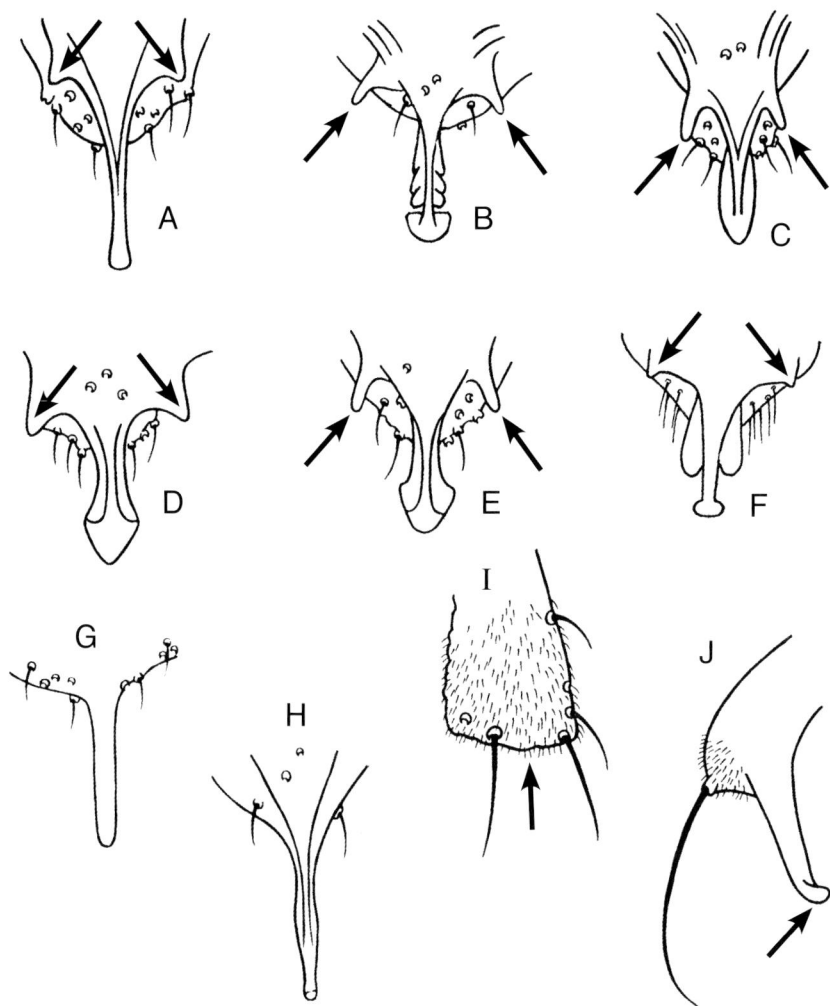

Fig. 96.   **A–F:** anal tergites of: A, *Polypedilum apfelbecki*; B, *P. bicrenatum* (showing the appearance of the anal point when viewed under high power); C, *P. pullum*; D, *P. quadriguttatum*; E, *P. scalaenum*; F, *P. tetracrenatum*. **G, H:** anal points of: G, *P. acutum*; H, *P. pedestre*. **I, J:** superior volsellae of: I, *P. apfelbecki*; J, *P. convictum*.

11(5) Superior volsella with a posterior lobe bearing at least 1 long seta (arrows, Figs 97A,B)—   (URESIPEDILUM), **12**

—   Superior volsella not as above, slender and curved (Figs 97C,D)— (POLYPEDILUM), **13**

12   Posterior lobe of superior volsella bearing 1 long seta (arrow, Fig. 97A). Hypopygium Fig. 229A—
Polypedilum (Uresipedilum) convictum (Walker)

—   Posterior lobe of superior volsella bearing 4 or 5 long setae (arrow, Fig. 97B). Hypopygium Fig. 229B—
Polypedilum (U.) cultellatum Goetghebuer

13(11)   Wings distinctly marked (Fig. 97E). Hypopygium Fig. 229C—
Polypedilum (Polypedilum) laetum (Meigen)

—   Wings unmarked or at most with very faint markings—   **14**

14   Abdomen pale, sometimes darkened distally—   **15**

—   Abdomen uniformly dark brown-black (pale brown in specimens treated with KOH)—   **16**

15   Anal point parallel-sided, rounded distally. Anal tergite rounded (Fig. 97F). Hypopygium Fig. 229D—   **Polypedilum (P.) acutum** Kieffer

—   Anal point tapered, longer and more slender. Anal tergite triangular (Fig. 97G). Hypopygium Fig. 230A—   **Polypedilum (P.) pedestre** (Meigen)

16(14) Antennal ratio 2.0 or more (p. 9). Hypopygium Fig. 230B—
Polypedilum (P.) nubeculosum (Meigen)

—   Antennal ratio not exceeding 1.7—   **17**

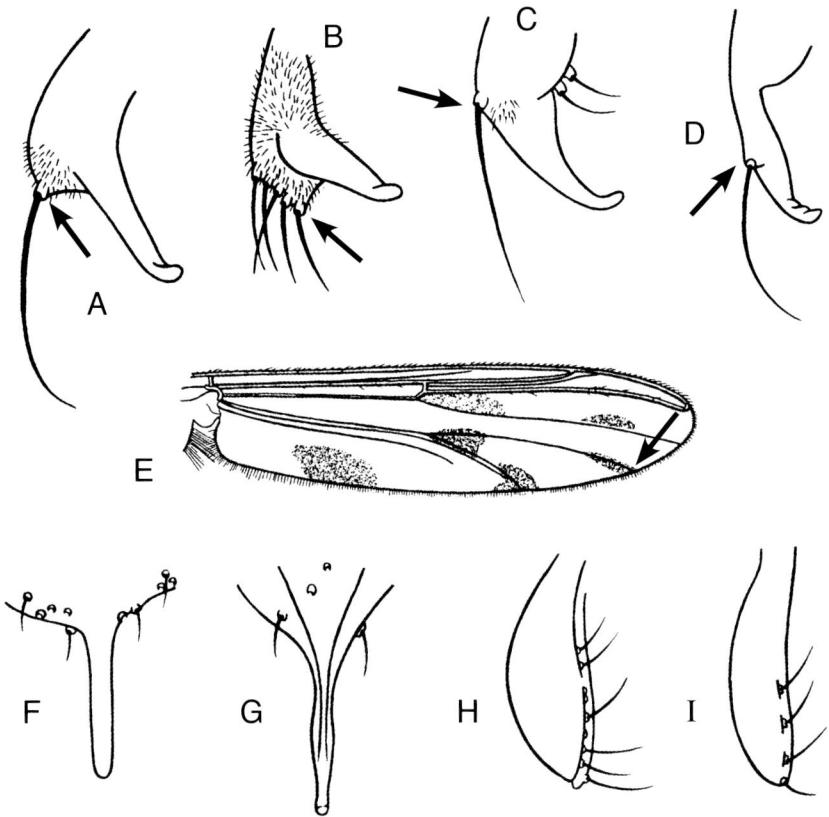

Fig. 97. **A–D:** superior volsellae of: A, *Polypedilum convictum*; B, *P. cultellatum*; C, *P. arundineti*; D, *P. albicorne*. **E:** wing of *P. laetum*. **F, G:** anal points of: F, *P. acutum*; G, *P. pedestre*. **H, I:** gonostyli of: H, *P. arundineti*; I, *P. albicorne*.

17   Gonostylus short and broad (Fig. 97H). Superior volsella slender, curved, the lateral seta arising in proximal half (arrow, Fig. 97C). Hypopygium Fig. 230C— **Polypedilum (P.) arundineti** (Goetghebuer)

—   Gonostylus long and more slender (Fig. 97I). Superior volsella robust and almost straight, the lateral seta arising in distal half (arrow, Fig. 97D). Hypopygium Fig. 230D— **Polypedilum (P.) albicorne** (Meigen)

Genus SAETHERIA Jackson

So far one species has been recorded, only from Ireland. It is very similar to *Paracladopelma* but the character given in the key to genera (p. 150) should suffice for its identification. Hypopygium Fig. 231A—

Saetheria reissi Jackson

Genus SERGENTIA Kieffer

The following key is mostly after Wülker *et al.* (1999).

1   Antennal ratio >3 (p. 9). Fore-leg ratio <1 (p. 14). Wing length usually well over 4 mm. Anal point spatulate. Hypopygium Fig. 231B—

Sergentia coracina (Zetterstedt)*

—   Antennal ratio <3. Fore-leg ratio >1. Wing length about 4 mm long or less. Anal point spatulate or parallel-sided—   **2**

*Another large species is widespread in the north of Britain, the male of which is unknown.

2   Anal point spatulate (Fig. 98A). Superior volsella of hypopygium sometimes with 1 seta. Hypopygium Fig. 231C—

Sergentia prima Proviz & Proviz

—   Anal point parallel-sided (Fig. 98B). Superior volsella without a seta. Hypopygium Fig. 231D—

Sergentia baueri Wülker, Kiknadze, Kerkis & Nevers

Genus STENOCHIRONOMUS Kieffer

1   Anal tergite with simple setae only (arrows, Fig. 98C). Gonostylus parallel-sided and broadly rounded distally. Hypopygium Fig. 232A—

Stenochironomus hibernicus (Edwards)

—   Anal tergite bearing broad, flattened setae flanking the anal point (arrows, Fig. 98D,E). Gonostylus tapered to the apex—   **2**

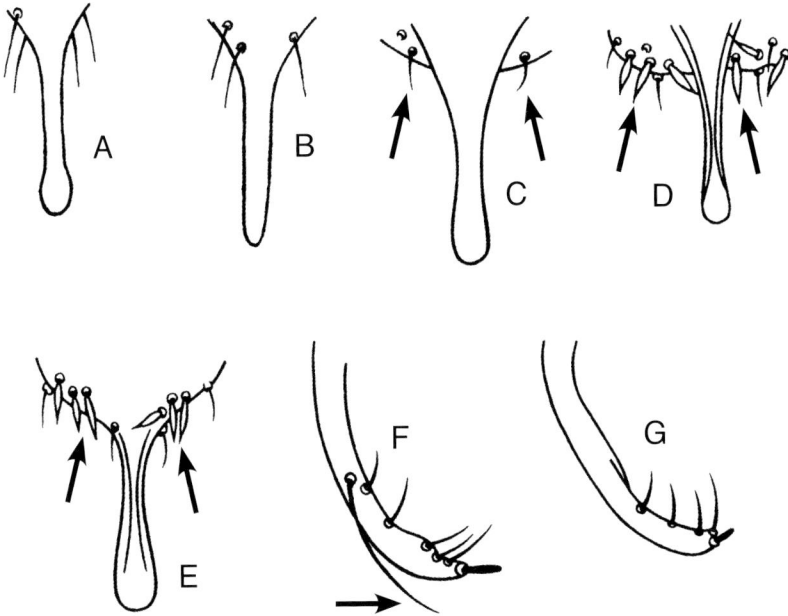

Fig. 98.   **A–E:** anal points of: A, *Sergentia prima*; B, *S. baueri*; C, *Stenochironomus hibernicus*; D, *S. gibbus*; E, *S. fascipennis*. **F, G:** inferior volsellae of: F, *S. gibbus*; G, *S. fascipennis*.

2   Anal point slender, scarcely expanded distally (Fig. 98D). Inferior volsella of hypopygium with 1 long lateral seta (arrow, Fig. 98F). Hypopygium Fig. 232B —   **Stenochironomus gibbus** (Fabricius)

—   Anal point broader, clubbed distally (Fig. 98E). Inferior volsella without a long lateral seta (Fig. 98G). Hypopygium Fig. 232C —
Stenochironomus fascipennis (Zetterstedt)

Genus STICTOCHIRONOMUS Kieffer

1   Wing membrane with several dark spots —   **2**

—   A single dark spot is present around cross-vein RM, *or* RM and adjacent veins are black, otherwise the wing is unmarked   **3**

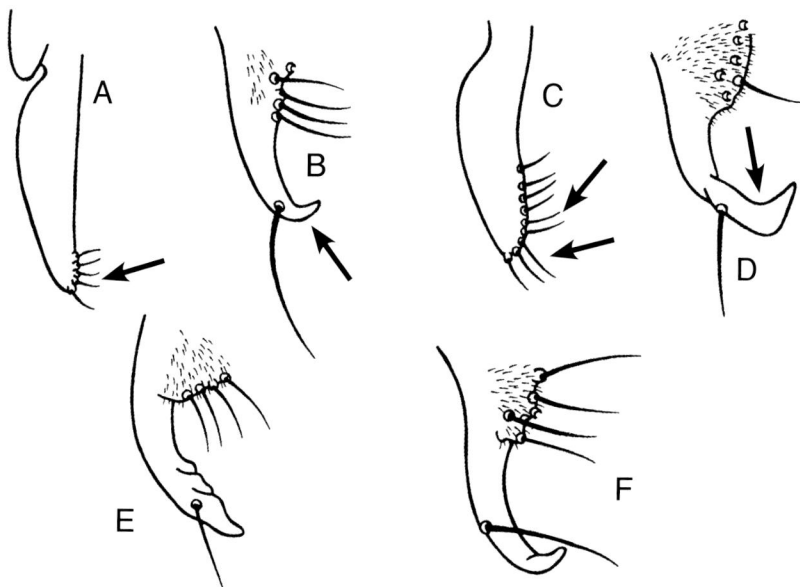

Fig. 99. **A, B:** *Stictochironomus pictulus*: A, gonostylus; B, superior volsella. **C, D:**
S. maculipennis: C, gonostylus; D, superior volsella. **E, F:** superior volsellae
of: E, *S. rosenschoeldi*; F, *S. sticticus*.

2   Gonostylus slender, with a few weak setae distally (arrow, Fig. 99A).
Superior volsella hooked apically, otherwise almost straight (arrow, Fig.
99B). Wing markings (spots) rather faint. Hypopygium Fig. 233A—
                    Stictochironomus pictulus (Meigen)

—   Gonostylus more robust, with a number of strong setae distally (arrows,
Fig. 99C). Apical half of superior volsella strongly curved (Fig. 99D).
Wing markings (spots) distinct. Hypopygium Fig. 233B—
                    Stictochironomus maculipennis (Meigen)

3(1) Superior volsella almost straight (Fig. 99E). Wing cross-vein RM and
neighbouring veins black; membrane unmarked. Hypopygium Fig.
233C—   **Stictochironomus rosenschoeldi** (Zetterstedt)

—   Apical section of superior volsella strongly curved (arrow, Fig. 99F).
Wing membrane with a small dark spot around cross-vein RM.
Hypopygium Fig. 233D—   **Stictochironomus sticticus** (Fabricius)

Genus SYNENDOTENDIPES Grodhaus

1   Abdomen mainly green, thorax black. Hypopygium Fig. 234A—

Synendotendipes lepidus (Meigen)

—   Abdomen predominantly dark brown-black—   **2**

2   Superior volsella robust, curved (arrow, Fig. 100A). Fore-tarsus with a setal beard. Hypopygium Fig. 234B—

Synendotendipes dispar (Meigen)

—   Superior volsella slender, straight except for the extreme tip which is hooked (arrow, Fig. 100B). Fore-tarsus without a setal beard. Hypopygium Fig. 234C—   **Synendotendipes impar** (Walker)

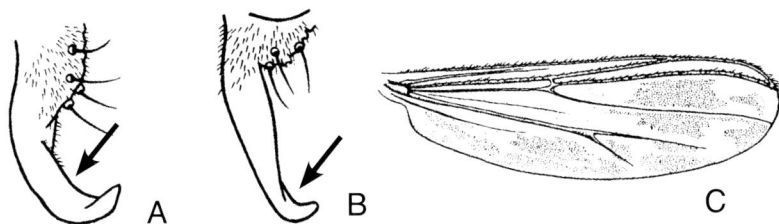

Fig. 100. **A, B:** superior volsellae of: A, *Synendotendipes dispar*; B, *S. impar*. **C:** wing of *Zavreliella marmorata*.

Genus TRIBELOS Townes

One species has been recorded from Britain. The characters used in the key to genera (see p. 152 and Fig. 79G) will serve to identify it. Hypopygium Fig. 235A—   **Tribelos intextus** (Walker)

Genus XENOCHIRONOMUS Kieffer

The only European species may be easily identified from its characteristic hypopygium (Fig. 235B)—   **Xenochironomus xenolabis** (Kieffer)

Genus ZAVRELIELLA Kieffer

Frequently parthenogenetic, the sole species is easily recognised by the numerous dark grey spots on the wings (Fig. 100C). Hypopygium Fig. 235C—   **Zavreliella marmorata** (van der Wulp)

Tribe PSEUDOCHIRONOMINI

Genus PSEUDOCHIRONOMUS Malloch

Only one representative of this genus occurs in Britain and Ireland. It is easily recognisable from the characters given in the key to genera (p. 146), notably the presence of long spurs at the apex of each tibia and widely separated eyes (without a dorsal extension). Hypopygium Fig. 235D—

Pseudochironomus prasinatus Staeger

Tribe TANYTARSINI

Genus CLADOTANYTARSUS Kieffer

1   Thorax with at least the black scutal stripes fused, usually all dark brown/ black; abdomen dark brown—   **2**

—   Ground colour of thorax yellowish or greenish with scutal stripes distinct or anterior scutum infuscated; abdomen green to brownish yellow—

3

2   Median volsella long, narrowed distally, with relatively few, shorter branched setae (arrow, Fig. 101A). Fore-leg ratio 1.5–1.76 (p. 14). Hypopygium Fig. 236A—   **Cladotanytarsus difficilis** Brundin

—   Median volsella short, parallel-sided, with more, longer, branched setae (arrows, Fig. 101B). Fore-leg ratio 1.8–2.0. Hypopygium Fig. 236B—

Cladotanytarsus atridorsum Kieffer

3(1) Yellowish with the posterior half of the thorax darkened. Antennal ratio (p. 9) about 1.5. Fore-leg ratio 2.0. Hypopygium Fig. 236C—

Cladotanytarsus pallidus Kieffer

—   Green with reddish or brownish to black scutal stripes—   **4**

4   Antennal ratio 0.7–1.0. Small species; wing length about 1.5 mm. Hypopygium Fig. 236D—   **Cladotanytarsus vanderwulpi** (Edwards)

—   Antennal ratio >1.1. Larger species; wing length 2.0–2.5 mm—   **5**

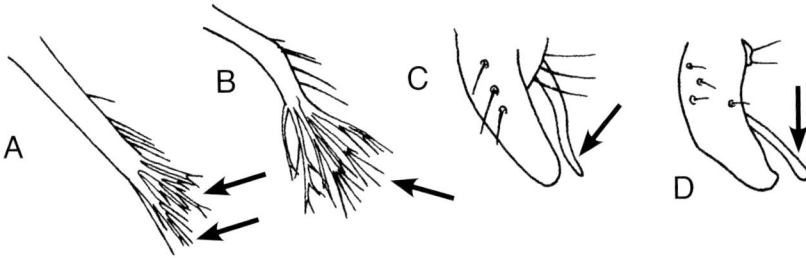

Fig. 101. **A, B:** median volsellae of: A, *Cladotanytarsus difficilis*; B, *C. atridorsum.* **C, D:** superior volsella and digitus of: C, *C. iucundus*; D, *C. nigrovittatus.*

5   Fore-leg ratio 1.5 or less. Hypopygium Fig. 237A —
                                 Cladotanytarsus molestus Hirvenoja

—   Fore-leg ratio >1.5 —   **6**

6   Digitus of superior volsella (Fig. 8D, p. 16) narrowed to the apex (arrow, Fig. 101C) —   **7**

—   Digitus of superior volsella knobbed at the apex (arrow, Fig. 101D) — **8**

7   Antennal ratio about 1.1. Fore leg ratio about 2.0 —
                                 Cladotanytarsus dispersopilosus (Goetghebuer)

—   Antennal ratio 1.13–1.38. Fore-leg ratio 1.57–1.84. Hypopygium Fig. 237B —   **Cladotanytarsus iucundus** Hirvenoja

8(6) Scutal stripes light brown or reddish. Hypopygium Fig. 237C —
                                 Cladotanytarsus mancus (Walker)

—   Scutal stripes black. Hypopygium Fig. 237D —
                                 Cladotanytarsus nigrovittatus (Goetghebuer)

Genus CORYNOCERA Zetterstedt

One species has been recorded from Ireland. Its hypopygium (Fig. 238A) is distinctive —   **Corynocera ambigua** Zetterstedt

Genus MICROPSECTRA Kieffer

1   Hypopygium with median volsella bearing dense spoon-shaped setae over the apical half (Fig. 102A). Black. Hypopygium Fig. 238B—
    Micropsectra radialis Goetghebuer

—   Median volsella with modified setae occupying less than the apical half. Green to dark brown—   **2**

2   Very small species (wing length <2.1 mm), pale green; scutal stripes scarcely differentiated. Hypopygium Fig. 238C—
    Micropsectra attenuata Reiss

—   Larger species (wing length >2.5 mm); scutal stripes distinct—   **3**

3   Anal point narrow, or sharply triangular (Fig. 102B)—   **4**

—   Anal point broad, parallel-sided and rounded distally (Fig. 102C)— **10**

4   Median volsella with a clump of broad, leaf-like setae distally (Fig. 102D). Hypopygium Fig. 238D—
    Micropsectra lindrothi Goetghebuer

—   Median volsella with spoon-shaped setae (arrow, Fig. 102E)—   **5**

5   Median volsella strongly curved (Fig. 102E). Hypopygium Fig. 239A—
    Micropsectra recurvata Goetghebuer

—   Median volsella more or less straight—   **6**

6   Lateral 'tooth' *t* of tergite IX well developed; anal point long and narrow (arrow, Fig. 102F). Superior volsella circularly rounded (Fig. 102G). Hypopygium Fig. 239B—   **Micropsectra groenlandica** Andersen

—   Lateral 'tooth' of tergite IX usually weak. Anal point less narrow (Fig. 102H); superior volsella tapered to a broadly rounded point—   **7**

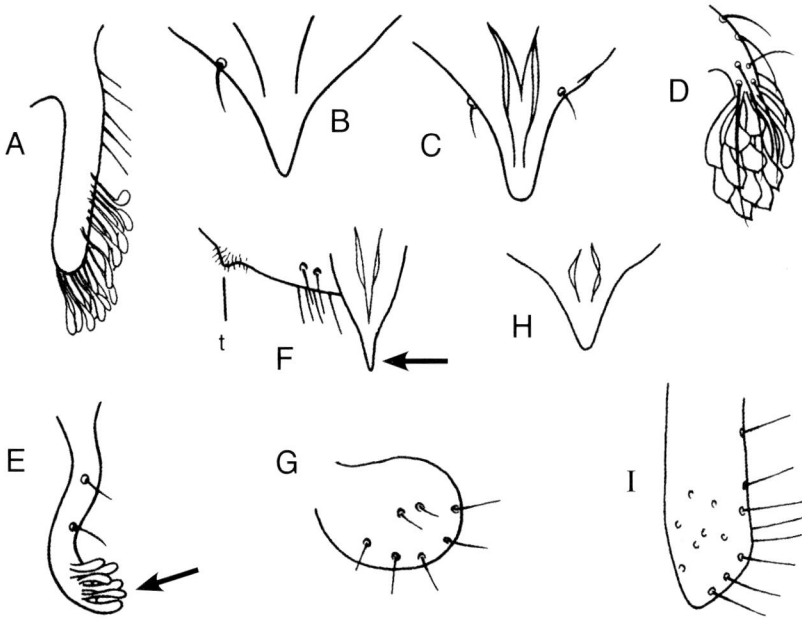

Fig. 102. **A:** median volsella of *Micropsectra radialis*. **B, C:** anal points of: B, *M. lindrothi*; C, *M. aristata*. **D, E:** median volsellae of: D, *M. lindrothi*; E, *M. recurvata*. **F, G:** *M. groenlandica*: F, tergite IX and anal point; G, superior volsella. **H:** anal point of *M. junci*. **I:** apex of gonostylus of *M. lindebergi*.

7   Abdomen mainly green, apical segments usually brown. Antennal ratio 1.0–1.3 (p. 9). Hypopygium Fig. 239C— **Micropsectra junci** (Meigen)

—   Entirely dark brown. Antennal ratio >1.3—   **8**

8   Gonostylus rather abruptly obliquely truncate at the apex (Fig. 102I). Hypopygium Fig. 239D—   **Micropsectra lindebergi** Säwedal

—   Gonostylus tapering to the tip—   **9**

9   Median volsella short (47–62 μm), not reaching the tip of the superior volsella. Hypopygium Fig. 240A— **Micropsectra notescens** (Walker)

—(9) Median volsella longer (74–89 μm), reaching well beyond the tip of the superior volsella. Hypopygium Fig. 240B—

Micropsectra apposita (Walker)*
and **Micropsectra contracta** Reiss*

*The males of these two species are indistinguishable, though the females are distinct.

10(3) Setae of inferior volsella spoon-shaped (as in Fig. 102E, p. 197)—   **11**

—   Setae of inferior volsella broad, strap-like (Figs 103A,B)—   **13**

11   Digitus long, extending beyond the superior volsella (arrow, Fig. 103C). Hypopygium Fig. 240C—   **Micropsectra bidentata** (Goetghebuer)

—   Digitus shorter, not reaching the margin of the superior volsella (arrow, Fig. 103D)—   **12**

12   Antennal ratio 1.0. Fore-leg ratio 1.25 (p. 14). Hypopygium Fig. 240D—   **Micropsectra atrofasciata** (Kieffer)

—   Antennal ratio 1.1. Fore-leg ratio 1.5—

Micropsectra subnitens Goetghebuer

13(10)   Flattened setae of median volsella uniformly tapered towards the fine apex (Fig. 103A), reaching almost to the tip of the inferior volsella. Hypopygium Fig. 241A—   **Micropsectra fusca** (Meigen)

—   Flattened setae of median volsella abruptly tapered distally, ending in a fine point (Fig. 103B), extending about half-way along the inferior volsella. Hypopygium Fig. 241B—   **Micropsectra aristata** Pinder

Genus NEOZAVRELIA Goetghebuer

1   Digitus *d* not exceeding the superior volsella *sv*; median volsella *mv* extending beyond the superior volsella (Fig. 103E). Hypopygium Fig. 241C—   **Neozavrelia longappendiculata** Albu

—   Digitus *d* projecting well beyond margin of superior volsella *sv*; median volsella *mv* short (Fig. 103F)—   **2**

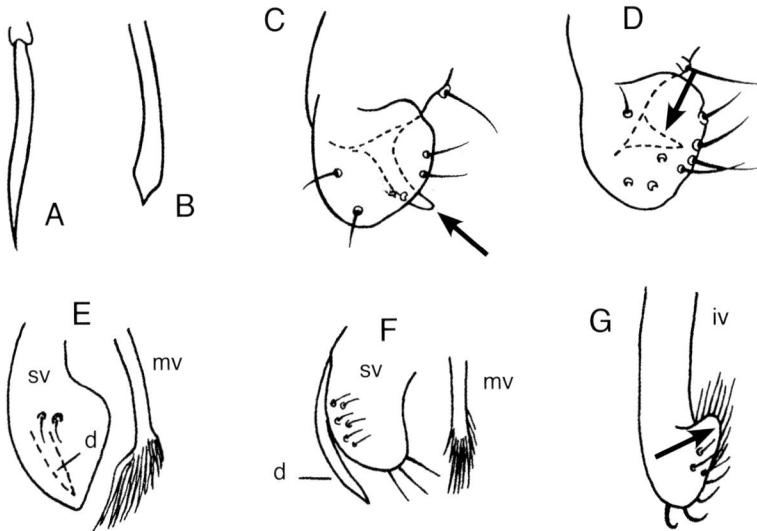

Fig. 103. **A, B:** lamellar setae of median volsellae of: A, *Micropsectra fusca*; B, *M. aristata*. **C, D:** superior volsella and digitus of: C, *M. bidentata*; D, *M. atrofasciata*. **E, F:** superior and median volsella and digitus of: E, *Neozavrelia longappendiculata*; F, *N. fuldensis*. **G:** inferior volsella of *N. fuldensis*.

2   Eyes hairy (p. 9). Inferior volsella not apically swollen. Hypopygium Fig. 242A —   **Neozavrelia luteola** Goetghebuer

—   Eyes bare. Inferior volsella *iv* with apex swollen to form an anteriorly projecting corner (arrow, Fig. 103G). Hypopygium Fig. 242B —
            Neozavrelia fuldensis Fittkau

Genus PARAPSECTRA Reiss

1   Gonostylus and gonocoxite about equal in length. Hypopygium Fig. 242C —   **Parapsectra chionophila** (Edwards)
            and **Parapsectra uliginosa** Reiss [see p. 165, Vol. 2]

—   Gonostylus about twice as long as the gonocoxite. Hypopygium Fig. 242D —   **Parapsectra nana** (Meigen)

Genus PARATANYTARSUS Thienemann & Bause

1   Median volsella apically with spoon-shaped setae. Hypopygium Fig.
    243A—   **Paratanytarsus tenellulus** (Goetghebuer)

—   Median volsella apically with leaf-like setae or setae unmodified—   **2**

2   Median volsella with a distal clump of flattened setae (e.g. Fig. 104A)—
                                                                          3

—   Median volsella with simple setae only (e.g. Figs 105I–L, p. 203)—   **9**

3   Median setae of anal tergite arising from elongate bases (arrow, Fig.
    104B). Hypopygium Fig. 243B—
                          Paratanytarsus bituberculatus (Edwards)

—   Median setae of anal tergite not arising from elongate bases—   **4**

4   Superior volsella digitus deeply divided into two lobes (arrow, Fig. 104C).
    Hypopygium Fig. 243C—   **Paratanytarsus intricatus** (Goetghebuer)

—   Superior volsella digitus not as above—   **5**

5   Median volsella with lanceolate setae extending beyond the inferior
    volsella (Fig. 104D). Hypopygium Fig. 243D—
                          Paratanytarsus penicillatus (Goetghebuer)

—   Median volsella with much shorter setae, not reaching beyond the
    inferior volsella—   **6**

6   Median volsella very short and directed inwards (Fig. 104E). Inner
    margin of gonostylus with a distinct bulge subapically (arrow, Fig.
    104F). Hypopygium Fig. 244A—
                          Paratanytarsus laccophilus (Edwards)

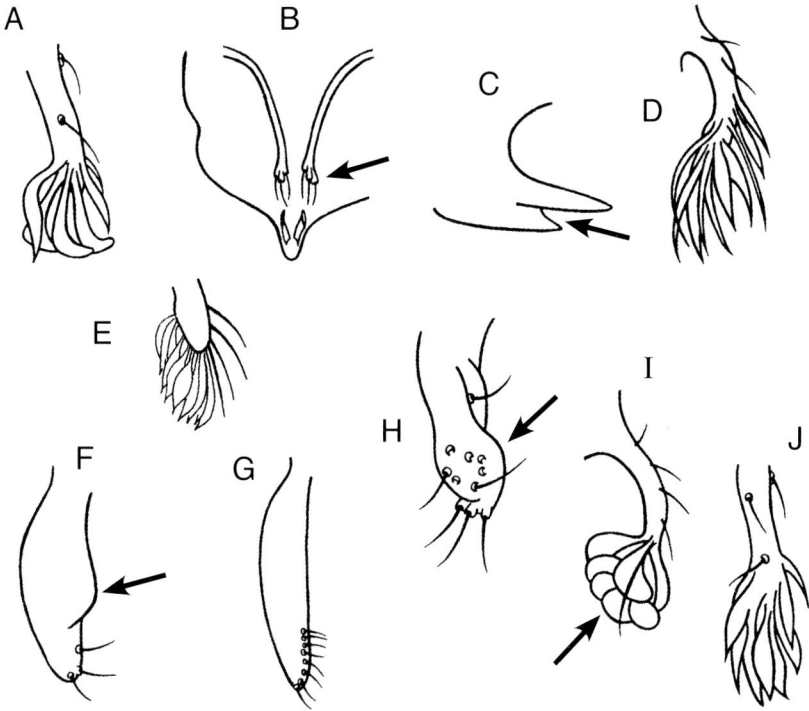

Fig. 104. **A:** median volsella of *Paratanytarsus intricatus*. **B:** anal tergite of *P. bituberculatus*. **C:** digitus of superior volsella of *P. intricatus*. **D, E:** median volsellae of: D, *P. penicillatus*; E, *P. laccophilus*. **F, G:** gonostyli of: F, *P. laccophilus*; G, *P. tenuis*. **H:** inferior volsella of *P. laetipes*. **I, J:** median volsellae of: I, *P. laetipes*; J, *P. tenuis*.

—(6) Median volsella longer, with setae exceeding the posterior margin of the superior volsella. Inner margin of gonostylus without a bulge (Fig. 104G)—   **7**

7   Inner margin of inferior volsella expanded in the distal half (arrow, Fig. 104H). Flattened setae of median volsella club-shaped (arrow, Fig. 104I). Hypopygium Fig. 244B—   **Paratanytarsus laetipes** (Zetterstedt)

—   Inferior volsella not as above. Flattened setae of median volsella straight or sinuous (Fig. 104J)—   **8**

8   Superior volsella roughly triangular (Fig. 105A). Median volsella straight. Hypopygium Fig. 244C—
                                        Paratanytarsus lauterborni (Kieffer)

—   Superior volsella more or less square (Fig. 105B). Median volsella long and bent medially. Hypopygium Fig. 244D—
                                        Paratanytarsus tenuis (Meigen)

9(2) Median volsella very long (90–120 μm) and flattened distally (Fig. 105C). Hypopygium Fig. 245A— **Paratanytarsus austriacus** (Kieffer)

—   Median volsella mv <60 μm long, not flattened distally (Figs 105D,E)— **10**

10   Inferior volsella iv strongly clubbed apically (Fig. 105D). Superior volsella elliptical to nearly circular (Fig. 105F)—   **11**

—   Inferior volsella iv not, or very slightly, swollen at the tip (e.g. Fig. 105E). Superior volsella with straight internal margin (arrows, Figs 105G,H)—
                                        12

11   Median volsella short (<40 μm), straight (Fig. 105I). Hypopygium Fig. 245B—   **Paratanytarsus natvigi** (Goetghebuer)

—   Median volsella longer (>60 μm), curved backwards (Fig. 105J). Hypopygium Fig. 245C—   **Paratanytarsus dimorphis** Reiss

12(10)   Superior volsella somewhat transversely rectangular (Fig. 105G). Inferior volsella frequently bent inwards. Median volsella with relatively dense and long setae apically (Fig. 105K). Hypopygium Fig. 245D—
                                        Paratanytarsus dissimilis (Johannsen)

—   Superior volsella rounded (Fig. 105H). Inferior volsella straight. Median volsella with relatively few, shorter apical setae (Fig. 105L). Hypopygium Fig. 246A—   **Paratanytarsus inopertus** (Walker)

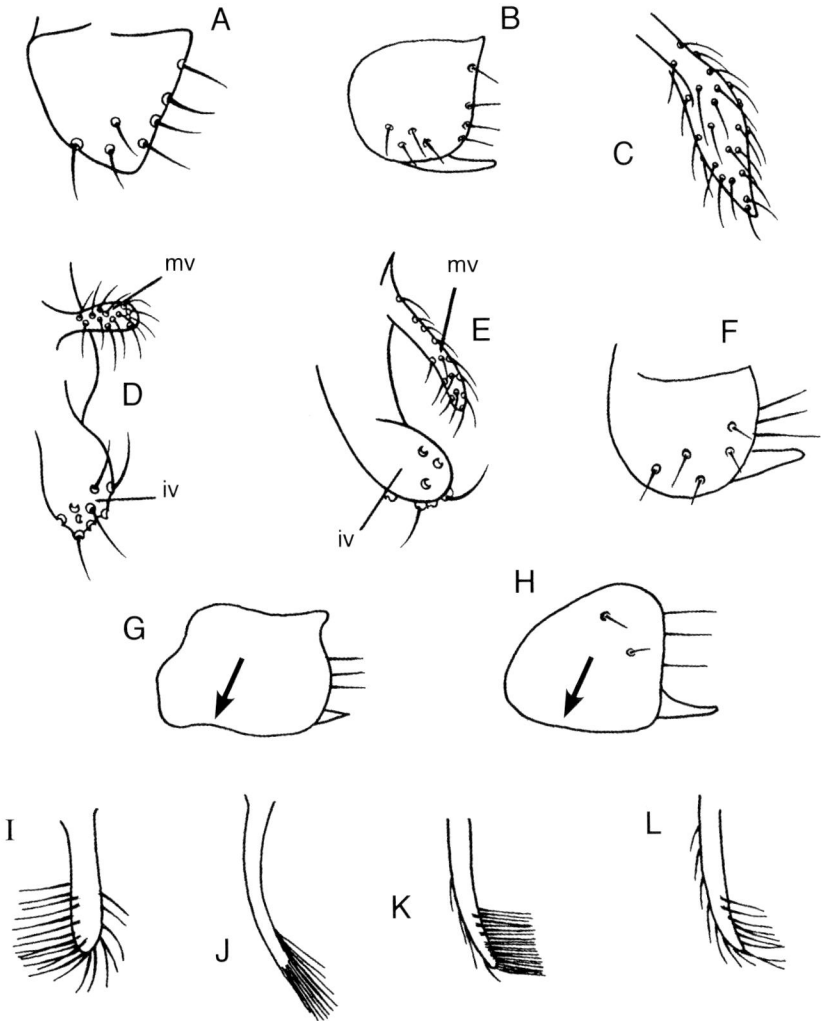

Fig. 105. **A:** superior volsella of *Paratanytarsus lauterborni*. **B:** superior volsella and digitus of *P. tenuis*. **C:** median volsella of *P. austriacus*; **D, E:** inferior and median volsellae of: D, *P. natvigi*; E, *P. inopertus*. **F–H:** superior volsella and digitus of: F, *P. natvigi*; G, *P. dissimilis*; H, *P. inopertus*. **I–L:** median volsellae of: I, *P. natvigi*; J, *P. dimorphis*; K, *P. dissimilis*; L, *P. inopertus*.

Genus RHEOTANYTARSUS Thienemann & Bause

1   Median volsella extremely long and narrow, with long setae reaching the end of the gonostylus (Fig. 106A). Hypopygium Fig. 246B —
Rheotanytarsus distinctissimus Brundin

—   Median volsella much shorter, with setae not exceeding the tip of the inferior volsella— **2**

2   Gonostylus not abruptly tapered distally (Fig. 106B)— **3**

—   Gonostylus abruptly tapered distally (Fig. 106C)— **4**

3   Anal point not conspicuously dark, with low, smooth-edged combs* (cf. Fig. 106I). Antenna with 12 flagellomeres. Hypopygium Fig. 246C —
Rheotanytarsus curtistylus (Goetghebuer)

—   Anal point black, with high and minutely toothed combs (see Fig. 246D). Antenna with 13 flagellomeres. Hypopygium Fig. 246D —
Rheotanytarsus nigricauda Fittkau

*The combs of the anal point in Tanytarsini are paired, longitudinal, usually smooth ridges (e.g. c in Figs 106H,I; also see Fig. 8D, p. 16). The allusion, in this case, is to the appearance (when viewed laterally) of a coxcomb, rather than a toothed comb. Clusters of spines are often present between the combs (e.g. Figs 107E,F,I, p. 207).

4(2)   Shaft of median volsella very long (Figs 106D,E), extending at least to the tip of the superior volsella— **5**

—   Shaft of median volsella not extending to the tip of the superior volsella— **6**

5   Median volsella flattened setae reaching to the tip of the inferior volsella. Posterior margin of superior volsella produced into a distinct 'beak' (arrow, Fig. 106F). Hypopygium Fig. 247A —
Rheotanytarsus photophilus (Goetghebuer)
and **Rheotanytarsus rioensis** Langton & Armitage [see p. 166, Vol. 2]

—   Median volsella flattened setae ending well before the tip of the inferior volsella. Posterior margin of superior volsella not or scarcely produced (Fig. 106G). Hypopygium Fig. 247B —
Rheotanytarsus pentapoda (Kieffer)

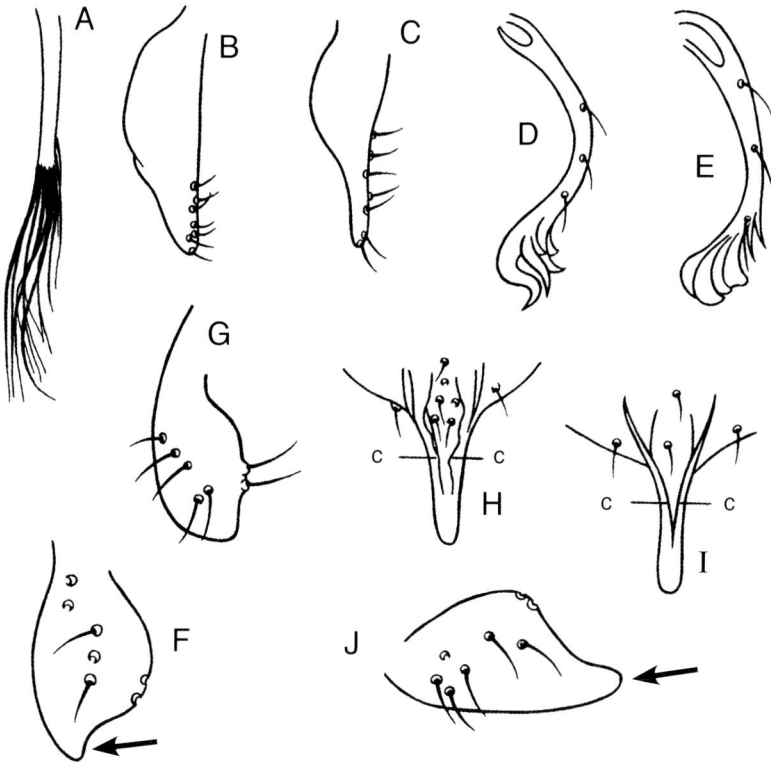

Fig. 106. **A:** median volsella of *Rheotanytarsus distinctissimus.* **B, C:** gonostyli of: B, *R. curtistylus*; C, *R. photophilus.* **D, E:** median volsellae of: D, *R. photophilus*; E, *R. pentapoda.* **F, G:** superior volsellae of: F, *R. photophilus*; G, *R. pentapoda.* **H, I:** anal points of: H, *R. reissi*; I, *R. muscicola* (c = combs). **J:** superior volsella of *R. reissi.*

6(4) Anal point rather broad (Fig. 106H). Superior volsella elongated apically (arrow, Fig. 106J). Hypopygium Fig. 247C—

                                  Rheotanytarsus reissi Lehmann

—   Anal point more slender (Fig. 106I). Superior volsella not as above— **7**

7   Thorax brown, scutal stripes and postnotum dark brown. Hypopygium Fig. 247D—   **Rheotanytarsus ringei** Lehmann

—   Ground colour of thorax green—   **8**

8   Gonostylus very strongly narrowed apically (cf. Fig. 106C, p. 205). Hypopygium Fig. 248A—   **Rheotanytarsus muscicola** Thienemann

—   Gonostylus less strongly narrowed apically (cf. Fig. 106B). Hypopygium Fig. 248B—   **Rheotanytarsus rhenanus** Klink

Genus STEMPELLINA Thienemann & Bause

1   Thorax black. Gonostylus very long, inferior volsella reaching to about one-third from its base. Hypopygium Fig. 248C—
     Stempellina almi Brundin

—   Thorax green with black scutal stripes. Gonostylus shorter, inferior volsella reaching to about half its length. Hypopygium Fig. 248D—
     Stempellina bausei (Kieffer)

Genus STEMPELLINELLA Brundin

1   Median volsella very slender (Fig. 107A). Anal point abruptly narrowed apically (Fig. 107D). Hypopygium Fig. 249A—
     Stempellinella edwardsi Spies & Sæther

—   Median volsella broader (Figs 107B,C). Anal point not abruptly narrowed apically—   **2**

2   Antennal ratio <1.0 (p. 9). Anal point slender (Fig. 107E). Hypopygium Fig. 249B—   **Stempellinella brevis** (Edwards)

—   Antennal ratio >1.0. Anal point broad (Fig. 107F). Hypopygium Fig. 249C—   **Stempellinella flavidula** (Edwards)

Genus TANYTARSUS van der Wulp

1   Tips of femora and tibiae with distinct dark rings. Anal point bearing three darkly chitinized combs* (arrows, Fig. 107G). Hypopygium Fig. 250A—   **Tanytarsus signatus** van der Wulp

—   Legs not ringed. Combs on the anal point not as above or absent—   **2**

*In addition to the longitudinal combs, a posterior, transverse comb is also present.

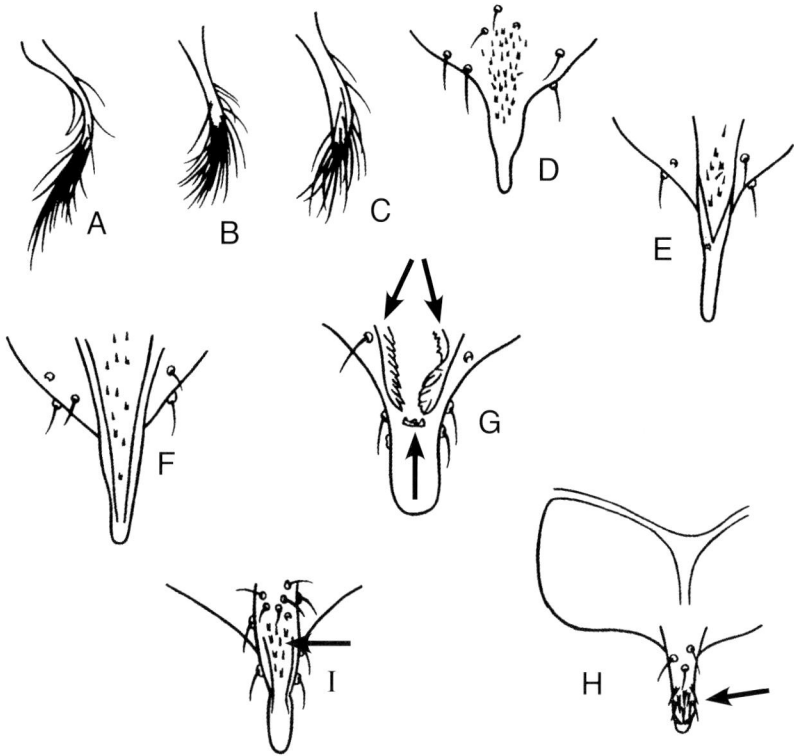

Fig. 107. **A–C:** median volsellae of: A, *Stempellinella edwardsi*; B, *S. brevis*; C, *S. flavidula*. **D–H:** anal points of: D, *S. edwardsi*; E, *S. brevis*; F, *S. flavidula.*; G, *Tanytarsus signatus*; H, *T. usmaensis.* **I:** *T. pallidicornis.*

2   Anal point with a subapical field of unusually long dark spines (arrow, Fig. 107H). Hypopygium Fig. 250B—   **Tanytarsus usmaensis** Pagast

—   Spines of anal point, if present, much shorter—   **3**

3   Dorsal surface of anal point bearing several clusters of short spines (e.g. arrow, Fig. 107I)—   **4**

—   Anal point without such groups of spines—   **31**

4   Anal tergite bands fused posteriorly to form a Y-shape (e.g. Fig. 107H, p. 207)—   **5**

—   Anal tergite bands well separated but occasionally linked by a broad, darkened median zone—   **9**

5   Inferior volsella *iv* and median volsella *mv* strongly curved, the latter very long (Fig. 108A). Hypopygium Fig. 250C—
                                    Tanytarsus sylvaticus (van der Wulp)

—   Inferior volsella and median volsella not strongly curved, median volsella shorter—   **6**

6   Gonostylus spatulate (Fig. 108B). Hypopygium Fig. 250D—
                                    Tanytarsus miriforceps (Kieffer)

—   Gonostylus not spatulate—   **7**

7   Digitus slender, strongly S-shaped; superior volsella roughly trapezoidal in outline (Fig. 108C). Hypopygium Fig. 251A—
                                    Tanytarsus pallidicornis (Walker)

—   Digitus more robust and less strongly curved; superior volsella obovate (Fig. 108D)—   **8**

8   Anal point combs reach nearly to the small, sharply-pointed tip (arrow, Fig. 108E). Hypopygium Fig. 251B—
                                    Tanytarsus gibbosciceps Kieffer

—   Anal point extends well beyond the combs and is more evenly tapered (arrow, Fig. 108F). Hypopygium Fig. 251C—
                                    Tanytarsus buchonius Reiss & Fittkau

9(4)   Digitus reaching at least to the margin of the superior volsella and usually well beyond—   **10**

—   Digitus short, not reaching the margin of the superior volsella—   **27**

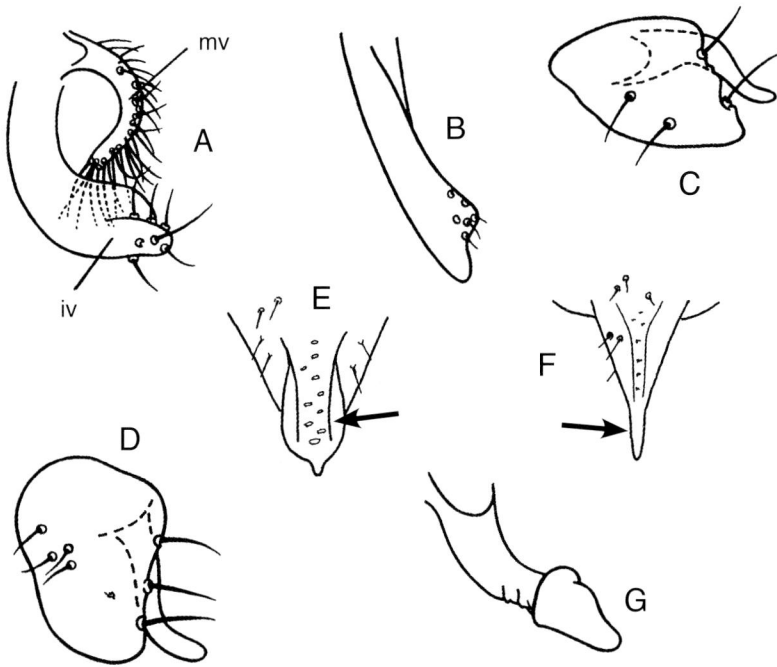

Fig. 108. **A:** inferior and median volsellae of *Tanytarsus sylvaticus*. **B:** gonostylus of *T. miriforceps*. **C, D:** superior volsella and digitus of: C, *T. pallidicornis*; D, *T. buchonius*. **E, F:** anal points of: E, *T. gibbosciceps*; F, *T. buchonius*. **G:** digitus of *T. brundini*.

10   Digitus helically twisted and distally flattened (Fig. 108G)—   **11**

—   Digitus not as above—   **12**

11   Median setae of anal tergite absent. Anal point with 5–10 groups of spines. Pale species without dark scutal bands. Hypopygium Fig. 251D—   **Tanytarsus curticornis** Kieffer

—   Anal tergite with 2 or 3 median setae. Anal point with 3–6 groups of spines. Scutal bands dark. Hypopygium Fig. 252A—

Tanytarsus brundini Lindeberg

12(10)   Median volsella very long, with distal setae extending beyond the tip
         of the inferior volsella (Fig. 109A,B)—   **13**

—   Median volsella much shorter, setae ending well before the tip of the
         inferior volsella—   **16**

13   Anal point long, microtrichia on tergite IX spreading to the setae at the
         base of the anal point (Fig. 109C). Hypopygium Fig. 252B—
                                              Tanytarsus longitarsis Kieffer

—   Anal point shorter, microtrichia on tergite IX stopping before the setae at
         the base of the anal point (Fig. 109D)—   **14**

14   Inferior volsella narrow, inner margin smoothly sinuous (Fig. 109E).
         Digitus with pointed tip (arrow, Fig. 109G). Hypopygium Fig. 252C—
                                            Tanytarsus telmaticus Lindeberg

—   Inferior volsella with inner margin projecting: somewhat hatchet-shaped
         (Fig. 109F). Digitus with rounded tip (arrow, Fig. 109H)—   **15**

15   Anal point short and wide at the base, U- or V-shaped (Fig. 109K). Setae
         on the median volsella irregularly arranged, mostly directed obliquely
         backwards (Fig. 109A). Hypopygium Fig. 252D—
                                          Tanytarsus lestagei Goetghebuer

—   Anal point nearly parallel-sided. Setae on the median volsella regularly
         arranged and curved inwards (Fig. 109B). Hypopygium Fig. 253A—
                                             Tanytarsus palmeni Lindeberg*

         *Ekrem (2004) has synonymised this species with *T. lestagei.*

16(12)   Anal point very broad (Fig. 109L). Posterior margin of the superior
         volsella strongly concave (arrow, Fig. 109I). Hypopygium Fig. 253B—
                                               Tanytarsus niger Andersen
         and **Tanytarsus anderseni** Reiss & Fittkau [see p. 167, Vol.2]

—   Anal point more slender (cf. Fig. 107I, p. 207; Fig. 110E, p. 213).
         Posterior margin of the superior volsella not strongly concave, usually
         distinctly convex—   **17**

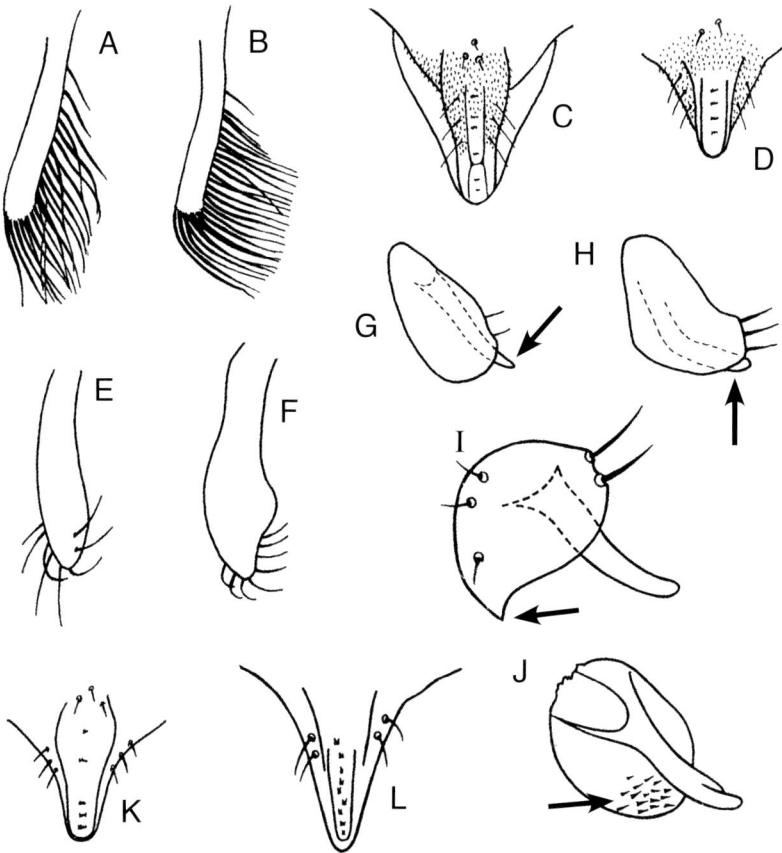

Fig. 109. **A, B:** median volsellae of: A, *Tanytarsus lestagei*; B, *T. palmeni*. **C, D:** anal points of: C, *T. longitarsis*; D, *T. telmaticus*. **E, F:** inferior volsellae of: E, *T. telmaticus*; F, *T. palmeni*. **G–J:** superior volsella and digitus of: G, *T. telmaticus*; H, *T. palmeni*; I, *T. niger*; J, *T. eminulus*. **K, L:** anal points of: K, *T. lestagei*; L, *T. niger*.

17   Superior volsella roughly obovate in outline and bearing a ventrodistal field of small papillae (arrow, Fig. 109J). Hypopygium Fig. 253C —
Tanytarsus eminulus (Walker)

—   Superior volsella differently shaped and lacking ventrodistal papillae — **18**

18   Superior volsella with a constriction which tends to set apart the posterior region as a distinct knob (arrow, Fig. 110A). Hypopygium Fig. 253D—
Tanytarsus ejuncidus (Walker)

—   Superior volsella not as above—   **19**

19   Superior volsella with an apical internal 'tooth' (arrow, Fig. 110B). Hypopygium Fig. 254A—   **Tanytarsus chinyensis** Goetghebuer

—   Superior volsella without a 'tooth'—   **20**

20   Superior volsella elongate, about twice as long as broad (Fig. 110C). Shaft of median volsella reaching the tip of the superior volsella. Hypopygium Fig. 254B—   **Tanytarsus medius** Reiss & Fittkau

—   Superior volsella usually less long, but if as elongate, the median volsella is very short—   **21**

21   Digitus broad and projecting well beyond the concave inner margin of the superior volsella (e.g. Fig. 110D)—   **22**

—   Digitus slender and projecting only slightly, if at all, beyond the superior volsella, which is strongly tapered—   **24**

22   Anal point, beyond the dorsal combs and groups of spines, long and very narrow (Fig. 110E). Hypopygium Fig. 254C—
Tanytarsus aculeatus Brundin

—   Anal point with a broad tip—   **23**

23   Groups of spines between combs (see couplet 3, p. 204) on the anal point mainly in a single row (e.g. arrows, Fig. 110F). Median volsella with a clump of broad, distally rounded, flattened setae (Fig. 110H). Hypopygium Fig. 254D—   **Tanytarsus palettaris** Verneaux

—   Groups of spines between combs on the anal point irregularly arranged (e.g. arrow, Fig. 110G). Median volsella with narrower setae terminating in several fine points (Fig. 110I). Hypopygium Fig. 255A—
Tanytarsus heusdensis Goetghebuer

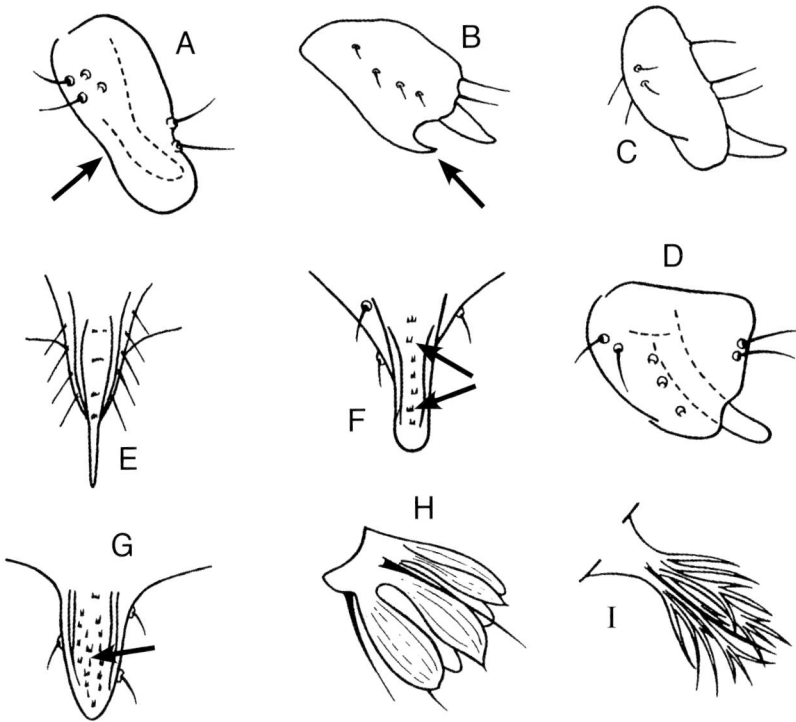

Fig. 110. **A–D:** superior volsella and digitus of: A, *Tanytarsus ejuncidus*; B, *T. chinyensis*; C, *T. medius*; D, *T. heusdensis*. **E–G:** anal points of: E, *T. aculeatus*; F, *T. gregarius*; G, *T. gracilentus*. **H, I:** median volsellae of: H, *T. palettaris*; I, *T. heusdensis*.

24(21) Anal tergite without median setae. Abdominal tergites with brown patterning. Hypopygium Fig. 255B — **Tanytarsus volgensis** Miseiko and **Tanytarsus mancospinosus** Ekrem & Reiss [see p. 168, Vol. 2]

— Anal tergite with median setae. Abdominal tergites without brown coloration — **25**

25   Inferior volsella clubbed distally (Fig. 111A). Beard of relatively long
        setae on the tarsus, beard ratio >6.0 (p. 14). Hypopygium Fig. 255C—
                                            Tanytarsus mendax Kieffer

—   Inferior volsella not clubbed. Beard of shorter setae, beard ratio <5.5— **26**

26   Median volsella very short, directed inwards, with 2–4 flattened setae,
        curved backwards (sickle-shaped) (arrows, Fig. 111B). Hypopygium Fig.
        255D—   **Tanytarsus occultus** Brundin

—   Median volsella longer, reaching to about the posterior margin of
        the superior volsella, with long, flattened setae (arrows, Fig. 111C).
        Hypopygium Fig. 256A—   **Tanytarsus striatulus** Lindeberg

27(9) Groups of spines on the anal point arranged more or less in a single row
        (e.g. arrows, Fig. 111D)—   **28**

—   Groups of spines scattered over the dorsal surface of the anal point (e.g.
        arrows, Figs 111E,F)—   **30**

28   Microtrichia not spreading from tergite IX between the combs of the anal
        point. Median volsella with long, narrow flattened setae reaching beyond
        the tip of the inferior volsella. Hypopygium Fig. 256B—
                                            Tanytarsus lugens (Kieffer)

—   Microtrichia present between the combs on the anal point. Median
        volsella with short setae—   **29**

29   Long axis of superior volsella more or less parallel with the body axis
        (Fig. 111G). Digitus absent. Hypopygium Fig. 256C—
                                            Tanytarsus gregarius Kieffer

—   Superior volsella orientated more or less transversely (Fig. 111H).
        Digitus present but very short. Hypopygium Fig. 256D—
                                            Tanytarsus inaequalis Goetghebuer

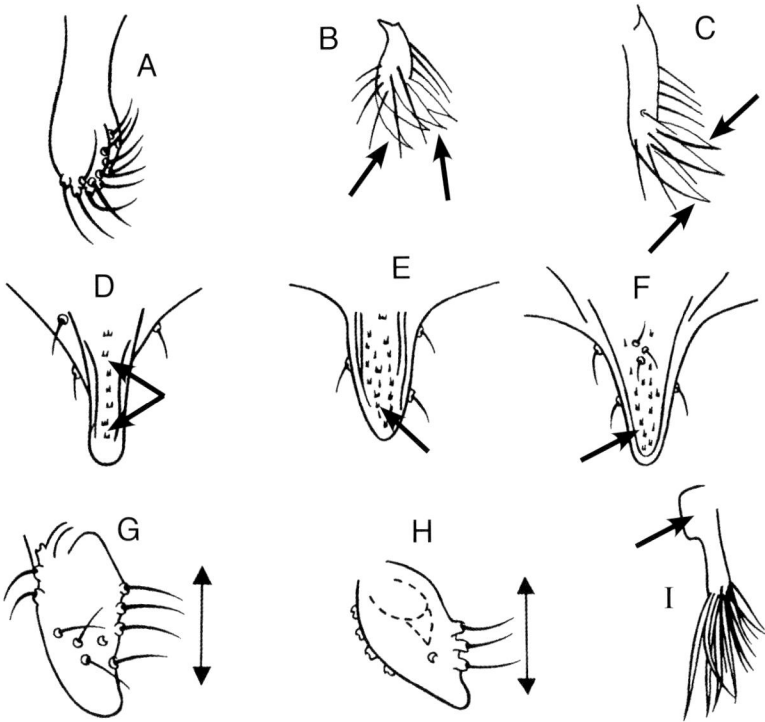

Fig. 111. **A:** inferior volsella of *Tanytarsus mendax*. **B, C:** median volsellae of: B, *T. occultus*; C, *T. striatulus*. **D–F:** anal points of D, *T. aculeatus*; E, *T. gracilentus*; F, *T. bathophilus*. **G, H:** superior volsellae of: G, *T. gregarius*; H, *T. inaequalis* (arrows indicate orientation in relation to the body axis). **I:** median volsella of *T. gracilentus*.

30(27)   Anal point broad (Fig. 111E). Median volsella with a short, but distinct, basal lobe (arrow, Fig. 111I). Hypopygium Fig. 257A—
                                    Tanytarsus gracilentus (Holmgren)

—   Anal point more slender (Fig. 111F). Median volsella without a basal lobe. Hypopygium Fig. 257B—   **Tanytarsus bathophilus** Kieffer

31(3) Median volsella with a hairpin bend in the middle so that the tip points towards the gonocoxite. Hypopygium Fig. 257C—

Tanytarsus recurvatus Brundin

— Median volsella straight— **32**

32 Inner margin of superior volsella produced into two distinct lobes: anterior *al* and posterior *pl* (Figs 112A,B)— **33**

— Superior volsella not as above— **34**

33 Posterior lobe *pl* of superior volsella at least as long as the anterior lobe *al* (Fig. 112A). Hypopygium Fig. 257D—

Tanytarsus excavatus Edwards

— Posterior lobe *pl* of superior volsella distinctly shorter than the anterior lobe *al* (Fig. 112B). Hypopygium Fig. 258A—

Tanytarsus nemorosus Edwards

34(32) Anal tergite bearing a cluster of 2–6 unusually long, dark setae (arrows, Figs 112C,D)— **35**

— Anal tergite without such a cluster of setae (e.g. Fig. 112E)— **36**

35 Superior volsella with apical internal angle acute (arrow, Fig. 112F); digitus narrow. Hypopygium Fig. 258B—

Tanytarsus verralli Goetghebuer

— Superior volsella rounded or emarginate posterior to the two marginal setae (arrow, Fig. 112G). Digitus usually sturdy. Hypopygium Fig. 258C— **Tanytarsus debilis** (Meigen)

36(34) Anal tergite with setae medially. Anal point without a group of setae medially dividing it into anterior and posterior sections, but with a pair of nearly parallel combs extending to its tip (arrow, Fig. 112H). Hypopygium Fig. 259A— **Tanytarsus lactescens** Edwards

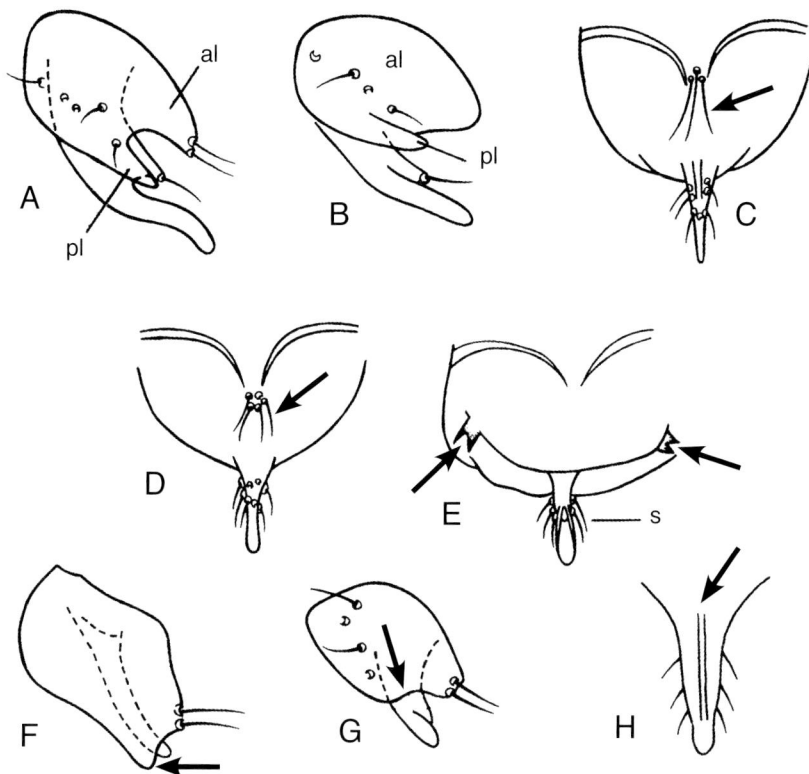

Fig. 112. **A, B:** superior volsella and digitus of: A, *Tanytarsus excavatus*; B, *T. nemorosus*. **C–E:** anal tergites of: C, *T. verralli*; D, *T. debilis*; E, *T. quadridentatus*. **F, G:** superior volsella and digitus of: F, *T. verralli*; G, *T. debilis*. **H:** anal point of *T. lactescens*.

—(36) Anal tergite without setae medially. Anal point without combs, but with a median group of setae *s* (Fig. 112E)—   **37**

37   Anterior tarsus bearded with long setae. Superior volsella quite deeply emarginate on its inner side (arrow, Fig. 113A). Lateral teeth of anal tergite large, usually bifurcate, but often difficult to detect in mounts (arrows, Fig. 112E, p. 217). Hypopygium Fig. 259B—
Tanytarsus quadridentatus Brundin

—   Anterior tarsus without a setal beard. Superior volsella with a straight or weakly concave inner margin (arrow, Fig. 113B). Lateral teeth absent from anal tergite. Hypopygium Fig. 259C—
Tanytarsus glabrescens Edwards

Genus VIRGATANYTARSUS Pinder

1   Dark brown species. Hypopygium Fig. 260A—
Virgatanytarsus triangularis (Goetghebuer)

—   Pale green, sometimes with light brown scutal stripes. Hypopygium Fig. 260B—   **Virgatanytarsus arduennensis** (Goetghebuer)

Genus ZAVRELIA Kieffer

The only species recorded for Britain and Ireland is easily recognised from its distinctive hypopygium (Fig. 260C). The anal point (Fig. 113C) is particularly characteristic—   **Zavrelia pentatoma** Kieffer

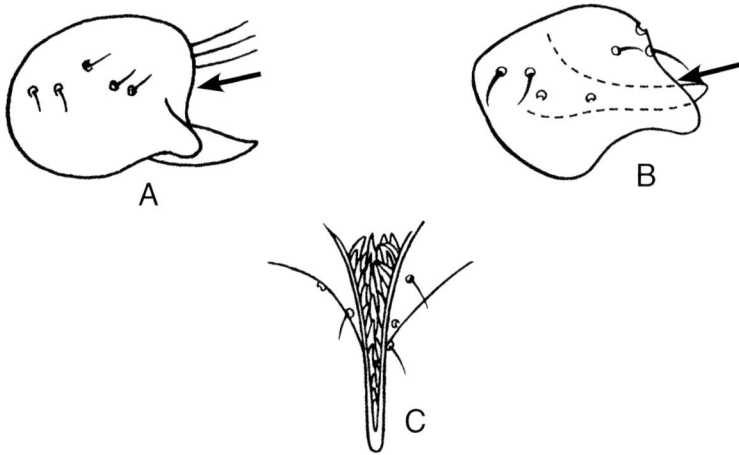

Fig. 113. **A, B:** superior volsella and digitus of: A, *Tanytarsus quadridentatus*; B, *T. glabrescens*. **C:** anal point of *Zavrelia pentatoma*.

ACKNOWLEDGEMENTS

Grateful thanks are due to M. Spies (Munich) for his extensive and invaluable communications on nomenclature, although the authors are responsible for any errors made in this publication. PHL also thanks Dr L. P. Ruse (Environment Agency, Reading) for sharing his material, containing many of the species that are new to the British Isles. Full acknowledgement of the help given in preparing the earlier FBA key to adult males of British Chironomidae is made in that publication (FBA Scientific Publication No. 37, 1978). LCVP wishes to restate his appreciation of the help provided by various colleagues at that time and for the continued help and collaboration of these colleagues and others, in a variety of ways since. He is especially grateful to PHL for the vast amount of effort that he has put into the preparation of this new key, and to David Sutcliffe for his skill and attention to detail in preparing it for publication.

REFERENCES

Albu, P. (1980). Chironomidae – Subfam. Chironominae. *Fauna Republicii Socialiste România, Insecta, Diptera* **11**, 1-320.

Ali, A., Ceretti, G, Barbato, L., Marchese, G., D'-Andrea, F. & Stanley, B. (1994). Attraction of *Chironomus salinarius* (Diptera: Chironomidae) to artificial light on an island in the saltwater lagoon of Venice, Italy. *Journal of the American Mosquito Control Association* **10**, 35-41.

Armitage, P. D., Cranston, P. S. & Pinder, L. C. V. (Eds) (1995). *The Chironomidae: Biology and Ecology of Non-biting Midges.* London. Chapman & Hall. 572pp.

Ashe, P. & Murray, D. A. (1980). *Nostococladius lygropis* (Edw.), a new subgenus of *Cricotopus* v.d.Wulp (Diptera: Chironomidae). In *Chironomidae: Ecology, Systematics, Cytology and Physiology* (Ed. D. A. Murray), pp.105-112. Pergamon Press, Oxford.

Bass, J. A. B. (1998). Last-Instar Larvae and Pupae of the Simuliidae of Britain and Ireland: A Key with Brief Ecological Notes. *Freshwater Biological Association Scientific Publication* **55**, 1-104.

Brundin, L. (1947). Zur Kenntnis der schwedischen Chironomiden. *Arkiv für Zoologi* **39**, 1-95.

Brundin, L. (1949). Chironomidae und andere Bodentiere de Südschwedischen Urgebirgseen. Ein Beitrag zur Kenntnis der bodenfaunistischen Charakterzüge schwedischer oligotropher Seen. *Report of the Institute of Freshwater Research, Drottningholm* **30**, 1-914.

Brundin, L. (1956). Zur Systematik der Orthocladiinae (Dipt., Chironomidae). *Report of the Institute of Freshwater Research, Drottningholm* **37**, 5-185.

Brundin, L. (1966). Transantarctic relationships and their significance, as evidenced by chironomid midges with a monograph of the subfamilies Podonominae and Aphroteniinae and the austral Heptagyiae. *Kunglica Svenska Vetenskapsakademiens Handlingar* **11**, 1-472.

Brundin, L. (1989). 4. The adult males of Podonominae (Diptera: Chironomidae) of the Holarctic region – Keys and diagnoses. In: *The Adult Males of Chironomidae (Diptera) of the Holarctic Region – Keys and Diagnoses* (Ed. T. Wiederholm), pp. 23-36. *Entomologica Scandinavica Suppl.* **34**.

Burtt, E. T., Perry, R. J. O. & McLachlan, A. J. (1986). Feeding and sexual dimorphism in adult midges (Diptera: Chironomidae). *Holarctic Ecology* **9**, 7-32.

Caspers, N. & Siebert, M. (1980). *Pseudorthocladius rectangilobus* sp.n., eine neue Chironomide aus dem Hünsruck (Deutschland) (Diptera; Chironomidae). *Mitteilungen der Schweizerischen Entomologischen Gesellschaft* **53**, 181-183.

Coe, R. L. (1950). Family Chironomidae. *Handbook for the Identification of British Insects* **9**, 121-206.

Cranston P. S. (1982). A Key to the Larvae of the British Orthocladiinae (Chironomidae). *Freshwater Biological Association Scientific Publication* **45**, 1-152.

Cranston, P. S. (1995). Introduction to the Chironomidae. In *The Chironomidae: Biology and Ecology of Non-biting Midges* (Eds P. D. Armitage *et al.*), pp. 1-7. London. Chapman & Hall.

Cranston, P. S., Ramsdale, C. E., Snow, K. R. & White, G. B. (1987). Keys to the Adults, Male Hypopygia, Fourth-Instar Larvae and Pupae of the British Mosquitoes (Culicidae), with Notes on their Ecology and Medical Importance. *Freshwater Biological Association Scientific Publication* **48**, 1-152.

Cranston, P. S. & Sæther, O. A. (1982). A redefinition of *Acamptocladius* Brundin, 1956 (syn. *Phycoidella* Sæther, 1971, n.syn.) (Diptera: Chironomidae), with the description of *A. reissi* n.sp. *Entomologica Scandinavica* **13**, 25-32.

Cranston, P. S. & Sæther, O. A. (1986). *Rheosmittia* (Diptera: Chironomidae): a generic validation and revision of the western Palaearctic species. *Journal of Natural History* **20**, 31-51.

Dejoux, C. (1968). Le Lac Tchad et les Chironomides de sa partie Est. *Annales Zoologica Fennici* **5**, 27-32.

Disney, R. H. L. (1999). British Dixidae (Meniscus Midges) and Thaumaleidae (Trickle Midges): Keys with Ecological Notes. *Freshwater Biological Association Scientific Publication* **56**, 1-128.

Ekrem, T. (2004). Immature stages of European *Tanytarsus* species. 1. The *eminulus–*, *gregarius–*, *lugens–* and *mendax–* species groups (Diptera, Chironomidae). *Mitteilung aus dem Museum für Naturunde in Berlin, Deutsche Entomologische Zeitschrift*, **15,** 97–146.

Ekrem, T., Reiss, F. & Langton, P. H. (1999). *Tanytarsus mancospinosus* sp.n. (Diptera: Chironomidae) from eutrophic lakes in Europe. *Norwegian Journal of Entomology* **46**, 79-87.

Fittkau, E. J. (1954). Die Gattung *Neozavrelia* Goetghebuer (Dipt. Chironomidae). (Chironomidenstudien II). *Deutsche entomologische Zeitschrift* **1**, 161-179.

Fittkau, E. J. (1955). *Buchonomyia thienemanni* n.gen. n.sp. Chironomidenstudien IV. (Diptera: Chironomidae*) Beiträge zur Entomologie* **5**, 403-414.

Fittkau, E. J. (1960). *Rheotanytarsus nigricauda* n.sp. Chironomiden-studien VI. *Abhandlungen naturwissenschaftlicher Verein. Bremen* **35**, 397-407.

Fittkau, E. J. (1962). Die Tanypodinae (Diptera: Chironomidae). (Die tribus Anatopyniini, Macropelopiini und Pentaneurini). *Abhandlungen zur Larven Systematik der Insekten* **6**, 1-453.

Fittkau, E. J. (1971). Der Torsionmechanismus beim Chironomiden-Hypopygium. *Limnology* **8**, 27-34.

Fittkau, E. J., Reiss, F. & Hoffrichter, O. (1976). A bibliography of the Chironomidae. *Gunneria* **26**, 1-177.

Goetghebuer, M. (1927). Diptères Nématocères. Chironomidae Tanypodinae. *Faune de France* **15**, 1-83.

Goetghebuer, M. (1937-1954). Chironomidae. In *Die Fliegen der Palaearktischen Region* (Ed. E. Lindner), pp. 1-138. E. Schweizerbart'sche Verlagsbuchhandlung, Stuttgart.

Hirvenoja, M. (1962a). Zur Kenntnis der Gattung *Polypedilum* Kieffer (Dipt., Chironomidae). *Suomen Hyönteistieteellinen Aikakauskirja* **28**, 127-136.

Hirvenoja, M. (1962b). *Cladotanytarsus*-Arten (Dipt., Chironomidae) aus Finnisch-Lappland. *Suomen Hyönteistieteellinen Aikakauskirja* **28**, 173-181.

Hirvenoja, M. (1973). Revision der Gattung *Cricotopus* van der Wulp und ihrer Verwandten (Diptera, Chironomidae). *Annales Zoologica Fennici* **10**, 1-363.

Hirvenoja, M. & Hirvenoja, E. (1988). *Corynoneura brundini* spec. nov. Ein Beitrag zur Systematik der Gattung *Corynoneura* (Diptera, Chironomidae). *Spixiana* Suppl. **14**, 213-238.

Hoffrichter, O. & Reiss, F. (1981). Supplement 1 to "A bibliography of the Chironomidae". *Gunneria* **37**, 1-68.

Jackson, G. A. (1977). Nearctic and Palaearctic *Paracladopelma* Harnisch and *Saetheria* n.gen. (Diptera: Chironomidae). *The Journal of the Fisheries Research Board of Canada* **34**, 1321-1359.

Klink, A. (1983). *Rheotanytarsus rhenanus* n.sp. A common midge of the lithorheophilic fauna in large lowland rivers (Diptera: Chironomidae). *Entomologische Berichten* **43**, 136-138.

Langton, P. H. (1984). *A Key to Pupal Exuviae of British Chironomidae.* Privately published by P. H. Langton.

224   REFERENCES

Langton, P. H. (1991). *A Key to Pupal Exuviae of West Palaearctic Chironomidae*. Privately published by P. H. Langton.
Langton, P. H. & Armitage, P. D. (1995). *Rheotanytarsus rioensis* (Diptera: Chironomidae), a new species of the *pentapoda* group from the Canary Islands. *British Journal of Entomology and Natural History* **8**, 11-17.
Langton, P. H. & Visser, H. (2003). *Chironomidae Exuviae. A Key to Pupal Exuviae of the West Palaearctic Region*. CD-Rom, ETI/STOWA/RIZA, Amsterdam.
Laville, H. (1971). Recherches sur les Chironomides (Diptera) lacustres du massif de Néovielle (Hautes-Pyrénées). Premiere partie: Systématique, écologie, phénologie. *Annales de Limnologie* **7**, 173-332.
Lehmann, J. (1970). Revision der europäischen Arten (Imagines ♂♂) der Gattung *Parachironomus* Lenz (Diptera, Chironomidae). *Hydrobiologia* **33**, 129-158.
Lehmann, J. (1971). Die Chironomiden der Fulda (Systematische, ökologische und faunistische Untersuchungen). *Archiv für Hydrobiologie* Suppl. **37**, 466-555.
Lehmann, J. (1972). Revision der europäischen Arten der Gattung *Eukiefferiella* Thienemann. *Beitrag Entomologie* **22**, 347-405.
Lehmann, J. (1973). Systematik und phylogenetische Studie über die Gattung *Thienemanniola* Kieffer und *Corynocera* Zetterstedt (Diptera, Chironomidae). *Hybrobiologia* **43**, 381-414.
Lenz, F. (1959). Die Metamorphose der Gattung *Cryptotendipes* Lenz. *Deutsche entomologische Zeitschrift* **6**, 238-250.
Lindeberg, B. (1963). Taxonomy, biology and biometry of *Tanytarsus curticornis* Kieff. and *T. brundini* n.sp. (Dipt., Chironomidae). *Suomen yönteistieteeellinen Aikakauskirja* **29**, 118-130.
Lindeberg, B. (1967). Sibling species delimitation in the *Tanytarsus lestagei* aggregate (Diptera, Chironomidae). *Annales zoologici Fennici* **4**, 45-86.

Mason, W. J. & Sublette, J. E. (1971). Collecting Ohio River Basin Chironomidae (Diptera) with a floating sticky trap. *Canadian Entomologist* **103**, 397-404.
Michiels, S. & Spies, M. (2002). Description of *Conchapelopia hittmairorum*, spec. nov., and redefinition of similar western Palaearctic species (Insecta, Diptera, Chironomidae, Tanypodinae). *Spixiana* **25**, 251-272.
Mundie, J. H. (1955). On the distribution of Chironomidae in a storage reservoir. *Verhandlungen der Internationale Vereinigung für theoretische und angewandte Limnologie* **12**, 577-581.

Mundie, J. H. (1956). Emergence traps for aquatic insects. *Mitteilungen der Internationale Vereinigung für theoretische und angewandte Limnologie* **7**, 1-13.

Murray, D. A. (1976). *Thienemannimyia pseudocarnea* n.sp., a palaearctic species of the Tanypodinae (Diptera: Chironomidae). *Entomologica Scandinavica* **7**, 191-194.

Murray, D. A. (1987). *Conchapelopia aagaardi* n.sp., a new species of Tanypodinae (Diptera: Chironomidae) from Norway. *Entomologica Scandinavica Suppl.* **29**, 161-166.

Oliver, D. R. (1971). Life history of the Chironomidae. *Annual Review of Entomology* **16**, 211-230.

Pagast, F. (1931). Chironomiden aus der Bodenfauna des Usma-Sees in Kurland. *Folia Zoologica et Hydrobiologica* **3**, 199-248.

Palmén, E. (1959). *Microcricotopus balticus* n.sp. (Dipt., Chironomidae) aus dem Brackwasser des Finnischen Meerbusens. *Suomen Hyönteistieteellinen Aikakauskirja* **25**, 61.

Pinder, L. C. V. (1974). The Chironomidae of a small chalk-stream in Southern England. *Entmologisk Tidskrift (Suppl.)* **95**, 195-202.

Pinder, L. C. V. (1978). A Key to the Adult Males of British Chironomidae (Diptera). *Scientific Publications of the Freshwater Biological Association* **37**, 2 vols.

Pinder, L. C. V. (1986). Biology of the Chironomidae. *Annual Review of Entomology* **31**, 1-23.

Reiss, F. (1964). Eine neue Chironomidenart aus dem Bodensee. *Beiträge für Entomologie* **14**, 63-70.

Reiss, F. (1968). Ökologische und systematische Untersuchungen an Chironomiden (Diptera) des Bodensees. Ein Beitrag zur lakustrischen Chironomidenfauna des nördlischen Alpenvorlandes. *Archiv für Hydrobiologie* **64**, 176-323.

Reiss, F. (1988). *Irmakia* ein neues Subgenus von *Demicryptochironomus* Lenz, 1941, mit der Beschreibung von vier neuen Arten. *Spixiana* **11**, 1-12.

Reiss, F. & Fittkau, E. J. (1971). Taxonomie und Ökologie europäisch verbreiteter *Tanytarsus*-Arten (Chironomidae, Diptera). *Archiv für Hydrobiologie* Suppl. **40**, 75-200.

Reiss, F. & Säwedal, L. (1981). Keys to males and pupae of the Palaearctic (excl. Japan) *Paratanytarsus* Thienemann & Bause, 1913, n. comb., with descriptions of three new species (Diptera: Chironomidae). *Entomologica Scandinavica Suppl.* **15**, 73-104.

Sæther, O. A. (1980). Glossary of chironomid morphology terminology (Diptera: Chironomidae). *Entomologica Scandinavica Suppl.* **14**, 1-51.

Sæther, O. A. (1995). *Metriocnemus* van der Wulp: Seven new species, revision of species and new records (Diptera: Chironomidae). *Annales de Limnologie* **31**, 35-64.

Sæther, O. A. & Schnell, Ø. A. (1988). *Heterotrissocladius brundini* spec. nov. from Norway (Diptera, Chironomidae). In *Festschrift zur Ehren von Lars Brundin* (Ed. E. J. Fittkau). *Spixiana* Suppl. **14**, 57-64.

Sæther, O. A. & Wang, X. (1995). Revision of the genus *Paraphaenocladius* Thienemann, 1924 of the world (Diptera: Chironomidae, Orthocladiinae). *Entomologica Sscandinavica Suppl.* **48**, 1- 69.

Säwedal, L. (1976). Revision of the *notescens*-group of the genus *Micropsectra* Kieffer, 1909 (Diptera: Chironomidae). *Entomologica Scandinavica* **7**, 109-144.

Strenzke, K. (1959). Revision der Gattung *Chironomus* Meig. I. Die Imagines von 15 norddeutschen Arten und Unterarten. *Archiv für Hydrobiologie* **56**, 1-42.

Svensson, B. S. (1986). *Eukiefferiella ancyla* sp.n. (Diptera: Chironomidae) a commensalistic midge on *Ancylus fluviatilis* Müller (Gastropoda: Ancylidae). *Entomologica Scandinavica* **17**, 291-298.

Thienemann, A. (1954). Chironomus. Leben, Verbreitung und wirtschaftliche Bedeutung der Chironomiden. *Binnengewässer* **20**, 1-834.

Tokunaga, M. (1937). Chironomidae from Japan (Diptera), IX. Tanypodinae and Diamesinae. *Philippine Journal of Science* **62**, 21-65.

Tuiskunen, J. (1986). The Fennoscandian species of *Parakiefferiella* Thienemann (Diptera, Chironomidae, Orthocladiinae). *Annales Zoologici Fennici* **23**, 176-196.

Tuiskunen, J. & Lindeberg, B. (1986). Chironomidae (Diptera) from Fennoscandia north of 68°N, with a description of ten new species and two new genera. *Annales Zoologici Fennici* **23**, 361-393.

Wiederholm, T. (Ed.) (1983). Chironomidae of the Holarctic region. Keys and Diagnoses. Part I. Larvae. *Entomologica Scandinavica Suppl.* **19**, 1-457.

Wiederholm, T. (Ed.) (1986). Chironomidae of the Holarctic region. Keys and Diagnoses. Part II. Pupae. *Entomologica Scandinavica Suppl.* **28**, 1-482.

Wiederholm, T. (Ed.) (1989). Chironomidae of the Holarctic region. Keys and Diagnoses. Part III. Adult males. *Entomologica Scandinavica Suppl.* **34**, 1-532.

Wilson, R. S. (1987). Chironomid communities in the River Trent in relation to water chemistry. *Entomologica Scandinavica Suppl.* **29**, 387-393.

Wilson, R. S. (1996). *A Practical Key to the Genera of Pupal Exuviae of the British Chironomidae (Diptera: Insecta).* Privately published by R. S. Wilson.

Wilson, R. S. & Ruse, L. P. (2005). A Guide to the Identification of Genera of Chironomid Pupal Exuviae Occurring in Britain and Ireland (Including Common Genera from Northern Europe) and Their Use in Monitoring Lotic and Lentic Fresh Waters. *Freshwater Biological Association Special Publication* **13**, 1-176.

Wülker, W. (1959). Diamesarien-Studien (Dipt., Chironomidae) im Hochschwarzwald. *Archiv für Hydrobiologie* Suppl. **24**, 338-360.

Wülker, W., Kiknadze, I. I., Kerkis, I. E. & Nevers, P. (1999). Chromosomes, morphology, ecology and distribution of *Sergentia baueri*, spec. nov., *S. prima* Proviz & Proviz, 1997 and *S. coracina* Zett., 1824 (Insecta, Diptera, Chironomidae). *Spixiana* **22**, 69-81.

INDEX AND CHECKLIST OF
GENERA AND SPECIES

Names of genera and/or species in square brackets indicate synonyms used by Pinder (1978), and immediately follow the names used in this revision. References to page numbers in Volume 1 are followed by Figure numbers (**bold type**) of hypopygia, contained in Volume 2. For sixteen species, **S** followed by page numbers in **bold** refer to brief notes given in the Supplement of Volume 2.